W9-BWR-146

25 YEARS · BUILT to LAST

F

# The Only Job Hunting Guide You'll Ever Need

The Most Comprehensive Guide for Job Hunters and Career Switchers, Updated and Revised

## Kathryn and Ross Petras

A FIRESIDE BOOK

Published by Simon & Schuster

New York London Toronto Sydney Tokyo Singapore

*FIRESIDE*

*Rockefeller Center*
*1230 Avenue of the Americas*
*New York, NY 10020*

*Copyright © 1989, 1995 by Kathryn and Ross Petras*

*All rights reserved,*
*including the right of reproduction*
*in whole or in part in any form.*

*FIRESIDE and colophon are registered trademarks*
*of Simon & Schuster Inc.*

*Designed by Irving Perkins Associates*

*Manufactured in the United States of America*

*10   9   8   7   6   5   4   3   2   1*

*Library of Congress Cataloging-in-Publication Data*

*Petras, Kathryn.*
 *The only job hunting guide you'll ever need : the most comprehensive guide for job hunters*
*and career switchers / Kathryn and Ross Petras.—Updated and rev.*
   *p.   cm.*
 *"A Fireside book."*
 *Includes index.*
 *1.  Job hunting—United States—Handbooks, manuals, etc.   2.  Occupations—United*
*States—Directories.   I.  Title.*
*HF5382.75.U6P478   1995*
*650.14—dc20*                                                    *94-47511*
                                                                      *CIP*

*ISBN 0-684-80236-8*

# Contents

# Preface

The idea behind this book is simple. You can get almost any job you want—provided you know what you're doing.

Of course, a great deal depends on luck, educational background, and circumstances beyond your control. But a great deal depends on you. On how well you write your resumes and cover letters. On how effectively you sell yourself in an interview. On how well you research job opportunities. These are the things you can control.

This book takes all of these factors in your control, each and every aspect of your job hunt from start to finish, and tells how you can do them effectively, quickly, and better than before.

It is based on years of job hunting experience, thousands of interviews, and hours of listening. This book is very comprehensive —it not only lays out the basics, it is crammed with tips and techniques that make a difference.

To some degree, each and every job hunt is the same. It is a series of steps, starting from the first step of setting a job objective, and ending with the last step of saying yes to a job offer. In between are such steps as researching, writing resumes and cover letters, answering ads, conducting mail campaigns, and going on interviews.

We've set out all this information chronologically, step by step, so that the book accompanies you on every step of your job hunt. But we've also arranged the book so that you can use it as an encyclopedia and look up what you need when you need it.

We've also included a comprehensive research section and an

even more comprehensive reference guide. We think this is maybe the single most valuable aspect of this book: the information on how and where to research your way into a job. As Americans, we've all been deluged by the information revolution. But all too few of us know how—and where—to find vital information. We show you how to use the information deluge to your advantage.

The job search is really about being noticed—for the right reasons. The average Fortune 500 company receives over 250,000 unsolicited resumes every year. A daunting fact. But remember, *someone* always gets an offer, no matter how many applicants there are for a given position. And the person who does is the person with the most organized, most effective job hunting technique.

Which is what this book is all about.

# 1 Setting a Job Objective

## INTRODUCTION

*Before* you begin your job hunt ask yourself a few questions—and answer them. What do you want to do? What are you trying to do? What kind of job do you want?

By answering these questions at the outset, you create a job hunting *goal*, a clear, targeted objective you use to focus your resumes, cover letters, and interviews.

Most problems that surface during the job hunt itself have their beginnings in decisions you avoided—or didn't make—before you started. Poor early planning or a lack of career focus leads to lackluster interviewing, a badly managed job hunt, and a bad track record later in your career. It's hard to be dynamic during an interview when you have only a vague idea of why you're there in the first place. For the same reason, it's even harder to get a job offer.

**EXAMPLE: A man in a stable state government job quit to enter an MBA program at a local university. Talks with friends and extensive reading had led him to conclude that private sector or nongovernment jobs were more rewarding financially and personally. After graduating, he interviewed at over 30 corporations with no success. Problem: His job hunt was scattered across industry and functional lines. He knew he wanted *a* private sector job, but had no idea of what *kind*. *Result:* He returned to state government after losing two full years and tuition costs.**

The best way to avoid the problems and decide on a career is through a step-by-step approach. By tackling all of your job uncertainties and career dilemmas in a methodical and deliberate manner, you can progress from indecision to a plan of action. And you avoid the second most common problem of job or career changers—hopping from idea to idea, with no real plan or direction in mind.

*The five basic steps to take are:*

1. *Self-assessment*—deciding who you are, what you like, and what you want.

2. *Job assessment*—researching the job/career areas that fit your interests and needs.

3. *Informational interviewing*—talking with people in the career areas that interest you.

4. *Weighing career alternatives*—determining whether to quit your job, whether to look for a job in a new area, or whether to stay right where you are in the same job or career.

5. *Career counseling*—meeting with career counselors, who can take you through the entire process from administering assessment tests to helping you assemble a job hunting or career changing program. This step can be taken at *any* time . . . or not at all.

In general, deciding what to do is usually harder than doing it, but decisions made early in your job search pay dividends later. As always, the goal is to become an informed, targeted job hunter—the type of person who gets job offers.

## GENERAL TIPS ON A STEP-BY-STEP APPROACH

■ **The key idea is to *organize* yourself so you can arrive at some decisions about your job or career quickly and with the least amount of ambivalence.**

A step-by-step approach breaks things down into parts or tasks and helps you avoid the major problem facing anyone looking for a job or thinking about a career change—a scattergun approach in which the person looks at almost anything that pays a salary. Although it may seem practical, it's not. Particularly in today's competitive job environment, employers can pick and choose. Applicants who are unfocused and untargeted don't present themselves as winners. They just sound as if they don't know what they're doing.

The time you spend on each step depends on how sure or unsure you are about your career objectives. Someone who *knows* she is a born stockbroker may take only a few minutes with the self-assessment and job-assessment steps. On the other hand, someone who is deeply dissatisfied with his current career may take much more time.

■ **Don't worry if you're caught deciding between two careers—you can manage a job search in two or even more avenues, as long as you're focused on a definite plan.**

A common mistake is to be overly vague about your goals: "I want to remain in the health field, as a hospital administrator or a social worker supervisor, or in the public health service or maybe overseas with an aid agency. . . ." It's better to have one clear goal, or two, or even three, and *concentrate* on them.

> **EXAMPLE: A person with a degree in international relations and no real idea of what he wants out of life can start by picking several *defined* careers in which to research and interview. For example, he can choose diplomacy (the State Department), international banking, and import-export firms.**

■ **Don't be afraid to change: The idea is to move into a job or career where you will flourish.**

As more information about possibilities and opportunities becomes evident, you may realize that your original plan needs changing. Fine. Change your plan. The best way to manage a job search is to be flexible, and to keep narrowing your goals until you form realistic job targets. Jumping from interview to interview with no real purpose but a hope of getting hired will get you nowhere. The bottom line is always to keep yourself organized and your job planning under control.

## STEP ONE: SELF-ASSESSMENT

■ **Chart your interests, values, skills and abilities, and personality type.**

Many people have been so busy working that they have very little idea of what genuinely interests them or motivates them beyond getting a paycheck. If you are unsure about what you want, be prepared to take some time and let your mind wander through various possibilities. Stop and think of what jobs or school courses you most enjoyed, what hobbies you have had, what kind of friends you prefer. In the beginning, try not to limit yourself; let yourself go and think of what you actually *like,* not what you *should* like.

> **TIP: A quick way of getting a feel for your interests is to fan through a college catalogue, particularly a night-school catalogue that includes job-related courses. Note which course descriptions you stop to read, which interest you enough to actually consider taking the course. If you have the time and money—*take* the course.**

> **TIP: What makes you *angry*? Many people get angry with things that concern them the most: An idea might be to find a job in that area. For example, someone who is upset and concerned over acid rain or other forms of pollution might consider looking for a job with an environmental agency; someone who feels passionately about Bosnia might consider a job with Amnesty International, the United Nations, or international human rights groups.**

■ **Be honest with yourself.**

What kind of lifestyle do you want? What kind of people would you like to work with? What really motivates you: competition, a job well done, helping others, analyzing trends? Or making money first and foremost?

> **TIP: Be careful not to overdo this phase of the job hunt. Many people spend half their lives trying to figure out exactly what motivates them with career counselors, career authors, and psychologists, but never get anywhere. Don't mistake self-analysis for action.**

■ **List key factors of your personality and job needs.**

Think back to where and when you have felt most satisfied. What job elements made you the happiest and most productive? What do you want to get out of a career and out of life? What do you want to be remembered for?

Self-assessment is difficult, and the major questions can't be sketched out in a few pages. Many people need professional help and outside perspectives. If so, consider:

1. Career counseling. See pages 24–30 for a full discussion.

2. Personality and vocational testing. See pages 24–26.

3. Books. Many books offer detailed methods of self-examination and ideas for discussion. A few of the better known are:

> *Wishcraft*
> Barbara Sher with Ann Gottlieb
> Ballantine Books (New York, 1983)
>
> *Do What You Love, the Money Will Follow*
> Marsha Sinetar
> Dell (New York, 1989)
>
> *What Color Is Your Parachute?*
> Richard Nelson Bolles
> Ten Speed Press (Berkeley, CA, 1995)

## STEP TWO: JOB ASSESSMENT

### What Kind of Job Do I Want?

Knowing yourself is only the beginning. Your ultimate goal should be to answer two questions: *What do I want to do? Can I reasonably expect to do it?*

Surprisingly, very few people can answer either question. You should start by facing up to them and trying to establish some answers. Given what you know about yourself or what you've learned during self-assessment, pick one or more job areas that seem to suit your personality and interests. Don't worry about practicality yet, just try to determine the areas you are drawn to.

■ **Research the jobs and careers that interest you.**

Go to the career section of your local library. This is the best place to find specialized magazines or trade journals that will give you an inside view of employment and hiring trends. (See Chapter 3, "Research," for details on researching job and career areas.)

■ **Stop to reassess your position.**

Ask yourself: *Do I still* really *want to do this? Would a new field or job provide me with advancement opportunities? Would I be happy? Would I be challenged and interested?* Again, don't be afraid to change your mind.

Even in the early exploratory stages, you'll find yourself narrowing down the list of possible jobs or careers. For example, a highly ambitious person might read in a management magazine that advancement in a certain career is too slow or too predictable; he or she might then be better off reading about other areas before committing to this career. This commonly occurs with very idealistic and imaginative people. They may get all caught up in the *romance* of being an art historian at a major museum and ignore the problems of low pay and low advancement potential until it is too late. Look before you leap into a new job.

> TIP: **Given the bad climate for middle managers, be careful when assessing advancement potential. Ask yourself:** *Regardless of what the company says, where does this job or career* really *lead?*

> TIP: **If unemployed, be particularly careful when assessing new jobs or careers. Low self-esteem may cause you to look at less challenging or competitive careers more readily than you normally would. A common mistake is to make a decision based on** *only* **one criterion: Will they hire me?**

By the end of your research, you should have several major career areas or job choices that you want to pursue in depth—preferably by informational interviewing.

---

## STEP THREE: INFORMATIONAL INTERVIEWING

■ **Informational interviewing—interviewing experts in the fields that interest you—is the best way of assessing other careers.**

By asking the right people about their jobs and companies, you avoid having the common complaint *after* the job hunt is over: "If only I had known. . . ." During this phase of your research, concentrate on getting a *feel* for the industry or the job itself. Sometimes the information you uncover can save you a great deal of time by giving you a true picture of your dream job.

> **EXAMPLE: A man had long dreamed of leaving his present field and entering the medical profession. Helping others, earning a stable and high income, and keeping away from the fractious worlds of law and business were goals that he thought would be met by a career in medicine. In fact, when he spoke with doctors and health-care workers in person, he discovered that high stress, lawsuits and insurance problems, overwork, and variable incomes were also common aspects of many medical careers. In this case, he chose to stay in his field and satisfy his desire to help others through volunteer work.**

### How to Interview

■ **Start the interviewing process by gathering personal contacts through friends and coworkers.**

Most people know someone you should talk to, or at least have a friend who does. Ask for that person's name, phone number, and position. Call and make an appointment to come in and talk about jobs. Stress that all you seek is information: You're not looking for a position now. This is important because it is necessary to put your interview targets at ease if you want the truth, and not some nervous response to keep you from asking them for a job.

■ **Cold-calling—contacting people you haven't met or been referred to—is another tactic to consider. Cold-call the companies where you don't have a personal contact.**

From the library, you can get the names of companies or organizations that interest you; now is the time to call them and ask to speak to the people who can give you specific information about the jobs and careers they provide. You can get the names of managers from friends, magazine articles, and annual reports.

> **EXAMPLE:** "Mrs. Jones, my name is Paul Jobseeker and I'm interested in eventually pursuing a career in your field. Your name was given to me as an example of one of the company's most successful managers. I'd appreciate it if you could give me a few minutes of your time to describe the pros and cons of the field. Would coffee next week be okay?"

> **TIP:** If you don't have names, call the company and say you're updating a mailing list or telephone directory and need the name and number of the marketing director, or whomever. It's usually best not to ask for names directly because many companies will not give out the names of individuals over the phone. You can check association listings or directories (see pages 305–377) for names and titles. Or you can attempt to track down the authors of magazine articles in professional journals. Usually, addresses and titles are listed. Then look up the name in the phone book and call.

Even though hundreds of people are doing it, cold-calling works: The trick is not to be discouraged by rejection and to keep on trying until you get someone to meet with you. Cold-calling can be intimidating and awkward—but it is still one of the quickest ways to get through to the right people. If you rely only on friends to give you names, it may take weeks; one day of cold-calling can yield two or three contacts.

> **TIP:** If cold-calling seems too intimidating, start with an informational letter campaign. Write to knowledgeable people in the field and give a date and a time when you will call.

■ **Take night-school courses in the area you've targeted.**

These courses are usually taught by professionals, one of whom might give you a referral, or you might make contacts through people in the class, who often work in the industry or know people who do.

## What to Ask

■ **During your informational interviews, ask your contacts about the best and worst parts of the job or career.**

Try to get them to tell you the truth and not a puffed-up version of how great things are. People inside the company have a tendency to tell outsiders only the positive aspects of a job. What a person says to the public and what he or she really feels can be two entirely different things, so tell him or her that the conversation is personal and completely off the record.

*These are some of the questions you should ask:*

1. Are there job opportunities available?

2. What kind of person fits in well?

3. What are the best and worst points of the job or career?

4. Does the company give you advancement opportunities?

5. Would you work in this profession if you could do it all over again?

6. What advice can you give me about getting into this business?

7. What training, education, skills, do I need?

8. Considering my background, what problems or advantages would I have that might affect my chances or performance?

9. Could you give me the names of other people to talk to, either in this company or the field in general?

■ **Be sure to get the names of other people to talk to.**

You need information from at least three or four people in the field in order to get a more balanced view and to build up a network of contacts. Also, if you're getting along well with the person, you should ask more specific and personal questions: What would you recommend *I* do to get a job? Do you think *I* have the right qualifications, background, experience?

## STEP FOUR: WEIGHING CAREER ALTERNATIVES

■ **The hardest part of job hunting comes after you have finished the research and informational interviewing:** *Now what do I do?*

You may only need a few hours or days or weeks to reflect on what you've researched or heard, but the average job changer takes six months to come to a firm career decision. Midlevel managers in depressed industries may take upward of eighteen months before moving successfully into a new job. Quite naturally, it's hard to be positive at this stage: You're usually weighing alternatives and wondering if you'll ever get hired or rehired. Over and over and over.

■ **Now is the time to assess how much experience or extra education may be needed to make a job or career switch, and to decide if it's worth it.**

Thoughts of what you want to do may change when you realize the entry requirements—that you may need extra schooling or training; that you may have to work for a long period in a low-level position—or when you discover that there is a lack of jobs in the area.

> **TIP: If you *really* want to have a particular career and are barred by a lack of education or experience, consider sneaking in through the back door. Try working at a lower level in the field while you go back to school or start working in a similar area to gain experience. You might be able to apply your current skills to a different kind of job in the same field.**

■ **One thing you shouldn't do is decide at the outset that the dollar cost of changing your job or career is too high.**

Many unhappy employees stay stuck in bad jobs because they're convinced that they can't afford a major career or job change, so they refrain from making any change whatsoever.

■ **As much as possible, avoid thinking of depressing scenarios.**

Concentrate on alternative methods of getting what you want. If you want something strongly enough, there is often a way of overcoming the odds against accomplishing your goal. By being negative or depressed, you lose sight of possible opportunities. Psychologists agree: Positive thinking works!

> **EXAMPLE: A man in his mid-thirties, with a wife and two children, realized that law, rather than a job in the housing industry, was his genuine interest. Instead of giving up the idea as wildly impractical, he began taking night courses at a local law school. After many grueling years he finally graduated and was offered a legal position in the same housing company.**

■ **If you want to enter a competitive field or position, but feel discouraged by the potential obstacles in your path such as the lack of money or time, face these problems directly.**

Go back and call the people you've interviewed and ask them for advice. Your contacts may know of shortcuts, means of funding, or other jobs in the field. Continue to expand your network until you have exhausted every possibility. Then, and only then, can you reasonably decide that you can't do something for "practical reasons."

Ultimately, a career decision boils down to two variables: (1) Would I like another job or career better? *Or:* Do I *have* to leave my current job? (2) If so, can I find a way of improving my situation without putting myself or my family at too much risk? There are no set rules on how to answer these questions—but these are some things you should ask yourself.

## Should I Quit My Current Job Before Getting Another One?

■ **The first question most people start with is: "Should I quit my current job?" In general, the answer is no.**

It's easier to find new employment when you are currently employed. Statistics show that it takes longer for unemployed people to find jobs. Like bank loans, jobs go to people who don't seem to need them.

■ **The real question to ask yourself is: *Should I start looking for a new job?***

Before making *any* kind of job or career change, look once again at the new position or career you've targeted. Compare it to what you are already doing. Many people find that their dissatisfaction with their current job or career is less of a problem than they had thought; their research has told them that alternative careers would be worse. Or at least not better.

Think long and hard about leaving your current job or career. *Remember:* You originally chose to do what you're doing now for good reasons. Are you sure those reasons are no longer valid?

*Before deciding to move, ask yourself several questions, particularly if you feel burned out or overly tired in your current job:*

1. *Would a vacation change my attitude?* Sometimes, temporary burn-out makes you feel negatively toward your employment in ways that are unjustified. This frequently occurs in high-stress positions. A vacation may recharge you and allow you to see things in a different light.

2. *Do I have a personal problem with my boss?* Tough or unfair employers can be dealt with directly or through grievance procedures *before* you quit a job in protest or disgust.

3. *Would more (or less) of a workload make me happier?* Sometimes the main problem with a particular job is boredom or overwork. Assess how a change in work responsibilities (e.g., hiring temporary help or taking on extra projects) might affect you.

4. *Would a lateral move be better?* Before jumping ship, consider the advantages of transferring within your current company. Especially in today's tough employment market, it's easier to stay in a place where your past record has more value. However, do not mistake longevity for tenure. Don't make a decision to stay on merely because upper management will reward your loyalty.

5. *Do I really want to change my situation?* A common problem you might face is having well-meaning friends and relatives convince you to leave a job for something better. Don't try something new unless you are *certain* that's what you want. Be careful of fads. Many dissatisfied managers switched into the faster-moving computer industry in search of quick promotions and big money, then the industry suffered a recession. Many of the same managers would have been better off remaining in their original fields.

6. *Am I glamorizing other jobs or industries?* Good research and contacts should answer this question. It's not unusual to convince yourself that things are much better at another firm or in another career. Make sure you know what the realities are before you consider leaving your current situation.

## Good Reasons for Leaving a Job or Career

There are many *good* reasons for leaving a job or career.

*You should strongly consider leaving if:*

1. *You've tried everything, but still are not excited by what you're doing.* A gold watch aside, the rewards for staying in a job or career you

really don't like are few. *Remember:* In today's competitive environment, you must be at your best. If you are unhappy, you won't work up to potential, and you may find that your loyalty to a company or career is rewarded with a termination letter. It's better to start thinking of alternatives *now.*

2. *Advancement is blocked, or you know you are in a dead-end job.* Coldly and rationally assess your advancement potential. If you are ambitious and know you are blocked by relatives in a family-owned business, or by a new management team coming in to replace the old, start thinking of moving. *Remember:* If you stay in a dead-end job too long, interviewers and recruiters won't necessarily think you're loyal, they may think you're unambitious and a slow mover.

3. *The company or organization is badly managed, losing market share drastically, or not responding to business or professional challenges.* Birds of a feather flock together. Don't remain a member of a management team that doesn't work, if you're convinced that nothing will be done to improve things. You will remain frustrated, and the longer you stay, the more closely you will be associated with failure. *Note:* This is also the case with lower-level jobs. One administrative assistant who had worked for ten years at a badly run firm was told during her interview: "How could you have stayed at that place? There must have been something you *liked* about its sloppy procedures." She wasn't hired.

4. *You're not adequately rewarded for your work.* This doesn't just mean salary. It might mean recognition, benefits, fair commissions, proper respect. First try to obtain satisfaction *within* the company. If things don't work out, consider leaving, particularly if you're convinced other firms will recognize your achievements. Also, it is sometimes difficult to "grow up" in a company and get substantial salary increases. You can be taken for granted and not be seen as the true professional you really are.

5. *You feel you* have *to try to fulfill your lifelong dreams.* Don't underestimate the power or importance of your own dreams. Even if you're relatively happy in your work, an unfulfilled entrepreneurial or creative dream can hurt you in your *current* job by making you feel bitter toward the company and yourself. If you're determined to do something special and know how and why you must do it, then make the break and take the risk of trying to accomplish it.

**EXAMPLE: A young coffee-shop owner in Georgia dreamed of an acting career. After years of being told to forget his im-**

practical dream, he hired a manager for his shop and went to New York. He failed miserably for five years, but was finally hired as a casting director's assistant. From there he began a slow move up the ladder, happy to have finally entered a field he truly loves. Today he is a successful Hollywood producer.

■ In general, *you* usually know if you should leave a job or a career and go somewhere else.

The considerations listed here are designed to objectify a decision that probably has been lingering inside you all along. The problem is getting it out. The best rule of thumb throughout a job hunt is: Be honest with yourself.

## STEP FIVE: CAREER COUNSELING

■ Go to a career counselor if you can't work out your career decisions or problems on your own, if you need help in planning your job hunt, or if you just want an independent opinion about you and your career.

Because jobs and careers are changing so rapidly, many people now go to a counselor for a "career checkup" whenever they are contemplating a major job or career move.

Career counseling is normally a three-step process. A good career counselor will help you assess yourself, help you decide on a career area, and then advise you on job hunting techniques.

### Career Testing: Interests and Aptitudes

■ As part of the counseling process, many career counselors administer psychological tests designed to measure interests and abilities, and with your participation they will analyze and interpret the results.

Many people only go to career counselors to take aptitude or personality tests, wrongly expecting to find some sort of easy "scientific" answer to a career or job dilemma. Of course, this is a mistaken assumption. Any test should be viewed *only* as a component of a total counseling session, and you should expect to work and analyze your situation independently, as well as with a counselor. All the same, there's something very compelling about career testing. Many experts and job or career changers find them helpful as a starting point.

Most common are the personality preference tests, which are designed to help you arrive at some answers you may have difficulty in finding on your own: *What do I like to do? Are there other fields or careers that I've overlooked where I might be happier or more productive? What kind of employee am I? What do I value in my work?*

> ■ **Two of the most commonly used tests, the Myers-Briggs Type Indicator and the Strong Interest Inventory, are multiple-choice tests that are designed to give you an idea of your personality, your interests, and possible career areas.**

Testing should be administered under the auspices of a career counselor or psychologist, who can offer professional counseling and guidance based on the results. The Strong test is a 325-question test that focuses on specific types of work and general interests as well as the individual characteristics that make up one's personality. Essentially, the test is a series of lists: lists of professions, school subjects, activities, and so on. As a test-taker, you are supposed to rapidly fill in your likes or dislikes in each category, or decide on preferences between categories—for example, whether you would prefer being a stockbroker or a warehouse manager, or are indifferent to both, or just can't decide. Your scores are then analyzed and matched against the scores of other people who are successfully involved in various professions and who have taken the test. Certain conclusions are drawn. For instance, even though you are currently a data processor, your responses may be found to strongly match those of veterinarians. This may prompt you to look more closely at this or related careers. This test is widely respected and is the principal vocational interest test given by counselors.

Whereas the Strong test is primarily concerned with career, the Myers-Briggs test concentrates on personality. The test is a three-section series of 126 questions that deal with choices between activities and attitudes, and between opposite or different words. It deals with how you behave, how you want to be perceived, and how you view yourself. For example, one question might ask if you would rather be considered a gentle person or a tough person; another might ask you to decide which of two words appeals to you more: "innovative" or "traditional."

When the test is scored, you will be designated as one of sixteen personality types, based on four scales of opposites: extroversion–introversion, sensing–intuition, judgment–perception, thinking–feeling.

The Myers-Briggs test has many satisfied customers, including top executives. The premise behind the test is that certain personality types do better in certain types of careers than others. Many people have found that it has accurately predicted or assessed their "unscientific" gut-level preferences in careers, or specific jobs within careers. In conjunction with the Strong test it is particularly valuable in helping you decide among career choices. Again, a good counselor will view the results of these tests *only* as a guide, not as the final word.

■ **An implicit danger with career testing lies in taking the tests too literally—some people feel compelled to explore careers in which they have very little interest, just because of the test results.**

This is where a good career counselor comes in: he or she can interpret your test results more abstractly and help you make a better career move that takes into account your particular situation. For instance, an unhappy stockbroker whose tests show a strong correlation with those of a research scientist might find some aspects of the results valuable without deciding to jump into molecular biology. A counselor can help him find other similarities in the same profession. In this case, the unhappy stockbroker ended up as a stock analyst, a career that contains certain elements of scientific research. It was far closer to his own interests in business and economics.

■ *Aptitude* **tests are not as commonly offered by professional counselors for a very good reason: That you perform well at some activity doesn't mean you should be doing it as a career.**

Many counselors prefer to assess known interests and feel that aptitude stems more from conscious motivation and less from natural talent. In other words, if you know what you like, you can usually find a way of doing it successfully, while an aptitude test may discourage you from even attempting to work in those areas that are not highlighted by the test results. There is some truth to this. One undergraduate student reported testing high on law and very low on science and mathematics. After majoring in prelaw programs, he finally decided to take a chance and study geology; today he is a successful environmental specialist who ended up marrying a lawyer instead of becoming one.

### Choosing a Career Counselor

■ **Choose a career counselor with the same care you would use in choosing a doctor or psychiatrist.**

Be careful of charlatans, people with quick, sure-fire techniques, and counselors who are linked with recruiters, headhunters, or job-placement firms. With the latter, if they're promising a job, the advice you get will depend on the openings they have on hand. You won't get the *independent* advice you need. Moreover, some job placement/counseling firms are fraudulent. These companies typically demand a large up-front fee for their services, which are often little more than a few brief sessions and a promise to circulate your resume.

Before committing yourself or your money to anyone, check the counselor's credentials, background, experience, and price per session. Most important, be certain that the two of you are compatible.

■ *Interview* **the counselor first.**

Make an appointment to have an exploratory session so you can get a feel for his or her techniques. Make certain you are being listened to as well as spoken to; a counselor shouldn't launch into a three-minute monologue ("This is what we can do for you") without first listening to your problems and questions. One common complaint and tip-off to disreputable or ineffective counselors is that they give a great high-powered sales pitch but then don't stop and pay attention to your needs. You need a dialogue, not an egotist's monologue.

*There are six questions to ask and rules of thumb to think about when interviewing a counselor:*

1. *Ask about his or her general approach.* You should feel comfortable with your counselor's approach and feel it is something you need. Some people prefer a trained psychologist or social worker, others prefer a personnel or outplacement specialist who has contacts in the Fortune 500. If you think you need career testing, be sure the counselor offers tests as a normal function—you want someone trained and experienced in analyzing the results.

2. *What does he or she view as a success?* Your definition and the counselor's definition should match but don't be swayed by someone who makes grandiose promises or guarantees you a job.

3. *What is the price per session?* The price of such consultations can vary enormously. The normal range is $30 to $75 per session. Most

counselors usually require a minimum of five sessions to investigate your problem. Some nonprofit organizations have counselors who charge on a sliding scale that is relative to your income. Be wary of exorbitantly priced counselors—usually you can get the same or better counseling services at lower prices.

4. *What other resources are available?* Good counselors are aware of what's out there in terms of jobs, careers, and career literature. Many are affiliated with groups that have career libraries, databases, and networks.

5. *What are the counselor's references?* Ask if the counselor is affiliated with any particular group, such as a university or corporation. Ask to see references, such as a list of previous clients, and see if it is possible to call any of these people.

6. *What are the career counselor's credentials and endorsements?* Credentials and endorsements aren't everything, but they do certify that certain standards have been met and maintained, especially for those who are members of the National Board of Certified Counselors.

*The major agencies or groups that certify career counselors are:*

The National Board of Certified Counselors (NBCC) and The National Career Development Association (NCDA)
(Both are divisions of the American Association for Counseling and Development.)
5999 Stevenson Ave.
Alexandria, VA 22304
—The major certifying agency for career counselors. Certified counselors all have degrees in the field or a related field from accredited schools and a minimum of three years' experience.
—Accredited counselors have the initials "N.C.C." after their names.

*Catalyst National Network of Career Resource Centers*
Catalyst
250 Park Ave. S.
New York, NY 10003
212/777-8900

*Directory of Outplacement Firms*
Kennedy & Kennedy, Inc.
Templeton Rd.
Fitzwilliam, NH 03447
603/585-2200
—Lists names and addresses of outplacement firms.

*Executive Employment Guide*
American Management Association
135 W. 50th St.
New York, NY 10020
212/586-8100
—Lists career counselors, including name, address, number, and specializations.
—Has extensive listings of executive search firms, employment agencies, and job registers.

Other state and national licensing associations:
—Most states do not regulate career counseling, although many regulate counseling and psychological services. In these cases, psychologists and social workers will have degrees and licenses that show state certification for counseling services. Some churches, universities, and civic groups maintain listings of reputable counselors; these listings are usually reliable.

## Other Types of Job/Career Counseling

The *John C. Crystal Centers* offer an interpersonal approach to counseling based on the best-seller *Where Do I Go From Here With My Life?* by John Crystal and Richard Bolles. In groups or as individuals, people are led through a unique series of in-depth exercises and counseling sessions designed to help them discover who they are, what they want to do, and then how to go about accomplishing it. The founder, John Crystal, is a former intelligence officer and businessman whose practical and theoretical approach to self-analysis and job hunting parallels his successful espionage and business experience during and after World War II. A network listing of successful job and career changers is maintained, and the centers offer lectures and talks by businessmen, entrepreneurs, and experts in career changing and self-motivation.

*For a complete listing of centers and courses, call or write:*

The Crystal-Barkley Corporation
152 Madison Ave.
23rd fl.
New York, NY 10016
212/889-8500

*Dale Carnegie Institute* offers specialized courses in public speaking and general topics that may be usefully applied to a job hunt; many Fortune 500 companies offer these courses to employees.

*For a complete listing of centers and courses, call or write:*

Dale Carnegie Associates
1475 Franklin Ave.
Garden City, NY 11530
516/248-5100 or 800/553-9003

## Computer Programs for Finding Career Direction

■ **You can get career help from computerized career counseling.**

Computerized career-counseling programs are for sale and can be helpful. They usually work via an interactive format that guides you, through a series of questions and answers, to a focused career decision.

Below we've listed a few programs currently on the market—call or check at your local computer software store for current prices and updates. Also, ask for a demonstration or a demo version to make certain the program will actually be useful for your purposes. Don't forget to check your local library, college career-placement office, or employment center as well: They may have these or other programs available for use for free or for a nominal fee.

*Career Design:* Sophisticated question-and-answer format. In a series of modules you gradually focus on your underlying career desires. Stresses self-motivated action rather than just passive analysis. For more information: Career Design Software, PO Box 95624, Atlanta, GA 30347. Tel.: 800/346-8007; 404/321-6100; $99.

*Career Opportunities:* A computerized career bank that includes the texts of the *Federal Career Guide, The Occupational Outlook Quarterly* (which discusses job trends and careers), and *Your Military Today* (which lists civilian employment opportunities in the military). Useful for browsing and computerized searching and information. For more information: Quanta Press, Inc., 1313 Fifth St. SE, 223A, Minneapolis, MN 55414. Tel.: 612/379-3956; $129.

*Peterson's Career Options:* Question-and-answer format. Leads you to various career options, with brief general descriptions of the careers. For more information: Peterson's, PO Box 2123, Princeton, NJ 08543-2123. Tel.: 800/338-3282.

# 2 *Resumes*

## INTRODUCTION

You can write an effective resume just as easily as you can write an ineffective one. In both cases, you are outlining your work experience, education, and skills on paper. The difference is that an effective resume sells you; an ineffective one merely recites the bare facts about you.

Telling prospective employers the facts is never enough. You have to market yourself as a product, position yourself, and target your campaign until you land a job. One of the strongest marketing tools you can use is a good resume.

## WHAT A RESUME SHOULD AND CAN DO

Remember two crucial facts as you begin to put together your resume:

Fact #1: You have only one chance to sell yourself with a resume—the first time someone reads it.

It takes less than a minute for a potential employer to scan a resume and decide yes, no, or maybe. In those few seconds, your resume must come across.

When you sell yourself on paper, you don't have a second chance to make a first impression. It isn't like an interview, in which you can correct yourself or amend responses according to the interviewer's reaction. With a resume, you put yourself on the line immediately. If it doesn't grab the person's attention, it can't sell you. Your resume must stand on its own.

Fact #2: A successful resume gets you an *interview*. Not a job.

This is an important distinction—a good resume makes someone want to meet you in person.

A resume is just one tool in your job hunt, a means to begin the process of selling yourself. An effective resume should make you sound like someone you would want to hire, someone you would want to find out *more* from.

A *targeted* resume takes both facts into consideration and helps you to overcome the odds. It sells you more efficiently because it deliberately positions you for a specific job. The work experience, achievements, and skills you include emphasize the abilities you need for that job. Relate your background to meet the needs of a prospective employer. You give him or her a *reason* to interview you because you have already answered a key question: Does this person have the qualifications and experience we need?

## HOW TO PLAN A TARGETED RESUME

■ **The first step toward developing an effective targeted resume is to zero in on your objective.**

Your objective can range from the very specific (a position as a junior sportswear buyer in a specialty store based in the Southwest) to the general (a middle-management position in marketing that would involve travel). Whatever the case, it is essential that you keep that objective in mind at all times. If you're vague about your job objective, your resume will wind up just as unfocused. In other words, the more clearly you define your objective, the more effectively you can focus your resume.

TIP: **If you have more than one objective, it is wise to write different resumes for each. That way you can tailor them to the specific needs of each job.**

■ **Approach your resume like a basic marketing plan.**

Your goal is to construct an effective means of selling your way into an interview. To meet this goal, you must take into account your intended audience—prospective employers. Everything about your resume should be designed to satisfy those people. Continually ask yourself what they would want to see, what qualities they are looking for in a prospective employee, what kind of experience is relevant to their needs.

*Engineer your resume in three main areas:*

• Style: choosing how to package yourself

• Contents: the essential parts of a resume

• Presentation: the actual writing, length, and appearance

## STYLE: THE DIFFERENT RESUME TYPES AND WHEN TO USE THEM

■ **There are three basic resume styles to choose from: chronological, functional, and a chronological/functional combination.**

Each resume style contains the same information—employment history, education, skills, accomplishments, and objectives—but the presentation of that data differs. The different styles work best in different situations. Following is a description of the three basic resume styles, a sample resume in each style based upon the same work history, and an explanation of when to use and when to avoid the different styles.

*General hints about selecting a resume style:*

• Don't choose a style purely on the basis of taste or appearance. Instead choose a resume style according to your situation (recent graduate with no employment experience, career switcher, etc.) and what aspects of your background you plan to stress.

• Because they serve different needs, one style is not necessarily worse or better than another. In general, however, we recommend avoiding the functional resume unless absolutely necessary. Use the chronological or combination style instead—on the whole, they have fewer drawbacks and come across more positively.

## The Chronological Resume

The chronological resume is the type most commonly used. The focus is on time and job continuity. Employment experience is presented in reverse chronological order, starting with the present (or most recent) job and going back in time.

In a chronological resume, you list job title, company name, the dates you held each job, and a brief description of your duties and accomplishments.

### Strengths

Because it is arranged by time, a chronological resume is the easiest to organize and write. It is also easy to read—a plus in selling yourself. It's difficult to go wrong with this choice since the chronological style is the standard, tried-and-true resume format.

### Drawbacks

Any gaps in your employment history, and short tenures, are immediately noticeable. Short of lying, you can't hide job hopping or periods of unemployment. Limited work experience can stand out harshly. And if your experience isn't logically related to your objective, you may have trouble demonstrating on paper why you're suited for the job.

### Who Should Use It

Almost anyone. It's best for people looking for a job in the same or a closely related field and people who want to stress their solid work record in one area.

### Who Should Avoid It

Job hoppers; people with long gaps of unemployment. Depending upon the specifics, career switchers and people with part-time or limited work experience might do better with the combination resume.

# SAMPLE CHRONOLOGICAL RESUME

Karen Charles
227 East 27th St.
New York, NY 10017
(212) 222-1111

## WORK EXPERIENCE:

Manager of Public Relations                                                    12/91–
   ABC Publications, Inc., New York, NY                          present
—Coordinate public relations and media relations for 15 top trade publications
—Designed and supervised promotion activities for successful trade workshop—resulting in
  heavier media coverage and a 28% increase in attendance
—Improved market share 23% through introduction of innovative publicity campaign, based
  upon editorial roundtable forums and tie-ins with major industry events

Public Relations Writer/Project Associate
   ABC Publications, Inc., New York, NY                          4/89–12/91
—Wrote brochures, direct mail letters, press releases
—Created new media kit format for different trade magazines
—Devised and implemented marketing plans for trade publication products

Producer of News Inserts
   WYYY-TV, New York, NY                                          9/87–4/89
—Produced news and feature stories requiring special production techniques
—Supervised control room staff and floor crew
—Acted as editorial director for taped commentaries of prominent New York individuals

Research Manager
   WYYY-TV, New York, NY                                          7/85–9/87
—Coordinated all research for nightly news show, documentaries and special news series
—Established guidelines and procedures for newly created information services department
—Designed and implemented computerized videotape library system

Associate Producer
   WYYY-TV, New York, NY                                          3/84–7/85
—Field-produced show segments; produced special features
—Wrote news and events copy; coordinated talent for on-set interviews

Production Assistant
   WYYY-TV, New York, NY                                          2/83–3/84
—Supervised editing of two-inch videotape and oversaw taping of international feeds
—Trained new personnel, operated character generator, and acted as graphics assistant

EDUCATION:
Bachelor of Arts, New York University, January 1983
Major: English Literature
Dean's List/Creative Writing Award

ACTIVITIES:
Member, American Women in Radio & Television
Member, Public Relations Society of America

## The Functional Resume

A functional resume focuses on functions, skills, and responsibilities. Instead of having job titles as headings, the resume is organized by functional titles that explain a general area of expertise.

Under each function heading, write a brief paragraph explaining your accomplishments in that area. The accomplishments don't have to be purely work-related; you can use examples from school and outside activities. Including company names and exact job titles in the descriptions is optional.

In a typical functional resume, dates are omitted. The emphasis is squarely on what you did, not when you did it. You can brush over gaps of time between jobs, length of time you have held jobs, and periods of unemployment.

## Strengths

You can tailor functional resumes to highlight the skills a particular job requires. Even if your job history doesn't strictly lend itself to the position you are applying for, a functional resume can help you bypass the problems of little or no formal work experience by concentrating on the knowledge you have acquired.

## Drawbacks

Because career counselors and books recommend functional resumes to cover up a spotty or unqualified job record, many employers red-flag them and immediately believe you are trying to hide something or cover up a weak employment background.

## Who Should Use It

Anyone who feels that showing dates would hurt their chances; frequent job switchers; people reentering the work force after many years; people who have been unemployed for a long period of time; people with little or no formal work experience.

## Who Should Avoid It

Almost anyone who can avoid using this style should do so, especially people who want to emphasize their employment stability to capitalize on the companies with which they have been affiliated.

## SAMPLE FUNCTIONAL RESUME

Karen Charles
227 East 27th St.
New York, NY 10017
(212) 222-1111

OBJECTIVE:  PUBLIC RELATIONS DIRECTOR for a television station, using my public relations experience, knowledge of television production, and managerial and administrative skills.

EXPERIENCE:

PUBLIC RELATIONS:  Manager of public relations for a top trade magazine publisher. Oversee all aspects of public and press relations for 15 publications and industrywide trade workshop. Designed and supervised promotion activities for successful trade workshop—resulting in heavier media coverage and a 28% increase in attendance. Improved market share 23% through introduction of innovative publicity campaign, based upon editorial roundtable forums and tie-ins with major industry events.

As public relations writer for the same publisher, wrote press releases, direct-mail brochures, and other promotional pieces.

Member of the Public Relations Society of America.

TELEVISION:  Producer of special inserts session for leading New York independent television station. Oversaw implementation of special effects and production techniques. Working knowledge of three-quarter-inch editing machines, character generator, and other television equipment. Field production and special segment production, including in-studio work.

Member of American Women in Radio & Television

ADMINISTRATION:  As public relations manager, supervise staff of 15. Coordinate and schedule all activities. $250,000 budget responsibility.

As research manager for the television station, oversaw research staff of three and directed them in all phases of newsroom research. Established all procedures for newly created information-services department. With news director, researched and purchased computer system for computerization of archives system.

EDUCATION:

Bachelor of Arts, New York University, January 1983
Major: English Literature
Dean's List
Creative Writing Award

## The Combination Resume

A combination resume uses elements of both the chronological and functional styles.

The bulk of a combination resume is functional, organizing your background by skills and function rather than by job title. A list of job titles and companies is given in reverse chronological order at the end.

This is the current hot resume style, recommended in articles and by career counselors, because it uses elements from both styles and crosses over well.

### Strengths

As with the functional resume, you can tailor an explanation of your job history to fit the job you're applying for. At the same time, you can show continuity in your job record.

### Drawbacks

Because descriptions of accomplishments are under functional headings, specific positions and titles are downplayed and specific job duties aren't spelled out. This can be confusing to the reader and can also look unwieldy—you have to take special care in layout.

### Who Should Use It

Career switchers who want to fit their past jobs to a different area; recent graduates with little formal work experience.

### Who Should Avoid It

People with strong, consistent experience in the same area as their objective; people who want to emphasize particular jobs and companies.

## BASIC COMBINATION RESUME

Karen Charles
227 East 27th St.
New York, NY 10017
(212) 222-1111

OBJECTIVE:  PUBLIC RELATIONS DIRECTOR for a television station, using my public relations experience, knowledge of television production, managerial and administrative skills.

SKILLS:

PUBLIC RELATIONS:

—As manager of public relations for a top trade magazine publisher, oversee all aspects of public and press relations for 15 publications and industrywide trade workshop.
—Designed and supervised promotion activities for successful trade workshop—resulting in heavier media coverage and a 28% increase in attendance.
—Improved market share 23% through introduction of innovative publicity campaign, based upon editorial roundtable forums and tie-ins with major industry events.
—As public relations writer for the same publisher, wrote press releases, direct mail brochures, and other promotional pieces.

TELEVISION:

—As producer of special inserts session for leading New York independent television station, produced news and feature pieces requiring special effects and production techniques.
—Extensive field production and special segment production experience, including in-studio debates and audience participation talk shows.
—Working knowledge of three-quarter-inch editing machines, character generator, and other television equipment.

ADMINISTRATION:

—As public relations manager, supervise staff of 15. Coordinate and schedule all activities. Profit and loss responsibility for $250,000 budget.
—As research manager for the television station, oversaw research staff of three and directed them in all phases of newsroom research.
—Established all procedures for newly created information-services department. With news director, researched and purchased computer system for computerization of archives system.

EXPERIENCE:

4/89–present    ABC Publications, Inc., New York, NY
                Manager of Public Relations
                Public Relations Writer/Project Associate

2/83–4/89    WYYY-TV, New York, NY
               Producer of News Inserts
               Research Manager
               Associate Producer
               Production Assistant

EDUCATION:
    Bachelor of Arts, New York University, January 1983
    Major: English Literature
    Dean's List
    Creative Writing Award

ACTIVITIES:
    Member:  American Women in Radio & Television
               Public Relations Society of America

## CONTENTS: THE CHIEF PARTS OF A RESUME

Regardless of format, a resume must cover certain areas of information. Those areas constitute the five key parts of a resume.

The length of each section, the information you include, and how you present it all depend on your background and objective.

### 1. Personal Data

Name, address, and telephone number.

These three basic facts are all your personal data section should contain; anything else is a waste of space. Don't bother with height, weight, marital status, or health. There is absolutely no reason to include any of those.

> **TIP: Put your name, address, and phone number in the upper *right-hand corner* instead of the middle of the page. When people flip through a stack of resumes, your name is immediately noticeable.**

### 2. Career Objective *or* Biographical Summary (Either Is Optional, but Recommended)

A brief summary of your immediate goals that targets your resume (with six lines the absolute maximum) or a brief summary of your achievements, skills, characteristics (60 words maximum).

Neither one of these is absolutely essential, but each is recommended. In both cases, these brief statements at the top of a resume can help you focus your resume, can help the prospective employer quickly get a feel for you, and, ideally, can help convince the prospective employer to read on. But while they may help accomplish the same thing and are located in the same spot on a resume, they're entirely different elements that work for different job hunters. Which one of the two you use depends upon your work experience.

If you're seeking your first job, are a recent graduate, or have limited job experience, you are probably better off using a *career objective*. If you have held numerous jobs and have a number of strong skills and achievements, plus a more extensive track record, opt for a biographical summary instead.

First, a quick look at a career objective: This is a statement designed to tell your target audience exactly what you're after. Many prospective employers flip through a stack of resumes, reading only the objectives. If there isn't an objective that grabs them, or there isn't an objective at all, they may scrap the resume.

In light of this: *Make it specific.* A general objective doesn't sell you; if anything, it weakens your resume. You should state succinctly *exactly* what you are looking for.

> **EXAMPLE:** *Objective:* **A position in human resources with a retailing company that will enable me to apply my 12 years of experience developing and overseeing training programs for retail management.**
>
> *Not:* **A position in human resources that will utilize my communications and business skills.**

Avoid mushy nonstatements like the second example. General phrases such as "utilize my business skills" mean nothing to a prospective employer. It comes across as if all you're doing is filling in the blanks. If the only objective you can come up with is this kind of bland statement, you're better off omitting the objective entirely.

You can skip the objective if you don't want to target your resume for a specific job. Also, if you have a well-grounded background that fits your job target and shows continuity and logical progression, you can omit a career objective without really worrying.

You should use a biographical summary instead if you're a more experienced job hunter—especially one with work experience you can brag about. Instead of a two-line statement explaining what you *hope* to do, you can write a statement telling what you *have* done—which will help convince prospective employers that you are a good choice for their company.

A biographical summary at the top of your resume should consist of several statements that clearly demonstrate your credentials or "fit" for the position you want. Even if you open with the job title you're aiming at, the focus is completely on your abilities.

In other words, unlike the "objective" the biographical summary does not describe the job you want. It describes what you can do.

As touched upon above, you can make your summary either a condensed sales message—in effect, a showcase for your strongest selling points—or a more targeted message, in which you name the position you're after, then follow up with the abilities you have that make you right for that position.

Here are two different ways of using the summary statement. In the first example, the resume writer is making the summary statement a condensed sales message—underscoring his achievements in a brief biographical sketch.

> **EXAMPLE: Extensive background as sales/marketing manager and as general manager, with P&L responsibility. Particular emphasis—improving cash flow and ROI, strengthening product lines, increasing inventory turns, turnaround situations, building organizations . . . and profits.**

In the second example, the same individual is taking much of the same information but focusing it slightly differently. He is making it a literal replacement of an "objective" statement by clearly pinpointing the position he's after and pulling up salient information from his resume to prove his credentials.

> **EXAMPLE: GENERAL MANAGER. Extensive background—improving cash flow and ROI, strengthening product lines, cutting costs, reducing inventory, building organizations . . . and profits.**
>
> **General Manager—P&L responsibility (two companies).**
>
> **Entrepreneur—organized $3 million company.**
>
> **Marketing Vice-President—$55 million company.**

As you can see, both types are, in effect, miniresumes—allowing the resume reader to quickly determine whether you fit his or her needs. This is why there is a danger to using summaries: Because you've (theoretically) put your strongest selling statement up front, the resume reader can decide whether you fit the bill *without* reading the rest of your resume. If you don't fit, you're out of luck.

The upshot? If you do write a summary, make sure it is as strong as it should be. If you're at all concerned or if you find you're unable to come up with a hard-hitting summary, drop it.

> **TIP: When writing summaries, be specific—for example, "Proven record of increasing market share," not "Successful marketing executive." Don't fall into vague statements that make you sound as if you have little to offer. Also avoid nonessentials, such as "highly motivated," or "success-oriented." What job seeker would say he wasn't?**

TIP: Because the summary is such a concentrated sales message, maximize the limited space by using sentence fragments, not complete sentences. Strip your language down to the bare bones. Rely on action words and descriptive lines to get your message across.

TIP: Write the rest of your resume *first,* then go back and write your summary. Often this will help shake loose the ideas you'll want to include in your summary.

## 3. Work Experience

Your past jobs and accomplishments arranged either by date or by function, depending on the format.

This is the real heart of a resume. The information you include and how you present it can make or break you. Take your time planning and writing your work history, always keeping your target audience and objective in mind. Tie your experience to your general objective.

If you've included a job objective on your resume, you *must* be able to back it up with the information in this section. Stress the achievements and jobs you've had that most underscore your ability to meet your objective. Take advantage of past experience that isn't directly linked to your objective by writing it up so that it relates *indirectly.*

EXAMPLE: A Houston morning talk-show producer wanted to make a move into the record industry. *Problem:* All of her work experience was exclusively in TV production. *Solution:* She played up the shows she had done about music, recording stars, and radio, emphasizing her interest in and knowledge of the field and supporting her objective.

EXAMPLE: A recent college graduate used his part-time job as a salesperson in a gourmet food shop to back up his ability to become an effective management trainee at a large industrial company. He explained that at the shop, he trained new personnel, managed it on weekday nights, oversaw the other part-time workers, and devised a new inventory system. Those specific examples demonstrated his ability to take on responsibility and stressed his innovative managerial skills—qualities that most management-training programs are looking for in new recruits.

*Where* you place certain facts about your work history can make a huge difference in how you are perceived. Use placement to emphasize the strongest aspects of your experience. Highlight the information that directly relates to your objective by positioning it prominently in your resume: at the top of lists or at the beginning of paragraphs.

In a chronological resume, emphasize your most recent job. List your accomplishments, your achievements, and your duties—four examples is a good number to aim for. A prospective employer will pay most attention to your recent achievements. The further you go into the past, the less information you should include—usually two or three key points are enough.

> **TIP: To make the work experience section of a chronological resume even more hard-hitting, write a brief paragraph that summarizes your responsibilities under each job title, *then* list three to four examples of specific achievements.**

You should apply the same general principle to a functional or combination resume. The function that is the most crucial to your objective should get the most detailed information; write less in the lesser function areas.

> **TIP: Don't stress the key areas of your experience (most recent job or strongest function area) at the expense of the rest of your work experience. If any part of your background looks sketchy, prospective employers become wary.**

## 4. Education
School, degree(s), year in which you earned your degree, major, any honors.

Generally speaking, the longer you have been out of school, the less space it should take on your resume. However, *if you're a recent college graduate or a student,* expand the education section by adding such information as dean's list, college activities, and awards. You can also include courses you think might stand in your favor. This works especially well if your major isn't directly applicable to your career objective, or if you have specific knowledge in another field that can enhance your candidacy.

**EXAMPLE: A young woman who was applying for an executive trainee position in retailing listed a few computer courses she had taken in college.** *Reason:* **She knew that buyer trainees had to use computers.** *Result:* **She was snapped up quickly.**

In addition, list education *before* work experience on your resume if you're a student or recent graduate seeking an entry-level position. Usually your work experience is limited, so prospective employers will place more weight on your educational background.

**TIP: If you were involved in a work/study program or co-op program, mention it briefly under "Education," but also include a description of the job itself under "Work Experience."**

**TIP: A phrase to include under education that impresses prospective employers is: "Earned XX% of college expenses." If you had a part-time, free-lance, or full-time job, you should add this phrase to your resume. It never fails to get a good reaction.**

## 5. Activities (Optional, but Recommended)

A brief list of outside activities, memberships, civic involvement, etc.

Don't write this category off as fluff. Extracurricular activities can play a big role in getting you an interview or a job. Not only do they differentiate your resume from others, making you come across as an individual, they can also strengthen your career objective.

Work-related activities underscore your expertise and professionalism. If you are a member of a trade or professional association, list it prominently. Also include any professional awards or honors you've received. If you've written any articles, you can list them here as well.

Be sure to list activities that reflect positive personal characteristics, such as volunteer work.

**TIP: Shy away from mentioning groups that are overtly political or controversial. The person reading your resume may have strong views—the opposite way.**

**TIP: List hobbies *only* if you have limited or no formal work experience and need to flesh out your skills and capabilities. If you have a few years of solid work experience to show, *don't* list hobbies, unless they mesh extremely well with the position you seek.**

*Note:* There should be *no* reference section in which you list the names of references—people who would speak in your favor. Except for very rare exceptions, there is absolutely no need to write out your references.

As for the common compromise, "References Available upon Request," don't bother. The person who reads your resume will assume you can provide the names of references if you're asked for them. There's no point in wasting space on the page saying so.

## WRITING A RESUME THAT SELLS

■ **The simplest way to begin drafting a resume is by making a resume worksheet, following the format you have chosen, and then filling it in.**

Start by listing your job duties. Flesh out your experience with summaries and examples of your accomplishments, skills, and abilities. This will give you a foundation upon which to build the substance of your resume and help you to organize your thoughts along the right lines. Always keep your job objective in mind, focusing on the qualities that a prospective employer would want for that job and how you can prove on paper that you have them.

At the same time, remember to play up the *general* qualities that employers like to see.

*Be sure to include:*

- examples of productivity/profit-mindedness

- patterns of accomplishment and upward movement

- examples that present you as a team player

- evidence of stability and direction

■ **Expect to write at least two drafts.**

The first draft will be your worksheet. Write more than you need, and don't worry much about phrasing and style. Cite as many examples and descriptions as you can. You can use the first draft as raw material and boil down the information to come up with the strongest facts to put in the final version. Edit with an eye to the reader and your job objective.

■ **Have friends and colleagues read and critique your resume.**

Make sure you have supported your objective, given enough specific information, and written clearly and interestingly.

> **TIP: Give your resume to someone in the same position as your career objective. That person will know what should be stressed and probably can give you some helpful advice.**

■ **One last point as you write, edit, and rewrite your resume: Don't forget that how you say something is as important as what you're saying.**

Someone with a weaker background can win an interview over someone more qualified, if that person is a better communicator. The key to writing a strong, effective resume is *presentation.*

Little things make a difference—length of sentences, the words you use to describe your experience, layout, and general appearance. Don't overlook anything. You want your resume to sell you, so make it as solid as possible in every way, from contents to presentation to appearance.

## FIVE BASIC GUIDELINES WHEN WRITING A RESUME

### 1. Be Brief

A resume should demonstrate your ability to communicate by summarizing and consolidating information clearly.

*Some guidelines:*

- Use short words. A resume isn't the place to demonstrate your impressive vocabulary. Avoid bureaucratese and jargon.

- If you have little experience or little to say, fine. Don't resort to puffery. When you puff up a resume, it shows.

- Use fragments instead of complete sentences. They read more quickly, take up less space, and force you to omit unnecessary words.

**TIP: Use bullets in the body of your resume to set off each piece of information under a heading.**

• Plunge right into your statements and avoid using "I." Say "Produced award-winning television commercials," not "I produced . . ." Everybody already knows you are the subject of the resume.

## 2. Be Specific

Try to come up with concrete *examples* of achievements rather than writing in terms of straight job duties or skills. Vague descriptions about your past jobs won't sell your experience effectively. Outlining specific results will. The more specific you are, the better you demonstrate your skills and accomplishments.

You want to underscore your ability to step into a job and begin producing results immediately. Listing the results you've already produced is the most convincing way to do this.

**TIP: Aim for ten specific accomplishments on your resume. This amount makes your background look solid.**

*Some guidelines:*

• Never include phrases such as "worked in a department that dealt with" or "worked for a company that." You should be specific about what *you* did, not what the company or department did.

• Avoid general comments such as "knowledge of," "helped with," "aided in." They make you sound like a nonachiever, someone who stood around and watched or lent an occasional hand.

• Whenever possible, use numbers or percents. Statistics stand out and make a resume look even more precise. Also, people are more inclined to believe numbers.

**EXAMPLE: Managed $2,000,000 procurement and supply budget and saved the company $250,000.**
**Supervised staff of 45.**
**Increased productivity 23%.**
*Note:* **Don't write out figures, especially when you are talking about money. Two hundred fifty thousand dollars doesn't jump off the page like $250,000 does.**

> **TIP:** If you are unsure about a number but still want to use one, avoid common numbers such as 50 or 100. Odd numbers sound less manufactured.

## 3. Be Active

Always use strong words that show action; avoid passive descriptions. Action words bring a resume to life. Most important, they make you seem like an achiever, a person who is a doer.

When you use action words in a resume, you underscore your skills and abilities subtly and succinctly. Certain words have the power to create a positive image, one that is implied as much as stated.

*Especially strong words . . .*

*. . . to emphasize your innovative and creative abilities:*

| | | | |
|---|---|---|---|
| conceived | devised | launched | produced |
| created | established | originated | set up |
| developed | initiated | planned | structured |

*. . . to emphasize leadership skills:*

| | | | |
|---|---|---|---|
| administered | delegated | headed | oversaw |
| authorized | directed | led | spearheaded |
| controlled | guided | managed | supervised |

*. . . to emphasize your contribution to productivity and growth:*

| | | |
|---|---|---|
| expanded | increased | strengthened |
| generated | | |

*. . . to emphasize efficiency and problem-solving skills:*

| | | |
|---|---|---|
| expedited | revamped | simplified |
| improved | revised | streamlined |
| reorganized | | |

*. . . and some good all-purpose words:*

| | | |
|---|---|---|
| completed | demonstrated | maintained |
| conducted | implemented | |

To further strengthen your resume, use strong adverbs and adjectives as modifiers. But use them sparingly. Too much descriptive language becomes annoying and looks slightly suspicious. If you overdo the glowing words, it looks as though you're trying too hard —and probably exaggerating.

*Some good modifiers to use are:*

| | | |
|---|---|---|
| actively | efficient | solid |
| comprehensive | far-reaching | strong |
| cost-effectively | innovative | substantially |
| dramatically | significantly | successfully |
| effectively | | |

> **TIP:** When you use a phrase such as "dramatically increased," be sure you include the figures or facts to back it up. Otherwise it may sound like an inflated claim.

## 4. Be Selective

Don't think that the more examples you list and the more information you pack into a resume, the more qualified you appear.

*Think* before you list job duties, skills, and accomplishments. Decide what aspects of your previous jobs apply to the position you want. By being selective, you target yourself and your resume more precisely.

Prospective employers want to determine your qualifications for a specific job. They don't want to wade through useless material to get to the pertinent information.

> **EXAMPLE:** "Able to build, motivate, and cultivate brilliance." This phrase, taken from an actual resume, is the type of comment you should cut to make room for concrete statements. The major problem—it isn't backed up with any specific examples. It also smacks of overstatement, something that adds nothing to the salability of the candidate.

If you clutter your resume with unimportant facts, examples, and claims of ability, you distract the reader from the information that sells you.

Focus only on the positive aspects of your background. Although you should be honest on your resume, you don't have to confess all.

## 5. Be Honest

Don't lie.

False statements and claims on your resume hurt more than they can help. At some point, your background may be checked or you may be asked to elaborate. Stick with the truth and you will have much less to worry about.

## PRESENTATION: THE RIGHT APPEARANCE

■ **A clear, readable typeface, cream, white, or off-white bond paper, and black print always look good.**

Stick with the basics and you can't go wrong. If possible, prepare your resume on a computer with a laser printer. It is less expensive than having it professionally printed because you don't need to order hundreds of copies. Instead you can print out as many as you need, when you need them. You can also update your resume whenever you want without doing as much retyping. If you don't have access to a computer, many word-processing services type, print, and store resumes for you.

Having your resume professionally printed is another option. It used to be the rule of thumb. This option has changed somewhat. It is still a good idea if you're planning to do a massive mailing—you don't have to print or run off hundreds of resumes yourself and you're assured of having resumes that are neat and professional looking. But there are drawbacks to having your resume typeset—it's costly to make changes; you usually have to order a large quantity; and people may think you're mounting a resume blitz. If you do decide to have your resume typeset, steer clear of anything but the standards in terms of paper color, typeface, and layout.

Whether you're doing it on your own or having it done professionally, remember that flashy layouts, colored paper, and ornate fonts are recommended *only* for creative positions. If you are applying to be an art director, an artist, or a photographer, and you feel the urge to show how clever you are with your resume, go ahead. But proceed at your own risk. Even in the creative fields, sometimes it is wiser to err on the side of conservatism. Your work should demonstrate how creative you are; your resume doesn't have to do that for you.

■ **Don't crowd information onto the page.**

Appearance is more than paper and type. It is also layout, an aspect of resume preparation that too many people downplay. Don't make that mistake—layout matters. If your resume is laid out poorly, people won't read it as carefully. Any artist will tell you that negative space is as important as positive space. *Translation:* Don't fill up the page with print. Leave space in between the major parts of the resume and between the paragraphs in those sections as well. There is nothing more difficult to read than a large unbroken block of text. It looks dull and threatening. Let your resume breathe.

## Length

■ **There are no hard-and-fast rules governing the length of a resume; make your resume as long as it has to be, no more and no less.**

Forget all the articles that say your resume *must* be two pages long or you *must* summarize 12 years' work experience in one page.

*A couple of qualifiers:*

- A resume should fill one page minimum. If you have little information to include, lay it out with a lot of spacing and wide margins.
- The trend is toward resumes more than one page long. Some career counselors say employers want to see more information than they need from prospective employees. But select your information judiciously and be sure it is relevant. Don't take this trend as an excuse to pad out a meager resume with extraneous details and data just so you can fill up space.

---

## SIX SPECIAL PROBLEMS AND HOW TO OVERCOME THEM

It can be difficult, but you can hide or disguise job-related problems on your resume. Following are six of the most common problems and what you can do about them.

### Problem #1: Being Labeled Overqualified

Two things on your resume can immediately flag you as being overqualified: too many jobs and too many *higher-level* positions.

To get around this problem, omit information on your resume and minimize the importance of certain jobs. The trick is to do both without undermining your qualifications.

*Some tips on how to do this:*

- Assess your background and determine what information is not crucial to support your career objective. Sometimes you can completely omit a few jobs—positions you held furthest in the past and lateral moves are safe cuts. *Remember:* You are trying to make your experience look like less than you actually have. The fewer positions you list, the less weighty your resume will seem.

- If you worked at the same company and received several promotions, combine two or more jobs into one. Don't bother listing each step.

- Picking up on job titles is a quick and easy way for a prospective employer to determine if you're overqualified. Don't give him or her the ammunition. Recognize which titles are triggers and replace them with equally descriptive but less imposing titles. For example, instead of referring to yourself as a vice-president, call yourself a department head.

- To avoid drawing attention to dates and job titles, use a combination or functional format. Focus on experience.

## Problem #2: Being Considered Too Old

Age discrimination is illegal in most cases—but it happens all the time. Sometimes otherwise ideal candidates are told they are "overqualified"; other times they are just not called back. To avoid the problem before it arises, consider *age-proofing* your resume.

*Try the following:*

- Adjust your resume accordingly by omitting or downplaying dates. Make certain to notice all the references to age in your resume: dates you attended school, dates you held jobs, military service, even the types of activities you list.

- Use a functional or combination format instead of chronological. If you prefer the chronological format, don't display dates prominently by setting them off. Bury dates in parentheses right after the job title. They'll attract less immediate attention.

- Eliminate mention of your earliest jobs. There is no point in advertising the number of jobs you have held, nor the number of years you have been working.

> **TIP: While we don't advocate lying, some people do knock a few years off their age. Warning: If you do that, be sure to be consistent. Take into account your spouse's age, your children's ages,**

how old you were when you graduated, and other important dates in your life. One man was convinced he had completely snowed his interviewer—he had dyed his hair, he knew his new (and more recent) year of birth, the revised date of his college graduation. But the interviewer looked a bit askance at him when he confidently blurted out the actual year of his wedding anniversary. Given his new age, he had apparently gotten married at the tender age of 14.

## Problem #3: Spotty Work Experience and Job Hopping/Jobs in Different Areas

Prospective employers often view spotty work experience as a negative signal: The person isn't a stable worker, can't hold a job, has no career direction.

You can fight against this perception. The key point in your favor is that despite your job hopping you do keep getting hired, so you must be doing something right. You want prospective employers to see the situation that way. Your resume should make them want to hear the reasons you changed jobs or career directions.

*Some ways of doing this:*

- If you held many jobs in a short time, use the combination or functional style resume to make the number of jobs and the duration of those jobs less obvious.

- Consolidate jobs under similar function headings or omit mention of certain jobs entirely. If you held a job for only a few months, feel free to drop it. Gaps of a few months don't look that questionable.

- Focus on achievements, but don't get carried away. If you held a job for only a short while, no prospective employer is going to believe you dramatically increased profits or turned around a failing division.

- Arrange your resume so that the reader can see a constant upward movement. You may have switched jobs, but you kept advancing.

- If you took a demotion, don't make it appear as such. Stress the different duties and different areas the job comprised.

- If you shifted career directions, emphasize the common bonds between the jobs you held in different fields. For example, if you went from retailing to computers, stress the computer literacy you needed to function as an assistant buyer. Downplay the non-computer functions.

## Problem #4: Odd Match Between Background and Objective

An employer has two chief concerns about a person attempting a career shift: Can this person's qualifications be applied to a different career, and is he or she committed to acquiring enough new knowledge to make it work?

When your experience is seemingly unrelated to your objective, you must figure out ways to convince a prospective employer that you have the qualifications and the background to fill the job.

By concentrating on the elements of your background that relate in any way to your job objective, you can skew your resume and present yourself as a strong candidate.

*Try the following:*

- Start by examining your past experience and recognizing any patterns in it that connect to your current job objective. Regardless of your primary duties, have all your jobs involved similar aspects—such as intense personal contact, communications skills, analytical ability? Did you volunteer to take on responsibilities outside of your job description, responsibilities that you can tie to your new objective? Play up anything that shows you have been interested in your objective for some time.

- Pay special attention to minor aspects of previous jobs that relate in any way to your new objective. Be creative in finding connections where it looks as if there are none.

    **EXAMPLE: You're trying to move into a sales position after having had experience as an audit accountant. Mention the extensive contact you have had with different kinds of people and how you have had to sell them on your presence in the company that was being audited.**

- In the descriptions of your jobs or functions, minimize or omit any specialized experience you can't tie to your objective.

- Stress leisure activities, even hobbies, that demonstrate your interest, abilities, or experience in your objective.

- Take continuing education or professional courses. Depending on the course, list under education or activities.

- Join professional associations and list them prominently. Even if you are a new member and have attended few, if any, meetings, it signals your interest in and commitment to this new field.

## Problem #5: Unemployed/Fired/Laid Off

Being unemployed when you're job hunting is a situation that is becoming more and more common and there is not the same stigma attached to it as there used to be. Still, problems exist. People often prefer to hire people who have jobs. It's not fair, but it's human nature: When a job candidate is holding a responsible position, prospective employers assume he or she is a solid, responsible person.

A well-designed resume can help you bypass some of the problems of being unemployed. It can hide your unemployed status or deemphasize it by focusing on your abilities and contributions to companies in the past.

*A few tips:*

- *Don't* explain on your resume why you were or are unemployed. Some people want to make sure prospective employers realize that they were laid off, not fired. They add a comment such as "Position was eliminated due to corporate cutbacks" at the end of a job description. This is a strategic error. Explanatory comments don't make you sound more qualified. If you feel the need to explain your present unemployment or any other gap in your record, do so in the interview or cautiously in a cover letter.

- In general, it's best to go with the combination or functional resumes. Either of these formats is more helpful when you're trying to concentrate on skills rather than dates and trying to make it less apparent that you're currently out of work.

- If you have a solid work record and you're looking for a job in the same general area, you *can* use the chronological format. Capitalize on your stability and consistency. These will outweigh your recent unemployment.

- Do free-lance or part-time work. Even if you only do a little, you can have a present job to put on your resume. For example, an unemployed attorney began taking on charity cases for no pay on a limited basis. That way, she could honestly state on her resume that she maintained a private practice.

- Ways to hide unemployment on your resume: 1) If you have a friend who owns his or her own business, ask if you can arrange a trade—you get a job title, he or she gets free assistance from you. This way you can legitimately list a job on your resume for the period in which you're unemployed. 2) If you left your last job on good terms, check with your employer to see if you can list the job as "current" on your resume.

## Problem #6: Reentering the Work Force

When you are reentering the work force after a short or long absence, your chief concern is to prove on paper that you have the right qualities and experience to fill a particular job—despite your time away.

Your resume must convince prospective employers that your employment gap hasn't affected your skills and ability to contribute and that you have maintained a level of professionalism.

One of the best ways to prepare a strong resume is to plan. Lay the groundwork for reentering the work force by becoming active *before* you start a formal job hunt. Keep abreast of developments in your field, join professional groups, recontact colleagues, take short courses.

*Some tips:*

- Begin by *honestly* assessing your background, paying special attention to the years you have been out of the job market. Think about everything in terms of marketability. Don't think that because you haven't held a formal job, you haven't had salable experience. Civic activities, leisure activities, hobbies, childcare— you can use any or all of them on your resume to show your abilities and experience.

- Use a functional or combination resume, so you can emphasize your abilities and nonwork experience as opposed to the time between your last formal job and the present.

- List on your resume any volunteer work you've done as if it were regular work. Be specific about duties and accomplishments.

- Include any brush-up courses or refresher courses you've taken.

- Be sure that you carefully target everything. Don't list activities just to prove that you've been active. If you can link only a few of them to your objective, fine. It's better to have a small amount of strong information, well presented and targeted, than lists of unrelated activities.

## RESUME EXAMPLES: BEFORE AND AFTER

To give you a clear sense of how to critique and evaluate your resume, what follows are some actual examples. We have commented on their strengths and weaknesses, then reworked them to make them as strong as possible.

# RESUME #1—BEFORE

<u>RESUME</u>

**[Comment: Titling the resume "RESUME" is absolutely unnecessary. The reader *knows* what this is. Omit.]**

Mark Wilson
129 Washington Street
Atlanta, GA
(404) 555-2222

Summary of Achievements

- designed the procedures for inventory control of components and finished products; implemented the system to reduce inventory costs.

**[Needs expansion—was the system successful? How much money was saved?]**

- coordinated and oversaw the regional implementation of a corporate obsolescence policy that resulted in a cost savings of over $250,000.

**[Good example—the dollar figure stands out.]**

- participated in "Administration Resources Seminars" and served on four integrated quality management teams.

**[All right, but would be better if it were explained what these programs/teams are.]**

**[Comment: The above section is a good place to emphasize the job hunter's top accomplishments, but it would be stronger if he began with a career objective statement, then used this summary to outline his strongest qualifications.]**

EXPERIENCE

May 1990     Tri-Lab Products, Inc., Duluth, GA
to Present
<u>Current Position</u>: Production Scheduling Supervisor, Production Control Department

Responsible for the supervision and coordination of scheduling the production of over 235 million pieces of consumer health products. Forecasting according to a "Just in Time" concept.

**[The information in this section is good, but it isn't presented as well as it could be. "Responsible for" deadens the section. Final statement needs clarification.]**

<u>June 1988 to April 1990</u>—Components Analyst/Scheduler, Production Control Department

**[Above date is buried, not consistent with the rest of the resume.]**

Responsible for the scheduling of all lines for a three-week sales cycle; planning and supervising a production group on a daily basis; expediting ingredients and components; organizing the obsolescence program.

**[Again, "responsible for" should go. Choice of verbs is good, but it would be better if they were in the active voice.]**

July 1987
to May 1988    Factors Walk Trading Co., Savannah, GA

Position: Export Assistant

Responsible for market research, product information, freight forwarding, and feasibility reports.

**[Because this job was not a recent one, the description can be this brief. But this needs work—action verbs, explanation of accomplishments.]**

August 1985
to June 1987    InfoNetwork, Inc., Atlanta, GA

Position: Researcher

Responsible for coordinating research study on consumer buying habits.

**[This should be put into the active voice.]**

**[Comment: Layout in this section needs work—job titles are buried, dates stand out more than company names or positions held. Job descriptions could be stronger.]**

EDUCATION
    Masters in Business Administration
        Emory University, Atlanta, Georgia
        Graduation: June 1989
        Major:   Industrial Management
        Thesis: "Just in Time" Inventory Management: Inventory and cost reduction through
                short-term integral planning

    Bachelor of Science
        Duke University, Durham, North Carolina
        Majors: Political Science and Economics
        Graduation: May 1985

**[Comment: Too much space given to above section. Layout could be consolidated.]**

REFERENCES
    Available upon request

**[Comment: Unnecessary section.]**

**General Comments About Resume #1**
**This isn't a bad resume—there are many strong things about it. But it could be much better.**
    **On the plus side: The writer has chosen good, specific examples of his achievements and has used numbers to underscore those examples. The "summary of achievements" section immediately points out his top accomplishments.**
    **The problems are chiefly layout and writing style. The layout is confusing and doesn't draw the reader to the most important information. The writing style could be punched up. The writer has taken several excellent examples and strong verbs and watered them down.**

## RESUME #1—REVISED

MARK WILSON
129 Washington Street
Atlanta, GA
(404) 555-2222

OBJECTIVE:  PRODUCTION/INVENTORY CONTROL MANAGER for a health & beauty aid
manufacturer

SUMMARY OF ACHIEVEMENTS
- designed and implemented inventory control system for health & beauty aid components and finished products, reducing inventory costs 21%
- coordinated and oversaw the regional implementation of a corporate obsolescence policy that resulted in a cost savings of over $250,000
- chosen by upper management to participate in "Administration Resources Seminars," and served on four integrated quality-management teams

EXPERIENCE
Production Scheduling Supervisor, Production Control Department
    Tri-Lab Products, Inc., Duluth, GA                                   (May 1990–present)
- supervise and coordinate production scheduling of over 235,000,000 pieces of consumer health products
- saved company over $110,000 in inventory costs by introducing "Just in Time" short-term planning method
- plan and forecast according to that method, maintaining minimum inventory and maximizing cost efficiency

Components Analyst/Scheduler, Production Control Department
    Tri-Lab Products, Inc., Duluth, GA                                  (June 1988–April 1990)
- scheduled all company product lines for a three-week sales cycle
- planned and managed production group on a daily basis
- expedited ingredients and components
- organized cost-saving obsolescence program

Export Assistant
    Factors Walk Trading Co., Savannah, GA                              (July 1987–May 1988)
- conducted market and product research surveys
- handled freight forwarding
- researched and prepared export feasibility reports

Researcher
    InfoNetwork, Inc., Atlanta, GA                                      (August 1985–June 1987)
- coordinated research study on consumer buying habits
- gathered and analyzed data

EDUCATION

  Masters in Business Administration
        Emory University, Atlanta, GA—June 1989
        Major: Industrial Management
        Thesis: "Just in Time" Inventory Management: Inventory and cost reduction through
              short-term integral planning

  Bachelor of Science
        Duke University, Durham, NC—May 1985
        Majors: Political Science and Economics

# RESUME #2—BEFORE

Veronica Carlin

| Permanent Address: | Temporary Address: |
|---|---|
| 208 Maple Avenue | 55 East 10th Street |
| Ridgewood, NJ 07450 | New York, NY 10003 |
| (201) 555-5555 | (212) 555-1234 |

OBJECTIVE          Application programming position with the opportunity for growth and advancement

**[Comment: A bit too general. Be more explicit about the kind of company; add a qualification statement.]**

OBJECTIVE

EDUCATION
9/91–Present

New York University
B.S. in Computer Science **[No abbreviation]**
Graduation Anticipated June 1995 **[Reword]**
Grade Point Average: In Major: 3.7/4.0
                              Overall: 3.5/4.0

**[Comment: Since this job hunter is still a student, this section belongs up top, but layout is poor.]**

WORK EXPERIENCE

Well-Known Computer Company                              Burbank, CA
   Programmer
      Summer Supplemental—1994
      —Using PL/I and IMS wrote software that generates and maintains a
        telecommunications network.
      —Tested software in test environment in which I had to modify and
        update a database.
      —The software I wrote and tested is now being produced.

Telecommunications Company                              Morristown, NJ
   Programmer
      Computer Science Internship—Fall 1993
      —Using SAS and RPF, wrote interactive software that simulates
        communication noise levels along power lines, and generates a table
        and graph for interpretation.

Electronics Co., Inc.                              New York, NY
   Summer 1993, Summer 1992
      —Office Clerical—Handled various office tasks including word
        processing and switchboard.

**[As phrased, this adds little to the resume. This should either be written to tie in with the objective and be presented as an example of the job seeker's work ethic, or be dumped.]**

[Comment: As this work history is set up, companies are highlighted and skills downplayed—a mistake. While the information given is specific and should be effective, this doesn't emphasize the job hunter's qualifications enough.]

## COMPUTER SKILLS

Hardware used:

| IBM 308X | IBM 370 | INTEL 8080 | VAX 785 |
|----------|---------|------------|---------|

Software used:

| ADA | ADF2 | APL | COBOL |
|-----|------|-----|-------|
| FORTRAN | IMS | JCL | LISP |
| MVS | PASCAL | PL/I | RPF |
| 360/370 ASSEMBLER | | 8080 ASSEMBLER | |

[An excellent addition to a technical resume and one that clearly shows the writer's expertise. Could be laid out to be more readable, but that is the only improvement this would need.]

## EXTRACURRICULAR ACTIVITIES

—member IEEE/ACM

[Comment: Mentioning trade association membership is a good idea, but this is buried under the long section heading. Writing out the association title would make it more prominent.]

## REFERENCES

Available upon request

[Comment: Again, a useless addition that does nothing for the resume.]

### General Comments About Resume #2

This is similar to many student resumes we've seen. The writer has made the mistake many people make: She follows a strict chronological format.

Because the job hunter is still a student her experience is limited to summer work, but her qualifications are quite strong. The resume would be much more effective arranged functionally, playing up her skills rather than the jobs she has held. Opening with a summary, followed by results-oriented highlights, then closing with a brief synopsis of the companies and dates would sell this job hunter more successfully.

## RESUME #2—REVISED

Veronica Carlin

Permanent Address:
208 Maple Avenue
Ridgewood, NJ 07450
(201) 555-5555

Temporary Address:
55 East 10th Street
New York, NY 10003
(212) 555-1234

OBJECTIVE
Application programming position in a computer or telecommunications company, giving me an opportunity for growth and advancement

EDUCATION
New York University
Bachelor of Science expected in June 1995
Major: Computer Science
Major Grade Point Average: 3.7
Overall Grade Point Average: 3.5
Earned 43% of tuition costs

EXPERIENCE
- Using PL/I and IMS, wrote software generating and maintaining a telecommunications network. Software is currently in production.
- Tested software in BTS test environment—requiring accessing, modification, and updating of database.
- Wrote interactive software using SAS and RPF, simulating communication noise levels along power lines and generating a table and graph, used by technical staff.
- Operated word-processing equipment and switchboard, and assisted office manager of an electronics company, to pay for college expenses.

| | |
|---|---|
| 1994 (summer) | Programmer <br> Well-Known Computer Company, Burbank, CA |
| 1993 (fall) | Programmer <br> Telecommunications Company, Morristown, NJ |
| 1992, 1993 (summers) | Office Assistant <br> Electronics Co., Inc., New York, NY |

## COMPUTER SKILLS

- Write and test software; working knowledge and experience in:

| | | | |
|---|---|---|---|
| ADA | ADF2 | APL | COBOL |
| FORTRAN | IMS | JCL | LISP |
| MVS | PASCAL | PL/I | RPF |
| 360/370 ASSEMBLER | | 8080 ASSEMBLER | |

- Hardware used:

| | | | |
|---|---|---|---|
| IBM 308X | IBM 370 | INTEL 8080 | VAX 785 |

## ACTIVITIES

Member, campus chapter of International Electrical and Electronic Engineering (IEEE).

## RESUME #3—BEFORE

CARL McMANUS    205 Wilshire Blvd.        Business: (213) 555-1234
                Los Angeles, CA 11111    Home: (213) 555-6789

**[Comment: Bad layout. Name doesn't stand out.]**

BUSINESS EXPERIENCE
L&B ADVERTISING—LOS ANGELES, CA 8/78–Present
>   Account Supervisor 9/89–present: Super Wine Coolers
>   —Manage strategic planning and execution for the multimillion-dollar, national introductory campaign of a new product line. This includes numerous duties, including market research and sales promotion activity.

**[This is his current position, yet he says next to nothing about it. Needs more description, more results.]**

>   Account Executive 8/82–9/89: A&A, Tip-Top, Suncool
>   —11/82–9/83: Managed A&A Inc. account, including successful introduction of A&A Aspirin and relaunch of A&A Cough Syrup. A&A's market share grew from 0.3% to 3.7% during this period.
>   —8/79–11/82: Responsible for both the Tip-Top hair-care and Suncool sun-care product lines. Accomplishments included the Suncool's tan accelerator new product introduction, the Tip-Top sweepstakes program, as well as development of direct response and gift-with-purchase promotions.

**[Could be punched up, made more active and results-oriented.]**

>   Assistant Account Executive 5/80–8/82
>   —Assisted on top national accounts including Tip-Top, Valkyrie Wine, Taylor's Toothpaste, SilkSense Hosiery.

**[Because this was in the past, this description should be brief.]**

KNIGHT & DAY ADVERTISING—LOS ANGELES, CA 8/76–5/80
Media Planner: Planned national broadcast and print advertising for Roast Beef Ranch, Sophisticated Lady Cosmetics, Vintage Wines, Amalgamated Chain Stores.

**[Format isn't consistent with above.]**

EDUCATION
1976    University of California at Berkeley
        Master of Science in Communications.
        Graduated 3.5 cume.
1974    University of California at Berkeley
        Bachelor of Arts in English/Sociology with honors.
        Graduated 3.6 cume.

1989–93   Selected to participate in advanced Agency Management Seminars
1988–91   Additional Graduate Courses: Public Relations, Sales Promotion, Business Writing

**[Could be tightened up. Grade-point average is unnecessary, because writer has been out of school for over a decade.]**

AWARDS AND HONORS
1976      Who's Who in American Universities and Colleges

**[Since there is only one "award and honor" and it isn't a professional award, this section should be omitted entirely.]**

## General Comments About Resume #3

**This job hunter is right in choosing a chronological format: it effectively shows off his stable work history and consistently upward movement.**

**The overriding problem with this resume is that his current job description is *much* too brief. In general, the writer has relied too much on listing account names and too little on outlining results-oriented accomplishments.**

**The layout is confusing, cluttered, and inconsistent, making it difficult for the reader to get through and digest the information.**

## RESUME #3—REVISED

CARL McMANUS
205 Wilshire Blvd.
Los Angeles, CA 11111
(213) 555-6789

EXPERIENCE:

<u>L&B Advertising</u>, Los Angeles, CA

1989–present ACCOUNT SUPERVISOR: Super Wine Coolers
- Managed strategic planning and execution of successful $18 million, national introductory campaign of new product line.
- Designed and coordinated multimedia consumer and trade promotions, market research, and extensive sales promotion—winning 3.4% share of market for product.
- Extensive client interaction, resulting in agency retaining the account despite outside agency competition.

1982–1989  ACCOUNT EXECUTIVE: A&A, Tip-Top, Suncool
- Oversaw successful relaunch of A&A cough syrup and introduction of A&A aspirin—during which A&A's market share grew from 0.3% to 3.7%.
- Directed Suncool tan accelerator national roll-out, planned and implemented the Tip-Top sweepstakes program, and developed Tip-Top direct response and gift-with-purchase promotions.

1980–1982  ASSISTANT ACCOUNT EXECUTIVE
- Assisted on top national accounts including Tip-Top, Valkyrie Wine, Taylor's Toothpaste, SilkSense Hosiery.

<u>Knight & Day Advertising</u>, Los Angeles, CA

1976–1980  MEDIA PLANNER
- Planned national broadcast and print advertising for Roast Beef Ranch, Sophisticated Lady Cosmetics, Vintage Wines, Amalgamated Chain Stores.

EDUCATION:

<u>University of California at Berkeley</u>
1976        Master of Science in Communications
1974        Bachelor of Arts in English/Sociology, with honors
1988–91     Additional graduate courses in: Public Relations, Sales Promotion, Business Writing
1989–93     Selected by supervisors to participate in advanced Agency Management Seminars

## RESUME #4—BEFORE

Leonard Paulsen
79 West 84th Street
New York, NY 10000
(212) 555-9999

OBJECTIVE:  General Manager
Extensive background—improving cash flow and ROI, strengthening product lines, cutting costs, reducing inventory, building organizations . . . and profits.
- General Manager—P&L responsibility
- Entrepreneur—organized $3 million company
- Marketing Vice-President—$55 million company

**[A good idea—combining objective with statement of qualifications in this way—but the objective is too general (general manager of what type of company?).]**

GENERAL MANAGER
U.S. subsidiary of major European multiproducts company (1979 to date)
P&L responsibility of $21 million division, reporting to President. Direct 40 people thru controller, sales warehouse, and service managers.
Products: Mopeds, bicycles, accessories

**[Good, brief summary of job responsibilities. But slang spelling "thru" is jarring.]**

- Established new U.S. market for mopeds thru comprehensive marketing and service program for the now-leading (and highest-priced) moped. Increased sales from 18,000 to 32,000 units, for 34% market share and 36% rise in profit contribution.
- Positioned company as significant new factor in bicycle business; changed supply sources, developed new product line, and created dealer sales programs. Sales jumped from 21,000 low-price units to 33,000 high units, with 31% increase in profitability.
- Cut number of warehouses from 5 to 2, without decrease in customer service and with $256,000 expense savings.
- Saved $110,000 in telecommunications costs and reduced waiting time on dealer calls from 9 to less than 1½ minutes at season peak.

**[This example doesn't come off well. It sounds as if the writer is trying too hard.]**

**[Comment: In general, a strong section. Good use of action verbs, numbers, and specific examples.]**

VICE-PRESIDENT, MARKETING
American Container Corporation, New York, NY (1973–1978)
Responsible for marketing strategies and sales programs of $55-million multiproducts company, reporting to President. Products: Garden products, sporting goods, apparel, specialty chemicals:

- As acting General Manager, improved market share of sporting goods company during poor market period. Reduced excess inventories. Set up new distribution system; prepared new catalogues; secured product publicity and set up successful consumer sweepstakes.
- Increased high-profit garden products company sales 18%, at lower selling expense. Repositioned product line, developed new products, redesigned packaging, and revised price structure. Established new sales organization.
- Turned around earnings of apparel company $1.3 million, despite poor market. Prepared business plan, trained sales manager, and developed two-tier sales organization and key-account sales program.
- Created innovative corporate-wide business planning system to enable divisions to prepare objectives-oriented action programs that could be monitored. Introduced inventory management program that cut inventory $900,000.

**[Comment: Again, generally well-written, but it gets a bit verbose. A few examples could be cut without weakening the effect.]**

GENERAL MANAGER

Bright Lights, Inc., New York, NY (1971–1973)

P&L responsibility of $5 million company, reporting to Group Vice-President. Directed 90 people thru two factory managers, controller, and two sales managers. Products: Lighting fixtures, home furnishings.

- Reversed long-term profit decline and loss, to profit. Slashed inventory 19%, cut product line 44%, with 5% sales increase from better balanced inventory. Negotiated union agreement and achieved cooperation during wage-control period.
- Repackaged profitable but slow-moving product line for first-year 77% sales increase, to $800,000. Established separate organization to capitalize on this opportunity. Product is an accepted leader.

VICE-PRESIDENT, OPERATIONS/MARKETING

Innovation Corporation, New York, NY (1968–1971)

As cofounder of $3 million multiproducts company, responsible for selected operations and all sales, reporting to President. Directed 30 people thru operations manager and 12 sales representatives thru two sales managers. Products: Furniture, boats, and marine accessories.

- Stemmed losses of $1.8 million boat company, as acting General Manager. Renegotiated financing; operated company on cash flow. Improved margins 9% with smaller factory force and sales organization.
- Improved furniture company margins by redirecting shift in product mix.
- Negotiated acquisition of two companies, as principal, and secured $715,000 working capital financing.

PRINCIPAL MANAGEMENT CONSULTANT

Avaco Services, Inc., New York, NY (1960–1968)

Responsible for management consulting projects in North America, Europe, and Middle East for leading management consulting organization. Directed four consultants. Products: Paints, plastics, packaged foods, construction materials, electronic components, real estate.

- Identified $10 million market for packaged food company and developed market-entry plans; secured 8% share in first year at targeted profit.
- Initiated plan to establish sales effort in $400 million market for construction company; firm is a leader in this market.
- Revised paint marketing and plant expansion program, for $1.2 million savings.

EDUCATION   M.B.A., New York University
            B.A., New York University

[Comment: Job hunter omitted dates purposefully—to avoid drawing attention to his age. But since preceding information is so dense, this section leaps out as sparse. It needs to be laid out differently to avoid drawing attention.]

PERSONAL   Married, 2 children
           Excellent health

[Comment: Personal section is unnecessary. Adds nothing to resume.]

## General Comments About Resume #4

A very strong resume and one that works well to sell the job hunter. It is a good example of a longer-style resume, one that leaves little information to the reader's imagination.

*Note:* Although this is technically a chronological resume, the writer has buried the dates in parentheses, drawing more attention to his experience and achievements and downplaying actual time. This works especially well for job switchers, career changers, and older job hunters who wish to avoid a functional resume but brush over time as much as possible.

To make this resume stronger, all it needs is fine-tuning and polishing. A clearer objective, the deletion of a few excessive descriptions, and the addition of one or two words—and the resume would be highly effective.

# RESUME #4—REVISED

Leonard Paulsen
79 West 84th Street
New York, NY 10000
(212) 555-9999

OBJECTIVE: GENERAL MANAGER for a multiproducts company
Extensive background—improving cash flow and ROI, strengthening product lines, cutting costs, reducing inventory, building organizations . . . and profits.
· General Manager—P&L responsibility
· Entrepreneur—organized $3 million company
· Marketing Vice-President—$55 million company

## EXPERIENCE:

### GENERAL MANAGER
U.S. subsidiary of major European multiproducts company (1979 to date)
- P&L responsibility of $21 million division, reporting to President. Direct 40 people through controller, sales warehouse, and service managers. Products: Mopeds, bicycles, accessories.
- Established new U.S. market for mopeds through comprehensive marketing and service program for the now-leading (and highest-priced) moped. Increased sales from 18,000 to 32,000 units—a 34% market share and 36% rise in profit contribution.
- Positioned company as significant new factor in bicycle business; changed supply sources, developed new product line, and created dealer sales programs. Sales jumped from 21,000 low-price units to 33,000 high units, with 31% increase in profitability.
- Decreased expenses $256,000 by cutting warehouses from 5 to 2 with no decrease in customer service; saved $110,000 in telecommunications costs.

### VICE-PRESIDENT, MARKETING
American Container Corporation, New York, NY (1973–1978)
Developed and managed marketing strategies and sales programs of $55 million multiproducts company, reporting to President. Products: Garden products, sporting goods, apparel, specialty chemicals.
- As acting General Manager, improved market share of sporting goods company during poor market period. Reduced excess inventories. Set up new distribution system; prepared new catalogues; secured product publicity and set up successful consumer sweepstakes.
- Increased high-profit garden products company sales 18%, at lower selling expense. Repositioned product line, developed new products, redesigned packaging, and revised price structure. Established new sales organization.
- Turned around earnings of apparel company $1.3 million, despite poor market. Prepared business plan, trained sales manager, and developed two-tier sales organization and key account sales program.

- Created innovative corporate-wide business planning system to enable divisions to prepare objectives-oriented action programs that could be monitored. Introduced inventory management program that cut inventory $900,000.

## GENERAL MANAGER

Bright Lights, Inc., New York, NY (1971–1973)

P&L responsibility of $5 million company, reporting to Group Vice-President. Directed 90 people through two factory managers, controller, and two sales managers. Products: Lighting fixtures, home furnishings.

- Reversed long-term profit decline and loss, to profit. Slashed inventory 19%, cut product line 44%, with 5% sales increase from better balanced inventory. Negotiated union agreement and achieved cooperation during wage-control period.
- Repackaged profitable but slow-moving product line for first year 77% sales increase, to $800,000. Established separate organization to capitalize on this opportunity. Product is an accepted leader.

## VICE-PRESIDENT, OPERATIONS/MARKETING

Innovation Corporation, New York, NY (1968–1971)

As cofounder of $3 million multiproducts company, managed selected operations and all sales, reporting to President. Directed 30 people through operations manager, and 12 sales representatives through 2 sales managers. Products: Furniture, boats, and marine accessories.

- Stemmed losses of $1.8 million boat company, as acting General Manager. Renegotiated financing; operated company on cash flow. Improved margins 9% with smaller factory force and sales organization.
- Improved furniture company margins by redirecting shift in product mix.
- Negotiated acquisition of two companies, as principal, and secured $715,000 working capital financing.

## PRINCIPAL MANAGEMENT CONSULTANT

Avaco Services, Inc., New York, NY (1960–1968)

Handled management consulting projects in North America, Europe, and Middle East for leading management consulting organization. Directed four consultants. Products: Paints, plastics, packaged foods, construction materials, electronic components, real estate.

- Identified $10 million market for packaged food company and developed market-entry plans; secured 8% share in first year at targeted profit.
- Initiated plan to establish sales effort in $400 million market for construction company; firm is a leader in this market.
- Revised paint marketing and plant expansion program, for $1.2 million savings.

EDUCATION:  Master of Business Administration, New York University
Bachelor of Science, Business Administration, New York University

# 3 *Research*

## INTRODUCTION

Research is one aspect of job hunting that everyone knows about, but most people could do it better. The typical problem is that too many people don't realize how many ways they can use research to help them find a job. It's much more than just compiling a list of business names and addresses or reading articles about a company before an interview.

Done correctly, research can assist you in every step of your job hunt: from writing a more targeted cover letter, to knowing key information that you can bring up during an interview, to laying the groundwork for effective networking. You can even find out about the existence of jobs where you thought there were none. In short, research is a way of making yourself more successful. It gives you the information you need to sell yourself effectively.

## USING RESEARCH TO STRENGTHEN YOUR JOB HUNT

You can strengthen your job hunt in seven vital areas through research.

Too many people walk into a library, collect a few company names and addresses, and walk out, convinced they've done enough research. They're making a mistake. Research can broaden your job hunt and increase your potential for landing a job.

*You should use research to:*

1. *Determine in advance which companies are good prospects and which aren't.* Although this is an obvious use for research, it's not often approached correctly. By reading articles in trade publications, talking with people at the company, reading corporate public relations literature, even by checking Who's Who directories and reading about the managers, you can get a good picture of the people and the company you might want to work for.

   The questions to answer: *Does this company have job openings in my area? Does it plan to have any in the future? Can I create a job? In* short: *Is this company a viable target?*

2. *Position yourself more precisely toward a company/industry/objective.* From day one in your job hunt, you will need to target yourself. The only way of doing that accurately is by knowing the particulars of a company's or an industry's goals, and then applying them to your own.

   The questions to answer: *What are recent trends or developments in the industry or company, and how can I use them to sell myself? Who is the ideal candidate, and how do I match up? Is my objective a realistic one?*

3. *Help sell yourself in an interview or letter.* This is one of the biggest payoffs of thorough research. It will help you take the general targeting information a step further and apply it directly to your letters, resumes, and interviews. By finding out about a company's management style, recent events and developments, and its policies and outlook *before* you contact them, you can increase your chances of fitting their criteria. You can refer to up-to-date information in your cover letter, skew yourself to match a company's style, anticipate their needs, and ask questions of an interviewer that will show off your knowledge.

   The questions to answer: *What in my background should I emphasize and what should I play down? How should I present myself, either in person or on paper?*

4. *Expand your list of potential employers.* A simple proposition, but one that's ignored by many job hunters. All it requires is an open mind. When you assemble a mailing list, take a few extra moments to check out related industries or companies. When you are reading

about a specific company or industry, make note of other companies, competitors, or ones in related fields. Through research, you might find job openings that fit your objective in companies or industries you hadn't considered.

The questions to answer: *What other industries hire people with my background? Have I overlooked any potential employers? How can I apply my work experience and/or educational background to different fields or companies?*

5. *Discover opportunities in the hidden job market.* This is one of the most rewarding outcomes of effective research: finding out about jobs before they are announced and, in effect, getting a jump on any other candidates. By following industry and company news and reading between the lines, you can pick up clues that can mean a job in the offing. Be on the lookout for information on impending mergers, proposed expansions, relocations. Take notice of items on a smaller scale: personnel moves, promotions, and the like. When someone is promoted, his or her old job may still be available. Also, a newly hired manager may want to hire new staff members to create his or her own "team."

The questions to answer: *Will jobs be opening up? Can I meet a specific need that will come up as a result of the company's move/merger/reorganization/expansion?*

6. *Create a job opening or position.* This requires more insight and more thought, but the rewards can be far-reaching. Relying mainly on trade publications, newspapers, and general business magazines, you can follow the news of a particular company or industry, read about its trends and developments, and put yourself in a position to *create* a job. A company that is relocating may need someone to scout out real estate; a company that is cutting back staff may hire an outplacement counselor; an expanding company may need someone to design training programs.

The questions to answer: *In what ways could my background fill a need of theirs? What evidence is there that the company needs a new position? How can I sell the company on both the position and myself.*

7. *Lay a foundation for networking.* Research can make it easier to set up a network of contacts. By checking directories, you can find out the names and locations of trade organizations; reading current trade journals can give you the names of the reporters who cover the industry, the people in your field who contribute articles or are interviewed, and the industry movers and shakers; reading re-

gional newspapers can give you the names of influential people in the immediate area. The possibilities are numerous and the effort required is minimal.

The questions to answer: *What trade associations are in my field, and how can I contact them? What trade events, conventions, or conferences are upcoming? How can I meet employees from the company that interests me? Who are the most prominent people in my objective position, and how can I reach them? Who can introduce me to people in hiring positions?*

You can accomplish all of the above by relying on a few simple sources: the *library,* your *computer, trade associations,* the *companies* that interest you themselves, and even *friends and colleagues.*

The trick, of course, is knowing what to look for in each of these sources of research information to meet your needs. The rest of this chapter will identify the research tools to seek out, the specific techniques you can use, the kind of information you can get, and the ways to apply it to your job hunt.

■ **Let's start with the basics, with a quick rundown of the research tools you'll be using—directories, trade publications and other business periodicals, computer databases, company material (annual reports, media kits, etc.), and more.**

Following is a brief discussion of these and other tools, lists of the most useful sources in each category, and tips on how best to use them.

## DIRECTORIES

■ **Directories—reference books of lists (or CD-ROMs of these books) —are a great, quick-and-easy source for finding the basic information you'll need in different phases of your job hunt.**

Directories are easily available, straightforward, and comprehensive. They're also an excellent starting point for researching your job hunt. They will help you to:

• *Contact companies.* With directories, you can pull together a resume mailing list by finding the company names, addresses, phone numbers, and even names of key executives.

- *Learn about networking possibilities and more.* You can get the names and addresses of trade associations as well as information on conventions and other professional and networking organizations and events—all of which can help you with job leads.

- *Find information to target your cover letter or use in an interview.* You can find financial statistics on companies, even biographical information on top executives in a company that will be interviewing you.

Most public libraries have the major directories you can use. In addition, some online services offer you access to several top directories.

There are a number of different directories you can use in your job hunt—corporate directories, which list major U.S. companies; state directories, which list companies in a particular state; industry-specific directories, which list companies in a specific industry; and more. In the following pages, we've run through the major directories you might use.

But first, a quick note: If you don't know the name of a specific directory you need or if you want to get a better idea of the many different directories that are available to you, your first step should be looking in a "directory of directories"—which, as you'd expect, is a directory that lists the names and publishers of thousands of other directories. One of the best:.

> *Directories in Print*
> Gale Research, Inc.
> 835 Penobscot Bldg.
> Detroit, MI 48226-4094
> 800/877-GALE
> Fax: 313/961-6083
> —This huge directory lists thousands of *other* directories and is available at virtually every public library. However, two things to be aware of: Information is often outdated. Be sure to check when the directory they're referring to was printed —generally speaking, you don't want to use anything over a year old. Second, in this publication, books that include lists are considered directories—and for your purposes, they're really not. Read the descriptive material carefully.

■ **If you want to use directories to put together a mailing list of companies, then you should look for *corporate directories*.**

Corporate directories will give you general information on thousands of leading corporations—addresses, phone and fax numbers, names of key executives, brief financial summaries, branch offices, number of employees, and the like.

> **TIP:** Many corporate directories offer indexing by SIC (Standard Industry Classification) codes (listed in the front of most directories) and by geographical location (state or Zip code). This can help you save time—by looking in the index, you can quickly see the companies that meet your needs.

> **TIP:** Whenever possible, doublecheck directory information—names, addresses, and telephone numbers. Even if the directory is marked 1995, the information in it is already a year old. Companies change addresses, merge with other companies, even go belly-up.

> **TIP:** Many directories offer their data on computer disks. This may be a help if you're planning to do your direct-mail campaign on computer. You can import names and addresses from the disk into your word-processing program and do a mail merge.

Here's a listing of some of the most useful (and most common) corporate directories that can help you put together a basic mailing list. These are *general* business directories, which means they list a wide range of different companies, not those in any one industry or state. They're best suited for people who want to apply to larger companies, or who are planning a broad job search.

One important point: In most cases, these directories are very expensive, often costing about $1,000. So you'll probably be using these in your library, either in hard copy or on CD-ROM, instead of buying them. Some of them, however, are available online. Check your online service to see if you can access any of them.

Some of the most helpful corporate directories are:

> *Dun's Million Dollar Directory*
> Dun's Marketing Services
> 3 Sylvan Way
> Parsippany, NJ 07054
> 800/526-0651
> —At virtually every library and also available online and on CD-ROM, *Dun's Million Dollar Directory* lists over 160,000 businesses—includes name, address, phone number, key executives, financial statistics. Often more useful than the below-listed *S&P* because it includes smaller companies, subsidiaries of companies, etc. One problem—corporate names are often abbreviated. If you use this, always call for the complete name of the company.

*Standard & Poor's Register of Corporations, Directors and Executives*
Standard & Poor's Corp.
25 Broadway
New York, NY 10004
212/208-8702
—Another library standard and also available on CD-ROM, the *S&P* consists of three volumes covering over 50,000 firms. Listings include brief financials, names, addresses of major executives, directors, new firms, etc. The key problems with using this to put together a resume mailing list—the *S&P* often only lists headquarters addresses, contains only major incorporated companies, and *doesn't* contain listings for subsidiaries or private companies.

*Ward's Business Directory of U.S. Private and Public Companies*
Gale Research, Inc.
835 Penobscot Bldg.
Detroit, MI 48226-4094
800/877-GALE
Fax: 313/961-6083
—Not at every library, but one of the best for job hunters, this covers over 107,000 businesses listed alphabetically and includes ranked listings with addresses—making it very handy to quickly pull together a mailing list.

*Corporate Yellow Book*
Monitor Publishing Company
104 Fifth Avenue, 2d Floor
New York, NY 10011
212/627-4140
—A good choice if you're targeting major public corporations and are thinking about buying a directory, this cost only $235 in 1994. Why is this a good bet? It lists over 38,000 executives and includes their *direct dial phone numbers*—a nice time-saver and a great way of contacting prospective employers.

*Standard Directory of Advertisers: Classified Edition*
National Register Publishing Co.
Reed Reference Publishing
121 Chanlon Rd.
New Providence, NJ 07974
708/256-6067
—The "Red Book," as it is usually called, lists companies that spend $75,000 or more a year on advertising. Given this slant, it includes names of advertising, marketing, and sales execs. Also includes an index of brand names.

> **TIP: If you're planning a resume mailing chiefly to well-known companies, you may want to use a less expensive alternative to getting addresses.** *The National Directory of Addresses and Telephone Numbers* **(Gale Research, Inc., 835 Penobscot Bldg., Detroit, MI 48226-4094, 800/877-GALE, Fax: 313/961-6083) has addresses and phone numbers of thousands of companies. A great inexpensive source of addresses and numbers that can save you library time.**

If you're planning to target *private* companies, check the directory listed below, as well.

*Directory of Leading Private Companies*
Reed Reference Publishing
121 Chanlon Rd.
New Providence, NJ 07974
800/323-6772

■ **There are other types of corporate directories that may be better focused for your job hunt, depending upon your specific needs.**

In some cases, the general corporate directories listed above may be a little *too* general for your job hunt. If you think that's the case, here's a brief rundown of corporate directories that are a little more focused.

If you're chiefly interested in manufacturing companies, check:

*Moody's Industrial Manual*
Moody's Investor Service
99 Church St.
New York, NY 10007
212/533-0300
—This lists about 3,000 publicly traded U.S. and international companies. (Moody's also puts out manuals for: Banking and Finance, Public Utilities, Transportation, Municipals.)

*Thomas Register of American Manufacturers*
Thomas Publishing Co.
1 Pennsylvania Plz.
New York, NY 10119
212/695-0500
—A 12-volume directory set that lists virtually all U.S. manufacturers—not only those publicly traded. A plus: It also lists products and product lines.

On the other hand, if you're after a job in the service industries, check:

> *Dun's Directory of Service Companies*
> Dun's Marketing Services
> 3 Sylvan Way
> Parsippany, NJ 07054
> 800/526-0651
> —This covers a range of service industries, including management consulting, executive search services, public relations, engineering and architecture, accounting, auditing and bookkeeping, health services, legal and social services, research, hospitality, motion picture, amusement and recreational services.

If you're thinking more about international jobs, you should check the following:

> *American's Corporate Families and International Affiliates*
> Dun's Marketing Services
> 3 Sylvan Way
> Parsippany, NJ 07054
> 800/526-0651
> 201/455-0900
> —This directory covers 1,700 U.S. companies and their 13,000 foreign subsidiaries, as well as 6,000 U.S. subsidiaries of international companies.

> *International Corporate Yellow Book*
> Monitor Publishing Co.
> 104 Fifth Avenue, 2d Floor
> New York, NY 10011
> 212/627-4140
> Fax: 212/645-0931
> —Covering the world's top 1,000 companies, this directory lists names of executives, direct dial phone numbers, etc.

> *International Directory of Corporate Affiliations*
> Reed Reference Publishing
> 121 Chanlon Rd.
> New Providence, NJ 07974
> 800/323-6772
> —This includes listings on U.S.-based subsidiaries of foreign companies and international subsidiaries of U.S. companies.

To get addresses and more on smaller companies, check *Dun's Million Dollar Directory* (listed above).

Finally, there are some other fairly general directories that may fit into your job hunt:

*Directory of Corporate Affiliations*
Reed Reference Publishing
121 Chanlon Rd.
New Providence, NJ 07974
800/323-6772
—This covers divisions and subsidiaries of 4,000-plus companies. Listings include financial statistics, officers, and—a plus for putting together a mailing list—names of officers at the divisions and subsidiaries.

*Dun's Business Rankings*
Dun's Marketing Services
3 Sylvan Way
Parsippany, NJ 07054
800/526-0651
—This is a compilation of ranked lists, by industry. The top 7,500 companies (both public and private) are ranked by sales and by employee number. Includes address, phone, etc., but doesn't include executives.

*Dun's Career Guide*
Dun's Marketing Services
3 Sylvan Way
Parsippany, NJ 07054
800/526-0651
—Another of Dun's guides, this lists employers, hiring areas, contact names, etc., arranged by state. A key problem—information is often overly general. For example, when listing the areas in which a company hires, this guide will list virtually every general business category—from accounting to administration to sales—which makes it not as helpful as one would hope. In addition, many large employers aren't included—making the state listings incomplete. Even so, it's worth a quick look if you've got the time.

■ **If you want to focus your job search on a specific geographical region or state, you probably will benefit from using** *state directories.*

As you probably can guess, state directories can help you put together mailing lists for a specific state. They're particularly handy if you're planning to relocate to another state and need to pull together an extensive list of companies, if you're targeting your job hunt by region, and if the companies you intend to contact *aren't* large enough to be included in the standard Dun's or Standard & Poor's type of directory.

You'll find state directories in the business sections of larger public libraries. Or if you're planning a very large mailing and would save time by owning a state directory, you can buy one—prices are often relatively low, typically from $45 to $200, depending upon the state and the number of companies contained. To make this simpler for you, we've listed most state directories in the Appendix, pages 351–377.

One problem: Many state directories focus only on manufacturing companies, an obvious drawback if you're targeting service companies. However, a number of directory companies put out service directories as well as manufacturing directories.

Some of the larger directories offer regional breakdowns or geographical indexing. In addition, some of them put out regional directories. One of these, at many libraries, is:

> *Dun's Regional Business Directory*
> Dun's Marketing Services
> 3 Sylvan Way
> Parsippany, NJ 07054
> 800/526-0651
> —This directory consists of different volumes covering different regions of the United States. It's a handy guide for quick regional information.

■ **For information about a *specific* industry, avoid the corporate directories and go straight to the industry-specific directory for your field.**

Industry-specific directories are a great way to quickly get information on companies that are only in the field you're interested in. For example, if you're looking for a job with a public relations firm, you could read *O'Dwyer's Guide to Public Relations* and get the names and addresses of most of the major PR agencies in the United States. For retailing, you'd look at *Fairchild's Financial Manual of Retail Stores*. And so on. In fact, industry-specific directories are available for virtually every industry—from advertising to biotech, from candy manufacturers to wholesale drugstores.

As with corporate directories, you can use these directories to put together a list of target companies and can also use them to get the names of contacts and to find out basic information about an industry or target company—financial statistics, number of employees, etc.

Another plus: Industry-specific directories often contain text about the industry, and sometimes contain forecasts or analyses that can help you understand where the industry is headed and information and listings on related industries and on associations.

As with most other directories, you can find many leading industry directories in the business section of the library, or check *Directories in Print,* listed above, or other directories of directories.

> **TIP: Many trade publications put out an annual directory or data book that lists top companies (sometimes with addresses). These are especially helpful because of the text that often accompanies these lists—roundup articles that talk about the different companies, sidebar articles that discuss up-and-comers, etc. In addition, you usually can buy these directories direct from the publisher at a fairly low cost. Call the specific trade publications for information.**

> **TIP: Use industry-specific directories to find fields and areas *related* to your target industry—suppliers, companies that service the industry, etc. These may give you employment targets you hadn't thought of.**

See the Appendix, pages 322–351, for lists of directories in twenty-seven different industries.

■ *Biographical directories*—which contain brief bios of corporate executives—are good sources for information for preinterview prepping and for better targeting yourself to a company, in general.

Biographical directories may give you background information on the executive who will be interviewing you. What can you expect to learn? Place and date of birth, education, club and other memberships, charitable and other activities, and the like. It gives you an insight into the person who'll be interviewing you—and may give you hints on what to include or not include in your resume or in your interview.

For example, if you notice that you have any similarities to the interviewer (same hometown, same associations, same school, etc.), you'll be able to mention them during your interview. On the other hand, if you learn that your interviewer is an active member of the local Republican party, perhaps it's best not to mention that you're a rabid Democrat.

You can use biographical directories even if you *aren't* being interviewed by someone listed in them. They work well to give you a picture of management style and corporate culture. Read about top officers at one company and see if there are similarities in their backgrounds. Did they all go to Ivy League schools? Are they members of the same groups and associations? Read between the lines and draw general conclusions. You can use these insights to better position yourself in your letter or interviews with the company.

The bottom line? Biographical directories give you inside intelligence that can help sell you.

Two of the most commonly found:

*Dun and Bradstreet Reference Book of Corporate Managements*
Dun's Marketing Services
3 Sylvan Way
Parsippany, NJ 07054
800/526-0651
—A directory completely devoted to bios, this covers executives from the vice-president level on up—a wider range than others. Profiles are fairly comprehensive, including address, phone, education and employment history, place of birth, memberships, civic and political activities. They offer nice intelligence to be used in your resume or interview.

Volume #2 of *Standard & Poor's Register of Corporations, Directors and Executives*
Standard & Poor's Corp.
25 Broadway
New York, NY 10004
212/208-8702
—The second volume of *S&P* includes the background information of over 75,000 key executives and directors at firms covered in the other volumes—business and home addresses, date and place of birth, memberships. One plus: This is often more widely available at public libraries than the *Dun and Bradstreet Reference Book of Corporate Managements.*

■ **There are other *directories that compile industry statistics* and often include company profiles and more. These can help you to begin getting information on an industry or company and may be particularly helpful if you're changing careers.**

These directories are useful because they give you a superfast way of tracking different industries. Which seem to be growing and why? Which are heading downhill?

Of course, you can't stop with these directories. You're best off adding to this very general research with more specific reading—

in business magazines and trade journals, for example. Still, these industrial directories are often good ways of getting a feel for an industry and for helping steer you away from dead-ends and into better choices.

Two of them are:

*Manufacturing USA*
Gale Research, Inc.
835 Penobscot Bldg.
Detroit, MI 48226-4094
800/877-GALE
Fax: 313/961-6083
—Covering over 300 manufacturing industries, this directory includes such information as industry statistics (people employed, number of companies, etc.), market trend analysis, product share information, state and regional analysis, occupations employed by each industry, leading companies in each industry, and employment trends. A good place to get a quick overview of a particular manufacturing industry—and it's relatively inexpensive ($159 in 1992).

*Service Industries USA*
Gale Research, Inc.
835 Penobscot Bldg.
Detroit, MI 48226-4094
800/877-GALE
Fax: 313/961-6083
—This directory includes analyses of over 300 service industries—including advertising, hotels, restaurants, sports, and entertainment. Industry analyses include statistics, product share information, geographical analysis, occupations employed, employment and leading companies. Also included is information on over 15,000 companies. Like *Manufacturing USA,* it's relatively inexpensive ($170 in 1992) and is a good source of quick overview information on different industries.

One final note: If you need a source for a range of information on different industries, you may want to try the *Encyclopedia of Business Information* (same address and phone as above). This one-volume directory is a convenient one-stop source—containing magazines, newsletters, databases, associations, books, etc., on a wide range of industries. One potential problem: Information is often outdated. Sometimes associations listed are defunct or have moved; magazines and newsletters have folded. But aside from this, it's a fairly decent starting point for quick research.

## TRADE PUBLICATIONS

■ **Nothing works better for you in a job hunt than trade publications —the magazines, journals, and newspapers that cover specific industries in depth.**

Every industry—from the largest and most prominent to the smallest and most obscure—has some sort of newspaper, magazine, or newsletter covering it; most have dozens. For example, the retail industry depends on *Women's Wear Daily;* jewelers read *Modern Jeweler;* the tire industry is mesmerized by *Rubber and Plastic News.* The list, variety, and scope are endless.

If you're not reading the appropriate trade journals already, start to do so as soon as you decide to look for a job and never stop. They're the easiest and fastest way to get an insider's view of the industry and they can help you in every aspect of your search—from writing cover letters to networking to finding job openings.

*By regularly reading trade publications, you can:*

- tap the hidden job market by anticipating job openings
- learn specific information about a company to use in your cover letter or interview
- gain salary information about your job objective
- get the names of people in your field who can serve as contacts
- fine-tune your job campaign by knowing industry trends

### Locating Trade Journals

■ **Your first step: Find out exactly what publications are put out in the industries you're pursuing.**

If you're unsure about the specific trade publications for your area of interest, or even if you already know some but want to find more, you should check one of the following directories. These list publications by specific business or industry, so you can quickly see what is available in your field. Short editorial profiles give you an immediate idea of the contents and how helpful the publication can be to you. Listings include name and number of the publisher as well as subscription information.

> *Business Publication Rates & Data*
> Standard Rate & Data Service, Inc.
> 3004 Glenview Rd.
> Wilmette, IL 60091
> 708/256-6067
> —Lists business, trade, and technical publications both in the United States and abroad.

> *Source Directory*
> Predicasts
> 1101 Cedar Ave.
> Cleveland, OH 44106
> 216/795-3000
> —Lists publications—technical, financial, business, trade.

> *Standard Periodical Directory*
> Oxbridge Communications
> 150 Fifth Ave., Ste. 302
> New York, NY 10011
> 212/633-2938
> —Covers over 85,000 publications in the United States and Canada.

■ **Don't choose only one publication; choose a few to read regularly.**

The depth of coverage can differ and you want to be sure you're getting the news that's on the cutting edge of the industry.

> **TIP: Try to find out which publication is the "industry bible" and pay special attention to it. (For example, in the auto industry, the weekly *Automotive News* sets the standards.) The stories it prints are the ones you'll want to remember to talk about in an interview and write about in targeted cover letters. If the publication issues industry awards, take special note of the winners. The companies that receive coveted industry awards like hearing about them.**

> **TIP: Get the publication of the major *trade organization* in your field. The information it contains is often invaluable—especially in terms of networking potential. Take special note of the people who write articles in the journal. They are usually well connected and make excellent contacts.**

## Getting the Most Out of Trade Publications

■ **Read trade publications** *creatively*.

The trade papers can give you a solid foundation in what's happening and who's who in the industry and can put you in a better job hunting position because you're keeping abreast of current events in the field. But you can take it a step further by asking: *How can what I'm reading help me get a job?*

*A few guidelines:*

- *Look at the stories for hidden hints on employment opportunities.* In trade publications, you can read about employment trends in the industry: which companies are hiring and which are laying people off. If you read between the lines, you can find first-rate, first-hand information that can give you an edge over other job candidates.

    **TIP:** For potential job leads, be sure to look for stories about the following subjects: *Expansion plans* (companies that are planning to expand often add new staff); *corporate relocations* (when a company moves, staffers often don't move with it—this may mean job openings in the new location); *new products or areas of business* (new business means new staff, in some cases). This is an especially good tactic for those with expertise in the specific area that a company is entering or in new product roll-outs.

    **EXAMPLE:** In *Women's Wear Daily,* a woman read about the unprecedented success of a retail chain. Because of its success, the company was planning to expand into new locations across the country. The woman realized that expansion meant the creation of new jobs. She sent the company a letter, congratulating it on its success and outlining her interest in being part of the expansion efforts in her region. She got an interview and a job *before* the company began any official recruiting.

- *Always be aware of how you can make practical use of the information you find in the trade publications.* Unlike the contents of the more general business magazines such as *Forbes, Fortune,* and *Business Week,* almost everything you read in the trade publications can be exploited to help you in some area of your job search. Pay special attention to the columns that briefly list new businesses, accounts, and clients. "Business Digest" or "New Business" columns can give you hot job leads.

**TIP: The "Executive Changes and Promotions" or "People in the News" columns can be helpful. Take note of the people who are with the companies you're interested in. See if you notice any trends: Are all the promotions occurring in one office or in one department? Is there a new department head?**

  **In some cases, you should drop a congratulatory note to whoever was promoted, even if he or she isn't in a hiring position. It's especially effective if you have something in common with that person: the same college, hometown, or associations. Mention your common ground, congratulate him or her, and briefly mention that you're applying for a job in the same company. Drop it there. Your aim is to have someone on staff who knows you and thinks well of you.**

**TIP: Most trade publications have an "Upcoming Events" or "Conventions and Trade Shows" column. It's wise to keep track of what's coming up in your area. It might be worth it to attend some seminars or meetings to make contacts.**

- *Don't ignore any segment of the trade publications.* Sometimes the most helpful information seems minor. Columns on advertising or media expenditures can let you know about new products or services a company is offering, or give you a feel for their financial standing.

  Even the masthead—which lists reporters, bureau chiefs, ad sales reps, etc.—can be exploited for your job hunt. You may want to call or write the reporter who covers your specific industry or specialty to see if he or she can give you any insight into the field. One word of warning: Many reporters won't want to be bothered. If you run into this, don't be a pest.

■ **Along the same lines, always read the want ads, even if you aren't planning to reply to any of them.**

- *Want ads aren't only useful as job leads. They're also great intelligence.* By scanning them regularly, you can determine trends—the hiring activity in your industry, the common salaries being paid, the types of positions that are available more often than others, the regions of the country that seem hottest in terms of opportunity.

TIP: **Before interviewing for a position, check to see if there's an ad for a similar position at a similar company—this may give you tips on what to say during your interview, points to highlight, and a rational salary and benefits package.**

■ **Be sure to read special issues that the trade publications put out.**

• *Most helpful for you—the Corporate Scoreboard, Top 100 Companies, or Directory issues.* These are handy quick references to determine which companies are doing well, which aren't, general financial stats, industry standings, etc.

Also find out about special issues that concentrate on a specific industry segment. (For example, *Advertising Age* puts out special Direct Marketing, Marketing to Minorities, and other issues.) By reading these special issues, you can get a real feel for the areas that are brushed over in regular issues.

TIP: **Check the regular display ads in the special-interest issues focusing on a specific industry segment to get the names of companies that service this aspect of the industry. The advertising is often as focused as the articles are and might give you ideas about other companies to target. And, of course, you should pay close attention to the classified ads in these issues as well. Recruitment advertising is often more plentiful in this type of issue.**

■ **Another good idea: Read Year in Review and Forecast issues.**

• *These can give you a cram course in an industry—which is especially helpful for first-time job hunters and career changers.*

And it's the simplest way of hitting the ground running where understanding an industry is concerned.

Year in Review issues, as you'd expect, usually come out in December or January and run down the most important events of the year in an industry: What companies folded? Who merged with whom? What new product roll-outs took off or bombed? What executives were big news? And the like. It's a great way of getting a thumbnail history of an industry's recent past—and of pinpointing companies that are on the move (or headed downward).

*Note:* For a list of trade publications broken down by industry, see the Appendix, pages 322–351.

## BUSINESS MAGAZINES, NEWSPAPERS, AND OTHER PERIODICALS

■ **It's a good idea to read basic business magazines and newspapers, in addition to trade publications. These can give you a general view of what's going on—where industries are heading, what's hot and what's not, and so on.**

This is a simple way of keeping up with what's happening in American business.

In addition to getting a general idea of industry trends, you can use business magazines and newspapers to locate information on the specific companies you're targeting. Often even smaller companies are covered in news stories—which can give you great ammunition for a cover letter or interview.

> **TIP: Don't limit your reading to articles about the company that you are interviewing with. Read about competing companies as well, so you will have a general idea about the climate of the marketplace.**

The following general business periodicals are good sources:

*Barron's*
Dow Jones & Co.
200 Liberty St.
New York, NY 10281
212/416-2759
—While chiefly an investment tool, *Barron's* is useful for determining the financial stability of a company or companies, and for getting a feel for industry forecasts.

*Business Week*
McGraw-Hill, Inc.
1221 Ave. of the Americas
New York, NY 10020
212/997-3608
—A good all-around business source for tracking industries, up-and-coming companies, etc.

> **TIP: Its annual directory, *The Business Week 1000*, is handy if you're planning a mailing to top companies in an industry. Reason? Unlike the Fortune 500, *BW* lists addresses and phone numbers. A nice cheap directory.**

*Forbes*
Forbes, Inc.
60 Fifth Ave.
New York, NY 10011
212/620-2200
—Another great source for keeping up with business in general, tracking industries, etc.

**TIP:** **If you're planning a direct mail campaign, get your hands on Forbes's 400 Largest U.S. Private Companies issue (generally comes out in December). It's a help when putting together a mailing list: Many of the companies listed in here aren't included in typical directories—and Forbes lists addresses, telephone numbers, etc.**

**TIP:** **A great source if you're pinpointing up-and-comers (which often offer better employment prospects): Forbes's 200 Best Small Companies issue (generally comes out in November)— which, like the above, includes names, addresses, and telephone numbers. Very handy.**

*Fortune*
The Time Inc. Magazine Co.
Time & Life Bldg.
New York, NY 10020-1393
212/522-1212
—Yet another good all-around source of information on different industries, companies, etc.

**TIP:** **There's good information on up-and-coming companies in each week's "Companies to Watch" feature.**

*Inc.*
38 Commercial Wharf
Boston, MA 02110
617/248-8000
—Invaluable for targeting the fast-moving corporations that tend to do the most hiring.

**TIP:** ***Inc.*'s special issue on the fastest-growing small companies in the United States is a great source of names for a mailing list. Often these companies are the ones that offer the most job opportunities.**

*Industry Week*
1100 Superior Ave.
Cleveland, OH 44114
216/696-7000
—This semimonthly covers industrial management. As such, it's best for those involved in industry.

*Nation's Business*
U.S. Chamber of Commerce
1615 H St., NW
Washington, DC 20062
202/463-5650

*National Business Employment Weekly*
420 Lexington Ave.
New York, NY 10170
212/808-6791
—The text offers job hunting tips and strategies, but this newspaper is chiefly useful because it contains a week's worth of *Wall Street Journal* help wanted ads. In addition, it offers weekly special sections, including Engineering Weekly, Computer, High Technology.

*Wall Street Journal*
200 Liberty St.
New York, NY 10281
212/461-2000
—A business standby, the *Journal* is great for quick updates on industries and businesses. Another plus: It often has good job hunting articles aimed at upper managers.

**TIP:** As with trade publications, seek out special issues of business magazines. These may give you more focused information. Many of the general business magazines put out special issues in which they cover a specific industry more closely, or a professional group—such as managers. One way of finding out about special issues: Call the publications and ask for an editorial calendar. Or check the *Business Periodicals Rate & Data* directory at your library.

**TIP:** Another general business source, which can help you if your job hunt is centered on major U.S. companies that are traded on the stock market exchanges, is the investment guide *Value Line*. This is great for one-stop research of major companies and industries. Industry sections examine trends and discuss the general climate in the industry, giving you insight into employment possibilities. And company reports, which are updated quarterly, are easy to read and packed with information beyond the usual financial statistics and forecasts. It includes a look at the recent past, developments that have shaped the company, and its outlook for the future. Use *Value Line* to get a grasp of a company's management style, where it has been, and where it's headed. It's especially handy to glance through just before an interview.

■ **Use newspapers to help you with your job hunt.**

When it comes to newspapers, think geographically. Keep in mind that certain areas of the country are centers of a specific industry, so the major newspaper in that area will often offer more comprehensive coverage of that industry. For example, if you're aiming at banking, check *The New York Times;* film and entertainment industry, *Los Angeles Times;* automotive industry, *Detroit Free Press,* and so on.

> TIP: If you're thinking about relocating, start reading newspapers from the areas of the country you're thinking about. A big plus: Often the business sections of papers outside your current area can give you a better feel for employment and industry conditions in other regions. Even more practically, you can see want ads for different areas.

■ **Once you've picked several target companies, always check the major local newspaper of the area in which each company's headquarters is located and in which the company does the most business. Also check into state and regional business publications.**

Newspapers will often do in-depth coverage of a locally headquartered business because it's an important presence in the community. For example, if the company you're targeting is headquartered in Atlanta, the *Atlanta Constitution* will probably have more stories on the company than *The Wall Street Journal.*

Also check into the many state and regional business publications that focus only on business trends, companies, and business news for that specific area. For example, *Crain's New York Business* covers the New York metropolitan area. The *Los Angeles Business Journal* covers L.A. These regional business magazines are great sources of information and often offer information unavailable in other sources.

> TIP: Many state business publications put out an annual directory issue that lists top companies in the state, or a yearly book of lists that breaks it down further and lists the top ad agencies, top manufacturers, top real estate companies, etc. Either one is

helpful when planning a long-distance job search—you can easily pull together the names of top companies, often with addresses and phone numbers, sales figures and employee figures. Call and ask the magazine's circulation or editorial offices—single-copy sales are common.

To find the names of out-of-state newspaper and business publications, check:

*Gale Directory of Publications and Broadcast Media*
Gale Research, Inc.
835 Penobscot Bldg.
Detroit, MI 48226-4094
800/877-GALE
Fax: 313/961-6083
—Available at many libraries, this directory lists newspapers, magazines, and other periodicals by state and city—which makes it a quick and easy way to locate the pertinent newspapers and magazines for your target region.

*Ulrich's International Directory of Periodicals*
R. R. Bowker/Div. of Reed Reference Publishing
121 Chanlon Rd.
New Providence, NJ 07974
800/346-6049
—A library standby, *Ulrich's* is a good source of state business periodicals—check listings under the BUSINESS heading; state business magazines and newspapers will be listed there alphabetically by title.

For a listing of some major state and regional publications, see the Appendix, pages 351–377.

■ As mentioned before, in many cases, you'll want to find specific articles in the above-mentioned general business magazines and newspapers (and in trade magazines, as well). To do this, you can use periodical indexes—which categorize and list magazine and newspaper stories by subject. These indexes are available as bound books in the library, and often on CD-ROM or through an online service.

Often, you'll need very specific articles—articles on a particular company, perhaps, or on an industry segment. Save yourself time by narrowing your search to the exact magazine or newspaper issues that have the information you need.

At the library, you'll be able to use periodical indexes. These handle articles from a wide range of newspapers, consumer and business magazines, and technical journals, so they're useful for a wide variety of subjects. As mentioned before, you can use them to track down articles on industry trends and forecasts that can help you define your career objective and focus your job hunt; articles about related industries; and more.

The two business publications indexes that are commonly available and helpful are:

*Business Periodicals Index*
—Indexes about 300 magazines, including *Forbes, Fortune,* and *Business Week,* as well as the top trade publications.
—This is ideal for finding articles that give you a quick overview of an industry. Because of its focus and depth, this index should lead you to most of the articles you'll need. It's also useful for finding articles on general employment trends and career outlook articles.

*Predicasts F&S Index United States*
—Indexes over 1,000 trade journals, business and financial publications, newspapers, government reports, and more. Also gives you abstracts of articles. This index looks a little more complicated, but it's actually not difficult to use and can save you a great deal of time. Often the abstract gives you so much detailed information that you can bypass reading the actual article.

For newspapers, you can check *The Wall Street Journal Index,* which comes out monthly and covers both the corporate news and general news sections; *The New York Times Index,* which includes extensive business coverage; and the indexes of other major newspapers in the geographical area you're interested in.

> TIP: When you use newspaper indexes, limit your search to the past six months to a year. Otherwise you'll wind up spending too much time on stories that, by now, are old news. There is an exception to this rule, though: If a company was involved in a major news story (a takeover battle, massive cost cutting, a merger, a new product introduction) within the last two years, take the time to review that story.

■ **Whenever possible, use computerized CD-ROM indexes such as *ABI/Inform* or *Business Periodicals Index* to locate the articles you need.**

These are available at most libraries and can speed your search quite a bit over using the old-fashioned bound indexes. You can get more specific at the outset and type in the exact company name you want to find, the dates you're interested in, even the name of the person who will be interviewing you and more.

Searching a CD-ROM index is a simple process. You type in your search terms at the first screen (typically a company name or an industry name). The computer will come up with any articles on the subject. In some cases, you'll only have access to the basic index information (article name, periodical name, date, page length, etc.). In others, you can see an abstract. And in still others, you can get the entire article.

The most commonly available indexes: *ABI/Inform* (covers many magazines—trade journals and other business publications), *Business Periodicals Index* (covers major business publications, leading trade journals, etc.), *UMI Newspaper Index* (covers leading newspapers— *Boston Globe, New York Times, L.A. Times,* etc.), *Management Contents, Trade and Industry Index, PTS T&S Indexes,* and *PTS Promt.*

## COMPUTERIZED RESEARCH

■ **Beyond using a CD-ROM index at a library, you should consider using your home computer for help in researching your job hunt.**

You can use a computer to tap into many of the sources mentioned earlier in this chapter—from corporate directories to newspapers. And, frankly, if you can, it makes a lot of sense. It's a way of making your life and your job hunt simpler. For example, if you subscribe to an online information service (or if your library does), you can access much of the information described above on computer.

If you're signed up with Prodigy, Compuserve, or another online service, check to see what specific information is available to you. In many cases, you'll find access to many directories, articles from newspapers, magazines and trade journals, company reports, and industry analyses. In other words, virtually everything you can find in hard copy at the library, you can get in seconds on your computer screen.

You can also check to see what databases are available out there and that may help you in:

*Directory of Online Databases*
Gale Research, Inc.
835 Penobscot Bldg.
Detroit, MI 48226-4094
800/877-GALE
Fax: 313/961-6083
—This lists nearly 5,000 databases that are accessible via many common online information services companies. It's available at most major libraries and includes explanations of what each database offers, as well as the online services that carry them.

■ **The key asset to going online? Speed and accuracy. The drawback? Price.**

Computerized searches can save you a lot of time—but cost a fair amount of money.

It's a real tradeoff. Still, if you have access to researching online, it may make sense. Remember, when you research online, you can get as specific as you need to. For example, if you want only those articles over the past year discussing the sales and marketing department of Procter & Gamble, that's all you'll get. Not general articles on sales and marketing and not general articles on P&G. In this sense, online searching does all the focusing for you and weeds out the unnecessary information. Of course, the problem is your online searches are as efficient as your search instructions are. Your best bet? Practice. The more searching you do, the more precise you'll get. And don't give up.

> **TIP: If you're not online yourself but want to take advantage of it, check with your local library. Many libraries now offer special searching services—you tell them what you're after, they'll do the search for you. In some cases, there's a fee. In others, the service is free. If you're strapped for time or if you're uncomfortable working on computers, this may be a good option for you. Ask your reference librarian.**

■ **Two of the best uses for computerized research in your job hunt? To put together a targeted mailing list and to dig out information that can help sell you in a letter or interview.**

First, you can pull together a very specific resume mailing list that meets whatever criteria you want. You can quickly and easily generate a list of target companies based on such factors as product, geographical location, sales, and number of employees. An added timesaver: Once you've downloaded this list, you can import it into your word-processing program for use in a mail merge of letters and envelopes. It's quite a time-saver—you can pull a list of job leads via computer more quickly than you can physically flip through a directory and copy the appropriate pages; you won't have to type in all the addresses.

Second, you can get specific information on a company or companies to use in an interview or a direct mail campaign. By using precise search terms (dates, company names, specific department names, etc.), you can get your hands on those articles in major magazines and smaller newspapers and trade journals that will help you position yourself in your interview or direct mail letter.

■ **One final way you can use your computer for job hunting research: If your computer is equipped with a CD-ROM reader, you may want to buy one of the previously mentioned directories and many other sources on CD-ROM.**

Most of the major directories and many other sources—such as business information (SEC reports, financial statements, brokerage information, etc.) and periodical indexes—are available on CD-ROM.

Like online searching, using CD-ROMs can streamline your research—typing in search criteria and generating lists based on those parameters. The only drawback: Because CD-ROMs are disks, the information on them isn't necessarily as current as that which you'll get online. However, many vendors (such as Disclosure, mentioned below) send updates.

> **TIP: Frankly, buying CD-ROMs for your job hunt only makes sense if you're planning a major mailing—say of 500 to 1,000 letters —to companies that will be included in these directories, since CD-ROMs remain fairly expensive at publication time.**

Some leading CD-ROM vendors:

Dun's Marketing Services
3 Sylvan Way
Parsippany, NJ 07054
800/526-0651

Disclosure, Inc.
5161 River Rd.
Bethesda, MD 20816
301/951-1300 or 800/843-7747

Standard & Poor's
25 Broadway
New York, NY 10004
212/208-8702

## TRADE AND PROFESSIONAL ASSOCIATIONS

■ **Most people know that trade and professional associations are great bets for networking. But they're also a good source of information for you in the research stage of your job hunt.**

We talk about how you can use trade and professional associations to network in the following chapter. But you can *also* take advantage of trade associations to help you with the research in your job hunt.

*A trade association can offer a number of helpful tools, such as:*

- Membership lists or directories—which you can use to find new contacts

- Journals and magazines—which sometimes include help wanted ads, give you an idea about the industry, or lead you to new contacts (people who've written the articles, etc.)

- Job services—many associations run job banks, resume services, job hunting workshops, and more for members. Some are even available to nonmembers

To find the names of associations in your field of interest, check:

*Encyclopedia of Associations*
Gale Research, Inc.
835 Penobscot Bldg.
Detroit, MI 48226-4094
800/877-GALE
Fax: 313/961-6083
—This is the most common directory of associations, available at virtually every library. One tip in using this: Be sure to check under multiple headings or check the Key Word index.
—Sometimes the industry headings are somewhat vague. For example, computer associations are listed under data processing.

Other sources:

*Associations Yellow Book*
Monitor Publishing Co.
104 Fifth Ave.
2d fl.
New York, NY 10011
212/627-4140

*Business Organizations, Agencies, and Publications Directory*
Gale Research, Inc.
835 Penobscot Bldg.
Detroit, MI 48226-4094
800/877-GALE
Fax: 313/961-6083

*National Trade and Professional Associations*
Columbia Books
1212 New York Ave., NW
Suite 330
Washington, DC 2005
202/898-0662
—This one is a good choice if you want to buy a directory. It's
   an inexpensive—$65 in 1994—directory listing thousands of
   associations.

TIP: **Don't only seek out associations in your specific field. More general professional associations (such as the National Association of Female Executives or the American Management Association) often offer a wide range of helpful material. In some cases, they offer more career assistance or job services than the smaller associations. Some examples: The American Management Association puts out an *Executive Employment Guide* that lists search firms, job registries, etc. And the Association of MBA Executives (Association of MBA Executives, 227 Commerce St., East Haven, CT 06512, 203/467-8870) offers a listing of corporations in three states of choice for one functional area for only $10 each.**

For other associations, see the Appendix, pages 304–351.

## USING COMPANIES AS A RESEARCH TOOL: WHAT THEY CAN TELL YOU

■ **Once you know which companies you're interested in, you can turn to a primary source of information outside the library—the companies themselves.**

Generally, you should call the company switchboard and ask for the public relations, public affairs, corporate communications, or personnel office. It usually doesn't matter to whom you speak: You're only after general information, not contacts.

Contacting the companies where you'll eventually be applying for a job saves you time and effort. They can give you answers to questions about their operation that you need to know. Approaching them instead of searching out answers from secondary sources makes sense. Two of the best reasons for contacting companies are to doublecheck a mailing list and to get background information.

### To Doublecheck a Mailing List:

Always call the companies directly to find out the exact name and title of an executive. Don't depend on articles, directories, even company literature. Typos are common, executives leave positions, titles change.

Before you send a letter, call the company first and doublecheck the name, title, spelling. Whenever possible, also find out what floor the executive's office is on. That speeds things up and makes it more certain that your letter won't be delayed or wind up sitting in the mailroom.

Never call and ask to whom you should address your resume. General inquiries usually get you the name and title of a personnel manager. Instead, be specific. Don't make it apparent that you intend to send in a resume. Sound authoritative and ask for the name of the manager of a specific department or whoever is responsible for a certain division.

Be straightforward rather than elaborate. Some people recommend clever tricks such as asking for a false person and waiting to be corrected, pretending to be a supplier, or calling a different department and asking for information. These ploys often work—but they're usually not necessary.

**TIP: Try telling the truth when you're asked why you need an executive's name and title. For example, a woman putting the final**

**touches on her resume mailing list called each company to make sure that she had the correct information. Whenever someone asked her why she needed the executive's name or title, she said, "I'm updating a mailing list." It was the truth—and it satisfied everybody.**

## To Get Background Information:

Calling or writing for printed information is one of the best and most efficient ways to gain insights into the company's corporate culture: how it perceives itself and how it *wants* to be perceived.

It's simple to get information directly from a company. Forget all the articles that tell you to lie and concoct a story about the article you're writing or the informational interview you want to do. More often than not, all you have to do is contact the public relations or corporate communications department and ask them to mail you current literature about the company.

Ask for a copy of the annual report, a media or press kit, and, if you're interested in an entry-level job or training program, recruitment brochures.

## Annual Reports

■ **Be suspicious of annual reports.**

Because of federal disclosure requirements, corporate annual reports are honest, but very often the "real truth" is hidden behind a mass of healthy-looking figures and healthier-looking balance sheets. Unless you're an accountant and know how to factor the numbers in the footnotes—contingent liabilities and the like—look at the numbers only for trends. Are sales healthy and increasing yearly? Are provisions for discounts and returns stable? Are the basic relationships between revenues and profits stable or increasing? Has there been a major sale of assets that makes the overall picture seem better than it really is?

Even with trends, don't get a false sense of confidence if everything looks rosy. Many high-tech firms had great trends. The numbers kept going up, until the high-tech crash in the late 1980s when many companies fell into bankruptcy.

■ **It's best to read the annual report to get a *feel* for the company's direction.**

Inevitably, company divisions or plans are emphasized, certain attributes are talked about, and you will pick up clues on how to behave during interviews. For example, the 1984 General Electric annual report had all the normal fluff about paring down bureaucracy and creating a good environment, but concluded that its main goal was to expand. A year and a half later GE bought RCA.

■ **Read the management statements for corporate style as well as for facts.**

As always, be aware of buzzwords that signal trouble. For example, "We look forward to facing exciting challenges ahead" usually means that the company is in trouble and just wishes those challenges would go away.

> **TIP: Read the annual report along with a photocopy of *Dun's* or *Value Line*'s report on the company. In this way, you can read between the lines and make a realistic assessment.**

In addition, you can get tips about the company's corporate culture by looking at the photographs used to illustrate the text, by reading the quotations, and by seeing who figures prominently and why. Some corporations are top-heavy with financial types, others with marketing, and some with the original founding entrepreneurs. Each one has a different makeup that will affect *your* interview and *your* job.

> **TIP: By checking the list of corporate directors and officers for women's names, you can tell how far women have advanced in the company.**

## Media/Press Kits

■ **Media kits contain the information that companies want people to know, which makes them ideal ammunition for a job hunter.**

Because they're designed for reporters or potential clients, media kits typically include an annual report, reprints of favorable articles about the company, pamphlets about the company's business, products, or services, and recent press releases.

See what achievements they stress in their literature and mention them in your cover letter or interview. Cite specific examples of your own experience that mesh with theirs.

> **EXAMPLE: In its media kit, an ad agency constantly referred to the extensive training programs it offered to every level of management. A man applying for an account executive position mentioned in his cover letter that he was impressed by the emphasis on education. He added that he had been responsible for setting up training programs for new employees at his current agency. Although the programs he had set up were far less extensive, he had made his point. The account executive who read his letter thought the man would fit in perfectly.**

■ **Media kits can show you how to package *yourself* when you go for an interview.**

A lot of company literature is commercial puffery. But if you're savvy enough to know how to interpret them, media kits can give you a good idea of how well you'd fit into the company. For example, you should notice their appearance and layout. Is a particular media kit pushing a modern, sleek image or one that's more staid? Is the writing dry and technical or more like an advertisement? Do the pamphlets stress tradition and emphasize the company's long history? Or do they talk about groundbreaking, new ideas? Knowing the company's slant helps you to see if that's where you belong and how to present yourself to the company.

> **TIP: Compare media kits from different companies in the same industry. You will notice the subtle differences between them and know how to better target yourself.**

> **TIP: Sometimes what *isn't* included is as informative as what is. Pay attention to omissions.**

Take special note of any press releases that are included in the kit. They tell you what recent developments the company wants to publicize. If those developments are important enough to prompt the company to write a press release, they're definitely important enough for you to mention in interviews or letters, if only to show how much you know.

Piece together information and draw conclusions. Press releases and articles about new lines of business can mean the company is planning an expansion; new products or marketing ploys can signal a shift in management style.

> **EXAMPLE: In the media kit of one of the auto giants, a woman read a press release about the innovative aerodynamic styling that was being introduced. Since the company previously had been very traditional, she took that to mean that it was moving away from its old-fashioned image to a more aggressive stance in the marketplace. She applied for a job in purchasing, mentioning that she chose this company because it appeared to be more on the cutting edge of the industry than the others. By stressing the new corporate image that management had just started pushing, the woman got a job.**

## Recruitment Brochures

■ **Recruitment brochures give you the facts on training programs or entry-level positions and usually explain company divisions, recruiting methods, and employment policies.**

Beyond the very basic nuts-and-bolts information, recruitment brochures are just another sales tool for the company. Take them with a grain of salt. Approach them like the public relations material they are. As with media kits, read between the lines to get an idea of corporate style. See if the same words keep cropping up. Also take a look at the type of training programs offered: Are they highly structured, or do they keep talking about personal initiative and "intrapreneuring"?

Take note of the photographs in recruitment manuals, as well. Even though they are usually posed, pseudocandid shots, they give you a general idea of what the company likes in its workers. Are all the employees wearing corporate suits, ties, and button-down shirts, or are they dressed less traditionally? Are there many photographs of employees at "play"—playing sports, or at home?

■ **Realize that recruitment brochures are trying to present the ideal corporate image—and that you can play the same game when you present *yourself* to them.**

## USING FRIENDS AND COLLEAGUES TO GIVE YOU THE INSIDE STORY

■ **For the most accurate information on companies, industries, and jobs, speak with people you know.**

Friends and colleagues can give you the real lowdown. Tell them to give you the unvarnished truth. This isn't the time to mince words. Ask them pointed questions that will offer you a definite picture of the company: *How long does it take to get promoted? What about raises? Is there a distinct management style? Does there seem to be a model for the ideal employee?*

With the detailed information that you get from reliable sources, you can figure out how to best sell yourself to the company. Knowing about the company's atmosphere makes you better prepared.

■ **Don't shy away from subjects that might seem unimportant.**

Sometimes it's the little things that actually get you hired. Find out what sports teams they have at the company, if people go out together after work or if they go straight home. Every piece of information contributes to a clearer sense of the corporation and its environment.

# 4 *Networking*

## INTRODUCTION

Networking is an often overused term in job hunting, but frankly, it's overused for a very good reason. Networking *works*. It's another way of using friends and colleagues in your job hunt. It is more than just a casual conversation between people about jobs. It's a *focused* method of developing and building a pool of contacts: people who can provide career information that can lead you to a new and better job. It can range from career advice to being recommended for a job to being hired. Each person you speak with brings you one step closer to getting hired.

The idea behind networking is simple: Talking to people gets you jobs. Most job openings—estimates range up to 90%—are filled by word of mouth, before job advertisements and recruiters get into the picture.

The aim of networking is to move you into the center of a hidden job market even if you're starting well out of bounds. Beginning with a few people, you can work to develop and expand your list of contacts until you reach the ones who can hire you for the job you want.

**EXAMPLE: A man with no experience in property management started talking with friends about his eventual goal of working in the field. One of them advised him to take a real estate course at a local community college. There,**

he met a city employee who introduced him to a real
estate developer, who introduced him to several other
property owners. One told him how to get the right experience and hired him part-time. Two years later, he was
fully employed in the field.

*There are four basic steps to setting up a strong job finding network:*

1. building a base of contacts

2. expanding your contact base

3. getting and using referrals

4. following up

Don't expect immediate results, although it can happen. Instead,
spend time developing a circle of people who are aware of the kind
of job you want and the kind of job you can do. Concentrate on
getting your name and skills talked about, and almost inevitably you'll
get the right lead and a job. A good networking setup is like a chain
letter. The only difference is that networks work.

But remember, with so many people networking, a little more
tact and ingenuity are important today.

## STEP ONE: BUILDING A BASE OF CONTACTS

■ **Start by talking with friends or close business associates—people
with whom you feel comfortable.**

Don't worry if they're not employed in the field you're interested
in. They may know someone who is, or at least someone who can get
you closer to the right people.

*Remember:* You're trying to get *information* from these people, not
a job. Asking friends or close business associates for a job outright
can put them off and make you sound overanxious or desperate. It
also distracts them from their main function: to get you the names of
*their* friends and career information about your field.

■ **Base your approach on how well you know and trust each person.**

Let him or her know that you're looking for a job and that you'd
welcome advice, suggestions, and ideas. Bring up the subject of your
job hunt generally; then ask if you could sit down and discuss it later.

You want to make certain your friend has time to spend with you and is given the chance to give your job search some advance thought. Don't be afraid to call on people whom you haven't talked with for a while; most people are flattered when they are asked for advice.

During the discussion be as open as possible. Go into detail about the industries and companies that interest you, the plans you've made, and the status of your job.

> **TIP: With friends, be honest about your shortcomings. You may cause problems by neglecting to admit your personal limitations. One man couldn't handle the stress of his high-pressure sales job. He really wanted to find a job that was lower-key and based locally. He avoided discussing this aspect of himself with a close friend, who talked to his boss, who then hired the man based on his friend's recommendation. The man was flattered by the high base salary but was too embarrassed to turn down a job he wasn't up to doing, so he accepted it. He was fired 10 months later—and lost a friend.**

## STEP TWO: EXPANDING YOUR CONTACT BASE

> ■ **You should now be getting more confident and better prepared, and thus ready to contact people you know less well, such as those you've met at associations and professional organizations, people in different departments at your present company, and people in other companies or organizations.**

You never know *who* can help you. Talk to as many people as you can. Quantity matters as well as quality when you're setting up a network. The more people you're in touch with, the better your chances of winding up with a job lead.

> **TIP: Alumni groups and trade associations are good places to get contacts. (See the Appendix for a list of associations broken down by industry.) Alumni groups are particularly good sources if you went to a small, out-of-the-way, or unprestigious college. Inevitably, someone made it big and that person is usually happy to help someone else from the same background.**

> **TIP: Don't stop with job-related groups. Hobbyist clubs, night-school classes, etc., may be *better* networking sources, because you share a strong common interest with potential contacts. One**

applicant got a job through someone in his stamp-collecting club —he specialized in British stamps and so did the CEO of a local firm who needed an assistant.

■ **Regardless of who your contact is, *focus* your aims and your requests.**

Don't throw your job hunt into someone else's lap and expect that person to know how to help you. Be specific—even to the extent of making appointments with people to talk about your job search.

> **EXAMPLE: "I've decided to make a move from public relations to marketing. I'm particularly interested in working for a smaller company in packaged goods. Since you've been in marketing for so long, I'd appreciate your thoughts on the subject. Would Tuesday at twelve be a good time to meet for lunch or drinks?"**
>
> *Not:* **"I'm leaving my job in public relations and I'm looking for a job in marketing. Do you think that you could help out?"**

■ **Strive for a *concrete* result from each conversation.**

Don't make the all-too-common error of letting the conversation drift into vague advice: "To get a job in this industry you've got to be tough . . ." Get specific help, such as the name of another person to talk to, a meeting time when you can go over your resume, the names of companies that might be hiring.

In this sense, it's important for you to direct the conversation and let the person know exactly what he or she can do for you. The more explicit you are, the more help you'll be given.

> **EXAMPLE: "As you know, I speak French fluently, and I'm interested in combining that skill with my commercial banking background. Do you have any contacts in international banking?"**
>
> *Not:* **"I speak French. Do you know of any jobs around that might need that?"**

> **EXAMPLE: "Yes, I know filmmaking is a tough field to break into. But I read that many people start out by working on location shoots as unpaid assistants. Do you know how I could find that sort of opening?"**

## STEP THREE: GETTING AND USING REFERRALS

■ **The most important information you can get from people is the names of *other* people you can contact.**

Very often the second circle of contacts—or referrals—is the most useful to you in your job hunt. Make it clear to your contacts that you're not asking only for the names of people who can hire you, you're also looking for people who can help you in general. Ask them for the name of *anyone* who can be of some use, such as people who work at the companies that interest you, or who work in a position similar to the one you want, or who work in the general industry. Someone who isn't in a hiring position can often lead you to someone who is.

> **TIP: Keep a networking file on your computer or on 3 × 5 index cards with each contact's name and number, the date that you met or spoke, and the information that he or she has given you. Each time you're given the name of another possible contact, make a new card or entry with the name of the person who referred him or her. You should continue to update this file of contacts throughout your job hunt and after you've been hired.**

■ **Go through your card file or list of names and determine which referrals look as though they could help you the most.**

Although you should still be concerned with adding to your network, at this point it pays to be discriminating. Since these referrals may be people you haven't met personally, networking with them can be a little more time-consuming and often more stressful. Get the best payout by starting with the best names.

### How to Cold-Call Referrals

The hardest part of networking for most people is cold-calling referrals. You don't know them, they don't know you, and it can be difficult to ask strangers for advice. But sooner or later it pays off. Even if you're out of work and feeling down and out about it, resist the temptation to avoid calling. Surveys of the unemployed consistently show one thing: Those who keep calling get jobs.

■ **Start by trying to make it easier for yourself. Ask your personal contacts to write a letter of introduction; arrange an introductory**

**meeting; or place a call, mention your name, and say you'll be in touch.**

An introductory call or letter can pave the way for your call and ensure that you'll get through to the person with no difficulties.

If your contact phones ahead and tells the referral to be expecting your call, make certain that you do so *promptly*. Don't delay or decide at the last minute that you don't want to speak with the referral after all. Your contact is helping you; don't let him or her down. You could damage your chances for any further help and destroy a potentially valuable relationship.

> **EXAMPLE: An editor at *Vogue* magazine complained that networkers rarely follow up on her referrals. Once she had called editors at other magazines and told them to expect a call from a certain woman who had asked her for contacts. The woman never called any of them. Instead, months later, she sent in a resume to *Vogue*. The editor threw it away.**
>
> > *Note:* **This type of situation is surprisingly common. Once you've started getting referrals, you *must* follow through.**

More often than not, you'll end up calling a referral without a formal introduction, so be sure to ask your contact if you can use his or her name.

For those with a nonsales personality, cold-calling can be intimidating. You just have to jump in and do it: The first call is the hardest. Most people find it easier after calling five or more people. Ask your contact for the best time to call the referrals that he or she has given you.

> **TIP: Early in the morning, in the middle of the week, is usually the best time to call. For extremely important or very busy people try to call *very* early in the morning (before regular work hours). *Rule of thumb:* Don't call on Monday, Friday, lunch hour, or late afternoon if you can help it. People are either busy, tired, eating, or cranky. Think of how you would feel at those times.**

■ **On the telephone, be swift and get quickly to the point of your call, which is *only* to introduce yourself, to briefly explain why you're calling, and to arrange for a meeting.**

Always mention your mutual friend as soon as possible to legiti-mize your call and your request for time. If the referral sounds busy, acknowledge it and say you won't take much time.

> **EXAMPLE: "This is Mary Carter speaking. Sally Jones from XYZ Corporation tells me that you're the person I should speak to about _____ [a field of interest, an industry, a company]. She suggested that I call to see if we could get together. Would coffee on Thursday morning be conve-nient?"**

*There are two things you shouldn't do on the phone:*

1. *Don't ask about possible job openings—even if your source has told you there are some.* While the referral may be in a hiring position, this initial phone call is not the time to mention it. Putting people on the spot rarely works to your advantage. They get defensive; you get the cold shoulder.

2. *Don't ask for specific advice.* During your introductory phone call, be brief and courteous. You don't want to waste the referral's time, and you don't want to give the referral the clever idea that it might be easier to advise you over the phone. You want a *personal* meet-ing, not a five-minute pep-talk.

> **TIP: If the referral suggests that you come to his or her office, choose a time outside of regular working hours when possible. Avoid the probability of interruptions so that the person can devote more time and attention to you. Almost always, the earlier in the morning the better.**

## Meeting with Referrals: How to Get the Most Out of Them

■ **Get the referral interested in you without directly asking him or her for a job.**

In the back of your mind you want a job from the people you are meeting. You know it and it's very likely that the referrals know it, too. Just don't ask for one. Instead, mention your job hunt gener-ally, and your need for names, information, and advice specifically. Get the referrals *interested* in you.

> **TIP: Before meeting with referrals, call back your initial contacts. Thank them and explain that you're about to meet their friend.**

Ask them for ideas and suggestions on how to deal with them: their likes and dislikes, etc. Then tailor your style to fit their personalities.

■ **Summarize your objective.**

Even though on the phone you've already sketched out the information you're seeking, repeat it at the beginning of your conversation. Be specific and straightforward. Explain why you're there and what you hope to get out of the meeting.

> EXAMPLE: "As I mentioned to you over the phone, I want to move into direct mail copywriting. Jack Bryant said you're the best person to speak with to get an idea of the ins and outs of the industry. I'm especially interested in hearing about the new trends you see in direct marketing. . . ."
>
> *Note:* Not only have you explained once more the general information you need, you have also reestablished your common acquaintance.

■ **Be an active participant.**

Keep up your end of the conversation. Well-thought-out questions, a concise summary of your job hunt, and clearly defined goals show that you've prepared for the meeting and are in charge of yourself.

For example, explain where your job hunt stands. Let the person know what you've already done, where you hope to be headed, and in what areas you need guidance. Ask directed questions that invite an active response.

> EXAMPLE: "Because I've been staging conventions for 10 years now, I've gotten to know hotel management people and problems pretty well. How would you suggest I start a job search in hotel management with my background?"

■ *Personalize* **your questions when you can.**

Even if you are asking the same questions of a few referrals, shape them to fit each person's area of expertise. Make the referral understand that he or she can make a real difference to your job hunt. Give your referral a good reason for wanting to help you.

> EXAMPLE: "I've followed your company's innovative advertising for years now—both inside the industry and out. And I

**know the importance of your role in beginning the trend. Now that I'm unemployed, I've decided to target the best and most innovative companies I can find. Which companies do you feel share your approach?"**

■ **Don't underestimate the importance of your initial meeting with your sources.**

On the surface, this is only an informational interview, but it's still an interview. Treat it like one.

Even though you shouldn't be asking for a job or even a job lead during this interview, it is always a conscious goal. At some point, this referral will be in a position to hire someone or recommend someone for a job. You want that person to be you, so you should:

- act as though you were being interviewed for a job
- be positive and confident about your goals and your background
- never badmouth your current or most recent position or employer
- above all, show a genuine interest in your job search and in the meeting itself

> **TIP: If you've read articles that the person has written, or if you've read about his or her accomplishments in a local paper or trade journal, say so. Honest compliments never hurt. Just don't resort to empty flattery.**

Take notes throughout the conversation. You want to keep track of any concrete suggestions the referral makes. It's also a good idea to take notes on what questions or comments elicit the best response, advice, or information from your contact. You should use the best methods in other interviews with other referrals.

"Read" the other person for cues, and end the meeting when you think it's appropriate. As a general rule, it's best to keep initial meetings with referrals on the brief side—15 minutes to half an hour is usually long enough.

> **TIP: Right after the meeting, enter short notes about it in the contact's computer entry or on the file card: date, what you discussed, suggestions the contact made, names the contact gave you, etc. Refer to the card for a quick refresher just before you contact the referral again.**

## STEP FOUR: FOLLOWING UP

■ **Begin thinking about a followup *during* your meetings with contacts.**

Keep in mind: A meeting isn't an end; it's a beginning. You should make it possible to remain in contact with the person, even if he or she has answered all your questions for the time being. Before leaving a meeting, ask if you can call again at a later date. Better yet, give the person a definite time when you will call again.

■ **Set up a concrete reason for checking back with your contact— following up on suggestions, names you've been given, companies to apply to, research to do.**

When you have a reason for calling back, it makes it simpler and more logical for you to be keeping in touch. It also guarantees that you *will* follow up.

> **EXAMPLE:** "Ken, I appreciate the suggestions that you've given me on researching the different opportunities available in purchasing. I'll call you next Thursday to let you know how they've all worked out."

■ **After each meeting with a valuable contact, always take the time to send a short thank-you note.**

Networking interviews are similar to regular interviews. You'd send a thank-you note to a prospective employer; you should do the same for referrals and contacts. It's a good way to remind them of your meeting and you.

> **TIP:** Recap a particular part of your conversation—ideally one that highlights a skill or one of your previous jobs, or something especially interesting that the referral had said. A note that is more specific than a general thank-you is also far more memorable.

> **TIP:** Avoid the common mistake of writing a stilted and overly formal thank-you note. The note shouldn't be a form letter that you can send to each and every one of your contacts. *Personalize!*

■ **Regardless of how well a meeting goes, you have to take the initiative to further develop a relationship.**

Don't stop with a phone call or a thank-you note and assume that the ball is in the other person's court. You *cannot* count on your contacts to keep in touch with you. Maintaining a relationship is far more important to you than it is to them. It's up to you to strengthen the ties that you've begun to establish.

■ **Keep building on your initial meetings with contacts.**

To follow up, you must continually remind people of you and your job hunt. Call them and keep them posted; arrange further meetings when you need or want more help. Don't mistake being persistent with being pushy. It seems obvious, but it's a common mistake. Periodic calls maintain a relationship; constant ones destroy it.

*Two of the best ways of following up are:*

- calling with a specific question relating to your discussion
- calling to explain how their advice is working out

> **EXAMPLE: "The articles you mentioned were terrific. I'm writing to the people that were interviewed to arrange meetings with them."**

No one is too shy or unaggressive to follow up effectively. If you are uncomfortable on the phone, you can avoid it in the beginning by sending notes as a matter of course—thank-you notes or notes to suggest another meeting. Awkwardness over the phone could come across as diffidence—and that would do more harm than good. But don't avoid following up on your contacts altogether. Instead, turn to other methods of developing the relationship.

> **TIP: Send clippings of newspaper or magazine articles that might interest your contacts, along with a short note. The clippings show that you've been thinking of them; it's also a diplomatic way of reminding them of you.**

> **TIP: Use other people to follow up for you as well. Have your initial contacts speak to the referrals. Ask them for feedback.**

■ **Regardless of how you follow up, the key to making it work is doing it continuously for the duration of your job hunt and modifying your methods as time goes on.**

Don't keep calling people with the same news and the same information. Try to keep your approaches fresh and let your contacts know that you're not sitting still.

> **EXAMPLE: "At a trade association meeting last week, I ran into an acquaintance of yours, Leonard Carter. He asked me to send his regards when I spoke to you next. He also gave me some interesting leads."**

> **TIP: Some counselors recommend exchanging acquired knowledge with contacts. Job hunters are in a position to learn and absorb a great deal of information about an industry through their research and network. Share it with your contacts.**

Above all, fight against feeling awkward. It takes time to find a job. Everyone—including your contacts—knows that. Try to remain as confident and assured as you were at the beginning of the networking process. A positive attitude affects how others view you. People would rather help someone who they think is going to make it—it's human nature. Don't let your contacts see you discouraged. If it looks as though you've given up, they will too.

■ **Keep your network strong.**

As your network develops, start weeding out those people who haven't been helpful. It makes your network smaller, but it also makes it stronger. In later phases, it's pointless to spend time cultivating someone who can't make a contribution to your job hunt, your career, or your personal life.

## SPECIAL NETWORKING SITUATIONS

### Trade and Professional Associations

■ **Trade associations are a built-in, prefabricated network of industry sources.** *Use them.*

When you research your job hunt, you should compile a list of associations in your field. (As stated in Chapter 3, "Research," check *The Encyclopedia of Associations* to put together a list of associations in your field. Also see the Appendix for a list of the top associations in different industries.)

Most associations have meetings or special events that are open to nonmembers. Call the associations that interest you and ask about conventions, trade shows, and seminars. Have them send you whatever literature they have: newsletters, introductory brochures, and more.

### ■ Find out if the association has a membership roster or directory.

Most associations publish a list of members annually that can be a real asset to you when you network. In it, members are listed along with their corporate affiliation. Read through a membership directory *before* you go to an association meeting. It's a good way to get a feel for the association, the types of members it attracts, and how useful belonging to it might be.

### ■ Keep in mind that the chief resource of a trade association is its members.

In general, you should network within an association the same way you would with other people within your established circle of contacts. Start with light conversation and, when you feel the time is right, bring up your job hunt. *Remember:* You are looking for people to add to your network of contacts.

> TIP: According to some career counselors, association members often complain about the number of job seekers who are nonmembers attending regular meetings. Be careful about how you approach people. If you're at all pushy, you'll be contributing to the problem.

*When you approach people at an association meeting, there are two key concerns:*

1. The most important point to get across:
   *I'm asking you for information, not a job.*
2. The most important question to ask:
   *Do you know someone else I might speak with?*

### ■ Keep your ears open.

Associations are great places to hear current industry gossip— gossip that might mean a job lead for you, such as which company is starting layoffs, which picked up a major new client, which is cutting back in one section, which is launching a new product line.

Pay special attention to what seems like cocktail chatter. People often talk about how things affect them personally: "I've been in the office until 10:00 every night for the past two weeks because of the new product roll-out." What you hear may be good ammunition for you in your job hunt.

> **EXAMPLE: At an advertising club meeting, a woman heard two ac-count executives from a major New York agency chatting about a client and the difficulties they were having with him. Since she had also been involved in business deal-ings with the same client, she insinuated herself into the conversation and made some suggestions. She gained two valuable contacts, both of whom helped her find a job at their agency.**

■ **If you already belong to associations in your field, start making yourself more visible as a member.**

As with the rest of the networking process, the chief objective in being an association member is meeting new people. Capitalize on this built-in network by talking with people about your job hunt. Attend meetings regularly. Join committees. The more active you are, the more people you will come in contact with.

> **TIP: Join the *membership* committee, which will give you a good rea-son to contact new people in your field at different companies.**

## Professional Skills Classes/Continuing Education

■ **Classes, like associations, also provide you with a built-in network.**

Don't just talk with potential employers. It's often useful to trade job information with other job searchers. They may be going through interviews or experiences that you can learn from and can give you the inside scoop on interviewers at specific companies.

In the more casual atmosphere of night-school classes, some-times professors can be helpful. Often they work professionally in the field in which they teach and can direct you to people and companies.

Many colleges offer courses that feature industry notables lectur-ing each week. Many people think these courses are a waste of time. They're not. The lecturers are often more helpful than you'd think.

> **EXAMPLE:** A prominent Hollywood director ended his lecture to a film class by telling them that they should feel free to stop by his house and ask him for help when they were looking for work. A woman took him at his word and went to see him after graduation. The director told her that, even though he had lectured dozens of classes and told them all that they were welcome to come to him for help, she was the first one who ever did anything about it. He gave her a job as an assistant on his next movie.

## Networking at Company Hangouts

■ **Through your contacts, find out where company employees go at lunch and after work.**

Typically there is a nearby bar or restaurant where many employees gather. Often that kind of relaxed atmosphere is the ideal spot to meet people from the company, pick up information or gossip, and get a feel for a company or an industry.

> **EXAMPLE:** A trade magazine writer who wanted to move into newspapers started going to a local bar where the editors and staff of the local paper relaxed after work. Over several months, he became friendly with many of them and eventually told them of his planned career move. Since they already knew him and respected his skills, they offered to help him break into this very overcrowded field.

## Miscellaneous Methods of Getting Exposure

■ **Winning exposure is important: letting people know what you can do, and finding the right ones to hire you.**

*Other methods of getting exposure are:*

1. Writing and submitting articles for trade magazines or local newspapers on topics that may interest potential employers, that will show you to be an (employable) expert. *Bonus:* Authorship of articles also looks good on your resume.

2. Working as a volunteer for charity programs that your target company sponsors. Usually, other company employees also volunteer

their time, which provides a good, informal setting for making contacts.

3. If you are unemployed and can type, working as a temporary employee at the target company. (See Chapter 6.) Temping is a quick way to get inside a company and can give you contacts and knowledge of the company before any interviews or applications take place.

> TIP: **A good networking source for women is the National Association for Female Executives (NAFE), 3 Irving Place, 5th Fl., New York, NY 10003, 212/477-2200, 800/634-6233. It sponsors the NAFE network, 1,200 career-resource groups nationwide, offering a variety of programs, and also publishes a magazine.**

> TIP: **For those over 40, good networking sources are the 40-Plus clubs, located in many states and cities. They offer resources and assistance. Check your local phone book to see if one is in your area.**

# 5 Contacting Companies: Letters and Telephone Calls

## INTRODUCTION

At this point in your job hunt, you start reaching out for a very tangible goal—an interview.

There are three common ways you can get an interview: through a cover letter, a resume letter, or a phone call.

Cover letters are the most common of the three. At one time or another, virtually all job seekers wind up writing cover letters to accompany their resumes. The trick is knowing how to transform a cover letter from a bland introduction to a strong selling tool that grabs a prospective employer's interest. This chapter will tell you how. It will also explain how resume letters—hybrid resume/cover letters—can compensate for a problem background and convince employers that you are worth an interview. Last but not least, we will take a look at telephone calls, the most immediate way of reaching a company and possibly the most off-putting. This chapter will demonstrate how to take the terror out of cold-calling—by going step-by-step through proven telemarketing techniques, with sample scripts to guide you.

Each method works better at different times and for different needs. But, with each of them, you are introducing yourself to a company, stating your objective, and if you approach it correctly, *selling* yourself into an interview . . . and, eventually, into a job.

## COVER LETTERS

■ **Keep in mind what a cover letter actually is:** *a sales presentation.*

Before you start writing a cover letter, think about the roles of the receiver and sender. The prospective employer who reads it is your customer or client; you are the product or service offered. In light of that, avoid dashing off the all-too-typical letter that goes along with many resumes:

> Dear Mr. Smith: I am interested in securing a position at ABC Company as an accountant. Enclosed please find my resume. You will note that I have extensive experience as a tax accountant, including five years at a Big Eight firm. I would like to apply my experience to a career position in your company. I hope to hear from you in the near future. Sincerely . . .

A letter like this one says nothing but "here is my resume." It doesn't distinguish the writer from the hundreds of other desperate, dull job seekers. *But it could.*

Most job hunters wrongly view a cover letter as nothing more than a polite enclosure when sending a resume to a prospective employer. It's actually a great opportunity to fine-tune your job hunt and position yourself more precisely than you can in the resume. Instead of composing a broad, generalized letter that just explains your objective and asks for an interview, write about specifics: your qualifications, the job for which you're applying, the company.

*A well-written cover letter should:*

- direct a reader's attention to your strong points and away from your weaknesses

- highlight and expand upon the facts found in your resume

- give new, topical information that *isn't* included in your resume

- show how well you know the company and the industry to which you're applying

### Planning a Targeted Cover Letter

■ **The first step in writing a targeted cover letter is the simplest:** *Don't* **start writing.**

Take a few minutes to plan your letter before you write anything down. You'll save yourself time and effort in the long run. Begin by carefully reading your resume. Select at least three aspects of your work experience, achievements, or abilities to include in your letter that will demonstrate how well suited you are for the job. To come up with the strongest points, ask yourself:

1. *Does this example show how much I could contribute to the company?* It should. Choose something that illustrates what you've accomplished for previous employers, thus implying that you'd do the same for them.

2. *Are there concrete facts or numbers I can use to back up my claims?* It's best if you can justify everything you say about yourself with hard numbers, percentages, or facts. There's less of a chance that people will think you're embellishing your past work history—and you will come across as more of an achiever.

3. *Is this a subjective claim?* It shouldn't be. Writing that "I bring out the best in my employees" or "I am able to build and cultivate brilliance" tells the reader nothing about what you can actually do. Worse, it sounds as though you have so little to say about yourself, you're resorting to puffery.

4. *Is this skill or quality central to the job I'm trying to get?* The answer always should be yes.

## SAMPLE COVER LETTER

123 Elm St.
Canton, OH 44707

May 23, 1995

Marianne Deaver
Director of Marketing
XYZ Toy Company
1000 Rush Street
Chicago, IL 60610

Dear Ms. Deaver:

According to industry sources, XYZ Toy Company is planning to expand into the stuffed toy market. With XYZ's innovative product line and aggressive marketing, there is no question that the company dominates the domestic toy market. I'd like to join such a winning team.

As art director for a small toy manufacturer, I designed and oversaw production of a stuffed toy line that was responsible for 32% of our 1994 profits. This was the first time any one toy line generated such a large margin of profitability. In addition, I developed new packaging for the company's entire product line. Once the new packaging was used, sales to toy stores went up 24%.

I'd like to produce similar results for XYZ Toy Company. With my 15 years in the toy industry and my hands-on experience in both product and package design, I know I can contribute a great deal to your design department. I will call you next week so we can set up a mutually convenient time to meet.

Sincerely,


Edward A. Carruthers

## The Three Basic Parts of a Cover Letter

■ There are three basic parts to a cover letter: the introduction, in which you state your purpose for the letter; the sales pitch, in which you present your qualifications; and the wind-up and close, in which you aim for an interview.

Following is an explanation of each of the three parts along with excerpts from a successful cover letter.

### Part #1: Introduction

When a prospective employer opens your letter, he or she will have one immediate response—Why is this person writing to me?

Explain up front—you saw an ad, you are interested in the company, you heard that it was expanding. Be exact and accurate. This is the right time to use the research you've accumulated on a company or field. Let the reader see that you are knowledgeable by referring to industry trends, specific events, etc. Mention what the company recently has been involved in: product introductions, new clients, expansion plans, etc. This will demonstrate the level of your interest.

> **EXAMPLE:** "According to industry sources, XYZ Toy Company is planning to expand into the stuffed toy market. With XYZ's innovative product line and aggressive marketing, there is no question that the company dominates the domestic toy market. I'd like to join such a winning team."

### Part # 2: The Sales Pitch

The sales pitch is the guts of the letter—the point at which a prospective employer will decide if he or she is interested in reading your resume or meeting you in person.

To sell yourself, tell the employer your qualifications and give examples of your experience. Take care to sound very positive (but not pompous) about your skills and experience. This is no time to be modest.

The same elements that make a resume effective also work here: Use action words. Be brief. Be specific. Write about particular accomplishments to show your qualifications. Use facts and numbers to back them up.

> **EXAMPLE:** "As art director for a small toy manufacturer, I designed and oversaw production of a stuffed toy line that was

responsible for 32% of our 1994 profits. This was the first time any one toy line generated such a large margin of profitability. In addition, I developed new packaging for the company's entire product line. Once the new packaging was used, sales to toy stores went up 24%."

TIP: You also can touch on other, less central points: aspects of your background that make you more qualified for the job, but ones that don't require much explanation. This works especially well if you are a recent college graduate or are changing careers and don't have direct experience to prove how qualified you are. Use *any* information that adds ammunition to your sales message.

EXAMPLE: "As you will see on the enclosed resume, I have won numerous awards in graphic design, including a first-place medal from the Nevada Department of Tourism for their statewide poster contest."

## Part #3: Wind-Up and Close

Be sure to restate *in one sentence* what you can do for the company. Once you've made a strong case for yourself and your qualifications for the job, don't let the letter die down. Wind up your letter as positively as you opened it. Restate how interested you are in working for the company. Don't be coy. Honest enthusiasm comes across. Give them a pithy reason for hiring you, but don't get carried away and oversell yourself at this point.

Close the letter by aiming for an interview with the reader. If you are going for an aggressive or sales-type job, use a direct approach. Take charge of the followup by stating a definite time you will call: "I will call next Thursday, April 2, to set up a mutually convenient time for us to meet."

*Don't* use a direct method if you are uncomfortable with it, or if there is any doubt in your mind that you can effectively follow up on it.

Making commitments does more damage than good if you can't carry them out. Instead, use the common indirect closing line: "I look forward to hearing from you in the near future" or some variation.

TIP: Even though you're putting the ball in the reader's court by asking him or her to call, be as positive as possible. Say, "I *look forward* to hearing from you," not "I *hope* to hear from you." Sound as though you expect a call.

EXAMPLE: "I'd like to produce similar results for XYZ Toy Company. With my 15 years in the toy industry and my hands-on experience in both product and package design, I know I can contribute a great deal to your design department. I will call you next week so we can set up a mutually convenient time to meet."

## Developing a Cover Letter's Basic Framework

■ One of the hidden beauties of targeting your cover letter to your job objective is that, in the process, you create a multipurpose letter—a basic framework that you can adapt to fit almost any situation.

As soon as you've come up with a strong, workable letter, you can reuse its core contents and add to or subtract from it according to the specific job you're applying for, whether you are answering an ad or making a blind approach to a new contact. The basic letter will be the same, but you can personalize it by highlighting different parts of your background and making references to the particular company you're addressing.

The following two letters should give you an example of how easily you can adapt a basic framework to meet your needs of the moment. They were written under two different circumstances (one as a result of a personal contact's lead, the other in answer to a blind ad in *The New York Times*), but the writer was able to use much of the same material. Note how she made each letter sound unique and how she added more information in Cover Letter #2 to target herself even more precisely.

## COVER LETTER #1

**[In response to a personal contact's job lead]**

55 West 14th Street
New York, NY 10011

February 12, 1995

Ms. Diane Walker
Vice-President
National Public Relations Association
800 Third Avenue
New York, NY 10022

Dear Ms. Walker:

Ken O'Brien, the NPRA's director of marketing, tells me that the NPRA has an opening for a public relations writer and promotion coordinator. That's a position I'm very interested in.

**[The writer opens with the name of the contact, a sure way to get the attention of the reader. Following with the job and an expression of interest makes the purpose of the letter clear.]**

Public relations is an area in which I've a proven track record. Due in part to my direct-mail pieces, press releases, news stories, and brochures, the 1994 Advertising Society of America's Trade Show and Convention was the largest in its 30 years of existence. My releases were picked up by a wide variety of publications, including over 20 international newspapers—which brought in 72% more foreign registrants than before. In addition, print and television coverage of the conference increased substantially.

**[In her sales pitch, she gives specific examples of how she helped a similar organization achieve results. The implication: I'll do the same for you.]**

That's a little of what I accomplished for the Advertising Society of America. I'd like to do more— but this time for the NPRA.

**[She flatly lays out her proposition and restates her interest.]**

Enclosed are my resume and several writing samples. If you want a recent reference, feel free to speak with Barbara Baker, the Advertising Society of America's Manager of Public Relations (555-1234). I look forward to hearing from you.

**[Because the letter is the result of a personal referral, she gives the name of a reference to check. That gives the reader an immediate action to take, moving the writer one step closer to an interview.]**

Sincerely,

Laurel Garrett

## COVER LETTER #2

**[In answer to a blind ad in *The New York Times*—the position advertised was for a public relations person in a television production company.]**

55 West 14th Street
New York, NY 10011

Box T1234
New York Times
New York, NY 10108

February 12, 1995

Your advertisement in today's *New York Times* caught my attention and held it. I've been hoping to see a job opening that would combine my promotion and public relations experience with my hands-on knowledge of television production. This sounds like the one.

**[She follows the same pattern as in letter #1—opening with how she heard about the job and stating her interest in it.]**

Public relations is an area in which I've a proven track record. Due in part to my direct-mail pieces, press releases, news stories, and brochures, the 1994 Advertising Society of America's Trade Show and Convention was the largest in its 30 years of existence. My releases were picked up by a wide variety of publications, including over 20 international newspapers—which brought in 72% more foreign registrants than before. In addition, print and television coverage of the conference increased substantially.

**[Exactly the same as in letter #1.]**

The key to getting such a strong press response is knowing what the press wants—especially television. Three years with WXXX-TV taught me a great deal about the press, news coverage, and television production. As associate producer of a news feature show and producer of a special news inserts session, I learned what makes a good story and how to reach the public with it.

**[Paragraph added to emphasize television production skills—the other half of her qualifications. She skews the information to stress how a knowledge of production strengthens her skills in public relations.]**

Now I plan to merge my public relations and television skills. I accomplished a great deal for the Advertising Society with my press and promotion background. I'd like to have the opportunity to do the same for you.

**[Again, a quick summary restating skills and interest.]**

Enclosed are my resume and writing samples. I look forward to hearing from you soon.

Sincerely,

Laurel Garrett

## Five Rules that Sell You in Your Cover Letter

### Rule #1: Know Your Audience

■ **You are writing your cover letter for one audience only: prospective employers.**

Each member of your audience receives dozens, if not hundreds, of cover letters and resumes. You want your letter to be the one that grabs his or her attention. The only way to do this is to consciously direct your letter.

The key question in your target audience's mind as they read your letter will be: Is this person worth my time? The answer to their question should be "yes."

■ *Talk* **to your reader when you write.**

Your letter is a stand-in for you. You want your reader to feel that you are communicating directly with him or her, not reeling off a sales spiel.

> **TIP: Read your letter out loud to yourself and listen to how it sounds. Does it sound natural, or does it sound forced? Is there too much stilted language or bureaucratese? Remember that no matter what your writing style or the contents of your letter, it should sound natural *to you*.**

■ **Use your knowledge to skew your letter** *indirectly*.

If you know that a company is very formal and traditional, avoid using contractions, informal language, or jargon. If a company is informal or if you're familiar with the person to whom you're sending the letter, you can loosen up a bit—but still keep it businesslike. It's better to be a little too formal than vice versa.

■ **Create a mental image of your reader.**

Whether your image of the individual to whom you're writing is a correct one or not is immaterial. Use it simply as a device to make your letter more personal rather than dry and dull. You can base your mental image on what you know of the industry and the people in it—anything that will help you get a fix on the type of person you're trying to reach through your letter.

■ **Refer to events in the industry at large that would interest anyone in the field.**

Even if you don't know much about the specific company, you can still present yourself as an expert in the field by mentioning events in the mainstream of things. It also will make your letter seem more personalized.

## Rule #2: Create Interest

■ **The best way to get people's attention is to talk about what interests them.**

Open your letter with a sentence that leads the reader in. Instead of writing about yourself, mention an interesting fact about industry trends, a recent company development, or the contributions made by individuals like your prospective employer—anything that you think will catch the reader's eye and make your letter stand out from all the rest.

> **EXAMPLES: "Dynamic marketing has made TNC Industries the undisputed leader in the widget field. With the roll-out of the new X-14 widget, TNC has cornered the widget market."**
>
> *Or:* **"As architect of TNC Industries' innovative marketing plan for the roll-out of the new X-14 widget, you spearheaded the company's unprecedented growth."**
>
> **(Of course, the reader knows this already, but he or she won't mind reading it again. A positive, complimentary truism about the company's or an individual's performance works. Just don't gush. Right after this type of opening, get to your purpose in writing and what you have to offer immediately.)**

■ **Referring to published quotations by the addressee is one of the best ways to open a cover letter.**

Quoting your prospective employer shows that you've researched the company and, more important, will appeal to the ego of the employer. Everyone likes to know that his or her comments have been noted and appreciated.

**EXAMPLE:** "Your statements in the June 18 issue of *Institutional Investor* about Addison, Thomson and Phillips' long-term investment strategies were most interesting. I was especially intrigued by your views on corporate pension plans. . . ."

■ **Don't confuse being interesting with being overly clever and catchy.**

You want to come across as a professional, not as a professional hype artist. Steer away from inflated opening lines, obvious come-ons, and the clever little gambits you read about in books and articles (the "Here is a dollar bill. I'm not trying to corrupt you, just trying to get your attention . . ." scheme and others). If you've read about these tricks, chances are so has another applicant—or the prospective employer himself.

**TIP:** *Remember:* **You can grab someone's attention without being super-creative. An effective opening can be as simple as: "Sam DiMatteo suggested I write you," or "I understand you are looking for systems analysts." Your main concern is getting the person to read on.**

## Rule #3: Once You Have Their Attention, Keep It

■ **Don't open strongly, then fade out into a bland recitation of your work history.**

You want the reader to remain interested in your cover letter from start to finish. Always maintain a simple and confident style, continually striving to reinforce your strengths and underscore your achievements.

**TIP: Don't phrase everything exactly the same way. Vary your sentence structure and use clauses. Especially avoid the "I, I, I" syndrome—beginning every sentence or every paragraph with "I" ("I am interested," "I have experience in," "I have enclosed a resume," etc.). You come across as conceited or a bore—and either way, you lose.**

## Rule #4: Communicate Your Message Clearly

■ **Be sure you are getting your message across—that you want a particular job at this company.**

Always be sure that the reader knows exactly what type of position you're after. It sounds ridiculously simple, but a great many people get vague when it comes to stating their reason for writing. Be specific. Don't say "I am interested in a management position." Say "I am interested in a management trainee position," "a job as a district sales manager," etc. In general, the simpler the better. Omit unnecessary words, flowery language, and convoluted, difficult-to-understand sentences.

■ **Be sure not to lift exact wording from your resume.**

It makes your cover letter redundant, and leads the reader to believe you have little or nothing original to say about yourself. As a general rule of thumb, if you can't expand upon the information you've taken from your resume, it shouldn't be a major part of your cover letter.

> TIP: Never pad out your letter with nonremarks such as "I'm a people person" or "I have strong interactive personal skills" or other overused, meaningless clichés. You want your letter to be a precisely aimed sales tool. A short letter is better than a puffed-up one.

■ **Assume that your reader knows nothing.**

Spell out things with descriptive, detailed phrases. Qualify statements: *not* "I worked in production control for a package goods company," but "I was production control supervisor at the second-largest package goods company in the Southwest."

## Rule #5: Keep Hammering at Your Main Objective

■ **Make your examples as pithy and hard-hitting as possible.**

You want to stress how good you are at what you do. At all times the inference should be "I can furnish your company with similar results." Don't force the prospective employer to figure this out by reading between the lines; say it outright.

> EXAMPLE: Don't write "I revitalized the sales department" and drop it there. Go on and tell the reader *how* you revitalized the department and what the effects were. "Due to my streamlining of office procedures and introducing weekly staff meetings, department morale improved and

productivity increased. We posted a 26% rise in sales the
first month after I instituted my new measures."

TIP: Examples that show how you increased profits, cut costs, or
brought in more business are always winners. As you did in
your resume, use numbers and percentages in your description.

TIP: Use bullets in the body of your letter to highlight your key
achievements. They will leap off the page and catch the reader's
eye.

## Format Do's and Don't's for a Cover Letter

How it looks is almost as important as what it says. Keep in mind the
following do's and don't's when you're writing your cover letter.

■ *Do* keep your letter brief.

Stick to one page. It is an accompaniment to your resume, designed to pique a prospective employer's interest. It shouldn't be
overly explanatory or repeat information verbatim that can be found
on your resume.

■ *Don't* use large blocks of text.

Break up the cover letter into a minimum of three paragraphs.
You want the reader to be able to understand and digest the information in each section.

■ *Do* use the typical business letter format.

Even if the letter is informal in tone, the appearance should be
businesslike.

■ *Don't* send photocopies.

You shouldn't be sending form letters; each letter should be
personalized. If you are sending the same letter to hundreds of companies, you shouldn't advertise that fact. Always use a personalized
salutation. (If you're printing a number of letters, use the merge
feature in your word-processing program to drop in different names
when needed.)

■ *Do* **use personalized letterhead stationery, on stock that matches your resume if possible.**

Stationery should be white, off-white, cream, or eggshell (the same color as your resume), and the typeface and layout should be standard. If you don't have personalized stationery, use a good quality bond paper in the same weight and color as your resume.

■ *Don't* **address a cover letter "To Whom It May Concern," or "Vice-President of Marketing," "Personnel Director," or some other title.**

Call and find out the exact name of the person to whom you're sending the letter and the exact spelling. Also doublecheck the title —is it Director of Marketing, Marketing Director, Vice-President of Marketing? People are notoriously picky about titles. Be sure to get them straight.

■ *Do* **proofread your letter more than once.**

One typo in your letter, even the most minor, and you've cut back your chances of being called in.

## Using a Cover Letter to Handle Special Situations

■ **Sometimes you may need your cover letter to act *defensively* for you—to steer a prospective employer's attention away from rough spots in your background that you can't completely hide on your resume, like gaps in employment, a spotty work record, or lack of experience.**

A cover letter is the only chance you may have to convince a prospective employer that you are worth interviewing, in spite of apparent problems in your background.

■ **To make your cover letter compensate for past employment weaknesses, read your resume objectively.**

Anticipate the objections that a prospective employer might have about you, such as that most of your experience is in an unrelated field; your resume shows that you have been unemployed for the past six months; your experience is limited; you have held a number of jobs for only brief periods of time.

■ **Then choose examples from your background, both abilities and achievements, that *counteract* any objection a prospective employer might come up with.**

Either show how well qualified you are in spite of your drawbacks, or show that your drawbacks aren't really a problem at all by emphasizing specific accomplishments. *Remember:* You have more leeway in a cover letter than you do in a resume, and thus can include information about yourself that is only briefly outlined in your resume (minor job duties, outside activities, hobbies, special courses, associations, volunteer work, etc.).

*Common problems that can be handled in a cover letter include:*

1. *No or very limited work experience in the field.* Solution: Draw parallels between seemingly unrelated experience and the job for which you are applying. Focus on skills and functions rather than job titles. Expand upon hobbies, outside interests, or memberships that relate to the job.

2. *Reentering the work force.* Solution: Include examples of what you accomplished while you were out of the work force. It is especially good to mention brush-up courses you've taken or methods you've used to keep abreast of developments in your field.

3. *No previous formal work experience.* Solution: If you are a recent college graduate with only low-level, part-time work experience or none at all, play up educational achievements and extracurricular activities in your letter. Talk about specific courses you've taken that relate to the job, your grades in those courses, any honors papers or theses you wrote. Emphasize skills that any employer wants—efficiency, persistence, hard work.

4. *Series of lateral moves; resume shows little or no upward movement.* Solution: Choose examples of achievements that indicate advancement —if not in actual job title, then in expertise and abilities: you've learned new skills, you've taken on different duties, your responsibilities have increased. Use *action words* that underscore movement and growth.

■ **The one problem you *shouldn't* deal with in a cover letter is unemployment.**

Leave the subject of past or current unemployment alone—especially if you were fired. Going into a long-winded explanation only draws attention to a circumstance that you wish to put behind you. In general, you are better off stressing your qualifications and avoiding comments on the periods of your unemployment.

> **TIP: Functional resume users should be careful. Most prospective employers view a functional resume as an automatic tipoff to trouble: You are hiding a spotty record, you have limited work experience, etc. Even if these are false assumptions, you *must* write a cover letter that counters those suspicions head-on. Everything should stress your stability and depth of experience. *Especially important:* Since time is not mentioned in a functional resume, use time-oriented phrases in your letter: "With my 12 years' experience in [the industry or field]"; "After seven years of developing production control methods . . ." You aren't saying how long you held any particular job; you *are* attaching a time frame to general functions.**

## RESUME LETTERS

■ **A resume letter is a combination cover letter/resume that takes the place of a conventional resume.**

Like a cover letter, a resume letter targets your background very specifically to a particular job or a particular company. As you would in a resume, you present a prospective employer with a brief sketch of your complete background including employment history, education, and outside activities. But unlike either a cover letter or a resume, the resume letter allows you a great degree of latitude in terms of how to present yourself.

*Resume letters work best in these circumstances:*

- when you *don't* have the logical qualifications for the job
- when you are changing careers and want to avoid using a functional resume
- when you have little or no related work experience
- when you are a recent college graduate with a skimpy background
- when you have heard about a job opening, but there has been no formal announcement
- when you are testing the waters at a company, but don't want to make a formal application

In these cases—and whenever else you believe a resume would hurt your chances more than help—send a resume letter instead.

The following is a prime example of when to send a resume letter, and *not* a resume. The following resume should never have been sent out. The job hunter is hoping to change careers, but, on the basis of her resume, she will never get an interview, let alone a job offer, in her objective field.

# A RESUME THAT SHOULD NOT HAVE BEEN SENT

ANN DELMONICO

123 Main Street, Oxnard, CA 11111 (213) 555-3456

Objective

POSITION IN HUMAN RESOURCES: A job in which I can use my ability to influence others through superior communications skills and imaginative approaches

**[An immediate turn-off. This objective sounds ridiculous—pompous and clichéd. More important, what does it mean? This gives you no idea of what the job hunter wants, what she can do, what her qualifications are.]**

Experience

• Convinced superiors of necessity to revamp program of instruction and motivational strategies, and was chosen to oversee efforts of four professionals in this project affecting over 300 people per year. Commended for ability to develop rapport and enhancement of working environment.

**[How did she convince superiors? What was she doing at the time? What is this program she's referring to? Furthermore, how did she enhance the working environment? Again, this smacks of puffery and exaggeration.]**

• Named to supervisory board of one of California's top universities. Persuaded top officers to form financial committee, to which I was appointed, to better plan budgetary matters. Resulted in a four-year wage development and review plan, and a 39% cut in the employee attrition rate.

**[More detail needed. This should be tied in with objective and worded much better.]**

• With several others, founded local chapter of nationwide organization working against drug abuse, and have given over 75 presentations on that topic at high schools, colleges, and other educational and public institutions.

**[Good experience, but could be expanded, explained in more detail, and tied in to objective.]**

• Motivated over 900 people during the past five years. Received awards that reflected my ability to encourage people to achieve beyond what they believed they were capable of.

**[Again, much too vague and confusing. Where has she worked? How and why has she motivated people? And the statement "beyond what they believed they were capable of" sounds overinflated.]**

Employment History

Teacher in the City of San Diego school system, 1988–present
Instructor, California State University, 1987–1988
Instructor, Centenary Junior College, 1986–1987
Teacher, Immaculate Heart High School, San Diego, CA 1985–1986

[Much too sparse. We have no idea what she teaches or has taught and why that makes her qualified for a human resources position.]

### Education

B.A., University of San Diego (English), 1983
M.A., University of San Diego (English), 1985

---

As you can see, this resume does nothing to sell the job hunter to a prospective employer. The job hunter hasn't presented her background well; she hasn't demonstrated that she has the qualifications necessary for the job. And, regardless of how much this resume is revised, the job hunter still will have to stretch to tie in her unrelated background to her objective. Her best recourse is to write a resume letter in which she can stress her work with people, administrative skills, and interests.

# RESUME REWRITTEN AS RESUME LETTER

123 Main Street
Oxnard, CA 11111

June 18, 1995

Ms. Carol Menninger
Director of Human Resources
Western Technical Co., Inc.
555 Wilshire Blvd.
Los Angeles, CA 11111

Dear Ms. Menninger:

In the May issue of *Personnel Management,* I read about Western Technical's plans to expand its human resources department by expanding employee-counseling programs. I agree that counseling is becoming more and more important as mergers and takeovers change corporate culture. The human resources field is changing to accommodate a changing corporate picture, and I am interested in meeting the challenge of these exciting times.

I am especially interested in a position as an outplacement counselor, devising special programs to handle the needs of newly retired or laid-off employees. I believe my background as a teacher, counselor, and administrator is particularly suited for a human resources position with your company. Among my skills and qualifications:

—As a cofounder of a chapter of the nationally known Narcotics Anonymous, I laid the groundwork for existing procedures, set up and implemented public affairs programs, counseled new members, and designed educational presentations for the community at large.

—Over 10 years' experience teaching at both the high school and college levels has given me the ability to communicate with a wide variety of people. In addition, I have developed excellent organizational, presentation, and training skills.

—I also have experience organizing material and making presentations outside the classroom. For the past three years, I have spoken to large groups—in local high schools, colleges, and universities—about drug abuse and the various programs available to them.

—Most recently, I have combined my administrative skills and counseling skills while serving as a college instructor at California State University. There, I oversaw the redesign of a business education/motivation program—a program with over 300 participants a year. The two-year project won me a commendation—both for my program design and for the working environment I fostered during its development.

—My administrative skills are not limited to devising educational programs. As an elected member of the supervisory board of CSU, I worked to establish a long-needed financial committee and subsequently was appointed to serve on that committee. My involvement resulted in a four-year wage development and review plan and a 39% cut in the employee attrition rate.

—I hold both Bachelor of Arts and Master of Arts degrees from the University of San Diego.

With my combined experience as a teacher, counselor, and administrator, I believe I have a great deal to offer to Western Technical's human resources division. The programs you are planning to put into effect sound exciting and very similar to the projects I have implemented in the past. I would like to learn more about them from you and also discuss how I might play a part on the human resources team. I will call you early next week to set up a mutually convenient time for us to meet.

Sincerely,

Ann Delmonico

---

**The rewritten resume letter does it all—and does it better. The writer identifies herself as a focused job hunter with a clear goal, and with clear examples of how her experience relates to her goal. By writing a letter instead of sending the resume, she stresses her strengths, downplays her weaknesses, and sends a forceful message to potential employers.**

---

■ **By having detailed information in your resume letter that you couldn't include on a resume (such as outside activities or hobbies) and *excluding* information you normally would have put into it (such as company names or employment dates), you can play up only your strongest points and skip over the weak ones.**

In a resume letter, you can take a less-than-perfect background and make yourself sound almost perfect for the job. You can even strengthen your sales pitch by omitting mention of certain jobs entirely or glossing over years of unemployment. Despite the leeway you have, a resume letter is actually very similar to a basic targeted cover letter. It has the same three essential parts—an introduction, in which you present yourself and the reason you're writing; a sales pitch, in which you outline your background and qualifications; and a close, in which you give your sales pitch once more, then aim for an interview.

*To write a resume letter you should follow these steps:*

- Write your introduction like a typical cover letter. Open strong, explain your interest in the company and your job objective.

- Then move into your sales pitch. The simplest way to be sure you are including enough information is to break your sales pitch into two parts. The first will be the main thrust of your letter, the section that presents the key ingredients of your resume (either your work history or education). Pay most attention to giving *detailed* information about your work experience. List jobs or functions and support them with specific examples of your accomplishments.

- The second part of the sales pitch sets out the rest of your background: work experience that isn't as central; education; activities that make you more salable. The information you provide in this part of the letter should roughly correspond to the information you would put farther down in your resume.

*Remember:* Because you're not sending a resume to amplify the statements in your letter, your letter must include anything and everything that will affect your chances for a job. When you write and reread your resume letter, be sure you have covered your entire background and hit on all the key points.

The following sample resume letter is from a career changer who wants to make a career move from legal publishing to a corporate law practice—and who wants to avoid using a functional resume. Note how he uses the more flexible format of a resume letter to emphasize his abilities and downplay his limited experience as a practicing attorney. The associate job he describes is part-time, the private practice is very minor, but he presents them well, making his background appear more substantial, and well suited for a corporate law position.

## SAMPLE RESUME LETTER

714 East 14th Street
Savannah, GA 11111

February 15, 1995

Mr. Kevin Bartlett
Vice-President
BTI Insurance, Inc.
142 Peachtree Lane
Atlanta, GA 30303

Dear Mr. Bartlett:

I saw your advertisement seeking an attorney to join your legal staff in the June 28 *Atlanta Constitution.*

The position described interests me a great deal. My experience with insurance cases has been from the other side—representing litigants in negligence cases. As such, I would bring to the firm a unique perspective and one that would enable me to work successfully on behalf of BTI.

As a member of both the Georgia and North Carolina Bars and a privately practicing attorney, I have in-depth legal experience. Among my accomplishments and capabilities are the following:

- As a private practitioner, have successfully handled corporate law, domestic relations, and real property cases—and have recently begun expanding my practice to include malpractice and negligence.
- Have made court appearances in product liability and negligence cases. In addition, I have handled most other types of litigation, including commercial, landlord-tenant, and real estate.
- Extensive experience analyzing current legislation and case law, specializing in corporate issues.
- Brief-writing and research on cases involving estates, pensions, copyrights, malpractice, and insurance.

I became a member of the Bar in 1988, upon my graduation from Duke University School of Law. I received my Bachelor of Arts in Political Science from Duke in 1985.

The position you described interests me very much. I look forward to meeting with you.

Sincerely,


Louis A. Russo

## TELEPHONE CALLS

■ **Use the telephone instead of a letter any time you think that speed will make a difference.**

There will be times during your job hunt when a phone call will be necessary in lieu of a letter. Usually it's a question of time—you can't afford to wait for your letter to reach a prospective employer and the key strength of calling is immediacy.

*More specifically, you should telephone a prospective employer when:*

- a want ad lists a telephone number

- a contact gives you a hot lead and you must follow up quickly

- you have been given a personal referral

By using the phone, you can reach prospective employers ahead of other candidates or before a job has been filled. Prospective employers will get a strong impression of you because you are right there on the line.

But being "on the line"—literally and figuratively—is just what makes people uneasy about using the telephone. You are forced to make split-second decisions about how to answer certain questions. You have to know how to get and keep a listener's attention and how to adapt your sales pitch to the immediate situation.

The trick to making effective phone calls is first planning your sales pitch, then knowing how to present yourself. In this way you are *telemarketing,* selling yourself as a product over the telephone. Your ultimate goal is to give a sales presentation in person or, in this case, to get an interview.

> **TIP:** Another way of using the telephone to land an interview is by *cold-calling* prospective employers. As a general rule, cold-calling works *only* if you have a great deal of confidence. You have to sell yourself uninvited to employers and you need a thick skin to handle the snubs, obstacles, and outright rejections you will more than likely encounter. *Translation:* If you feel at all uneasy or uncomfortable about picking up the phone, asking for a specific person, and proceeding to ask for a job interview right then and there, don't do it. Stick with letters.

## Selling Yourself on the Phone: Telemarketing Techniques

■ **First recognize what a telephone call actually is: an interview.**

Although the goal of making a telephone call is to get you a face-to-face interview, the telephone call *itself* is a screening process of sorts.

When you call, the prospective employer will have one question in mind: "Why should I spend my time with you?" You have to answer that question—quickly. So you don't waste time on the phone frantically thinking of what to say, you should prepare for the call before you start dialing.

■ **Begin by choosing the selling points that will convince the employer that you are worth the time spent talking, and worth seeing for a formal interview.**

Ask yourself: *What are my qualifications for the job? What aspects of my background will make the prospective employer interested in me? What can I explain easily and concisely about my qualifications?* Select selling points that give the prospective employer a good reason for wanting to meet with you and learn more.

> **TIP:** It might sound obvious, but be sure to choose examples you can *talk* about, not ones that only look good on paper. Always be prepared to substantiate or expand upon any aspect of your background that you bring up.

■ **Once you've chosen your selling points, the next step in making your phone call effective is to figure out how to present them.**

Mentally rehearse the conversation: Go over the points you want to cover, the order in which you want to talk about them, and how you will deal with the possible problems and questions.

> **TIP:** If it makes you more comfortable, use file cards to jot down the key selling points that you want to cover. Use these as a kind of script. Do *not*, however, write out an actual script and read it over the phone. You will sound as if you're reciting a sales pitch. Worse, you can get too dependent on it and wind up blowing the entire conversation. *A true worst-case scenario:* A job seeker confidently rattled off his strong qualifications, complete with numbers and every conceivable detail that made him sound right for the job. Everything went perfectly—until the prospec-

tive employer asked a simple question that wasn't in the script. The job hunter's reply: "Uhh . . ." *The moral:* Remember that you're going to be involved in a *dialogue*. A dialogue involves two people.

> TIP: Practice your sales call by actually telephoning a friend or colleague. Rehearsing the situation can make the actual phone call more effective.

■ **The final step before placing the actual call is *research*.**

Do as much background prepping as possible—know about the company, the job title, the job's duties, the person you should speak with, and so on. The more you know, the more confident you'll feel —and the better you'll come across.

> TIP: Before you call a specific individual, doublecheck on how to pronounce his or her name. Mispronunciation won't cost you an interview, but it can be awkward. Call ahead and see how the secretary pronounces it. Or ask straight out—just don't say who's calling.

## Three Steps to Selling Yourself over the Telephone

■ **The most effective telephone call in a job hunt is one that is patterned after a typical direct-sales call.**

Like a cover letter, a telephone call has three distinct parts: the opening, in which you introduce yourself; the proposition, in which you present your credentials and aim for an interview; and the close, in which you seal the agreement (in this case, to meet).

## Step 1: The Set-Up

The best move you can make, and the one that most impresses prospective employers: *getting to the point quickly*. Get directly to your purpose for calling and you will make a good impression from the beginning. This also will set the stage for the rest of your conversation.

*Remember:* Prospective employers don't know who you are or why you are calling until you tell them, so introduce yourself and state the general nature of your call at once. It can be as simple as "Mr. Baker?

This is John Bancroft. I understand you are looking for a new product-control supervisor," or "I am calling in response to your ad in *The Sacramento Bee.*" Don't be afraid of no-frills openings. Your aim is to get an interview, not entertain the prospective employer with your gags, or sound as though you're selling magazine subscriptions.

> **TIP: Whenever possible, use a mutual contact's name or refer to an article or ad. References will give your call more weight and credence. This is especially important if you are cold-calling.**

> **TIP: In general, avoid hoaxing your way into meeting a prospective employer. Too many people have tried the "I'm writing an article for the trade paper and want to interview you" approach. Not only is it a bit hackneyed, it can annoy the very person you're trying to impress.**

As when you're networking, make sure the other person has the time and inclination to speak with you at the moment. If you sense hesitancy, suggest you call again later or on another day. Your pitch won't go over well if the sales target is preoccupied.

> **TIP: If you are cold-calling, *always* try to reach a prospective employer when his or her secretary is least likely to pick up the phone and screen the executive's call. Before eight-thirty in the morning and after five-thirty at night are best bets.**

## Step 2: The Proposition

State your proposition flatly: You are interested in seeing the prospective employer in person to discuss a job.

Don't get fancy. You won't gain a thing by sounding like a fast-talking huckster. Plain speaking works better in this situation. But don't stop there and expect a warm welcome. You have to give the person a *reason* for wanting to meet you.

> **EXAMPLE: "I'd like to arrange a mutually convenient time to speak with you about a position at TNC Industries. With my 10 years of experience in production control, I'm sure I can contribute a great deal to your company."**

After stating your proposition go directly into your sales pitch, in which you briefly outline the highlights of your background that make you right for the job. Don't be too detailed or overly informative. You *don't* want this phone call to turn into the job interview. It's supposed to be a teaser—deliberately designed to intrigue the prospective employer.

List a few of your strongest achievements, then circle back to your key goal: *an interview.*

> **EXAMPLE:** **"To give you a rough idea of my accomplishments, I most recently saved my company—a major cosmetics manufacturer—over $200,000, by designing and putting into effect an inventory control system. I also coordinated and directed the local application of a corporate obsolescence policy. This resulted in a cost savings of over $100,000, the highest regional savings in the company. I'll go into more detail about the programs and tell you more about my background when we meet."**

At some point in this part of your conversation, you may have questions fired at you by the prospective employer—especially if you are calling in response to an ad or a formal referral. Answer questions succinctly and honestly, but again keep in mind that your real goal is an interview, not a job offer. In light of that, be as brief and general as possible. Take special care not to box yourself in and avoid saying anything that could *exclude* you from getting an interview.

> **TIP: Since you can't see the person with whom you're speaking, you can't pick up on body language and hidden cues that would clue you in on his or her reactions. Because of that, stick with safe answers—avoid absolutes and criticisms.**

Be *especially* wary when you're asked about salary expectations or salary history.

More often than not, employers ask questions about money to screen out "overqualified" candidates. By answering a salary question with a hard figure, you can be pricing yourself out of the market. You should sidestep these questions by turning them back toward the most important point at hand: setting a time for a formal interview.

> **EXAMPLE:** **(*If you're asked what salary you expect*) "I'd like to discuss salary with you after we've met and I have a better understanding of the job and what it entails."**
>
> **(*If you're asked what you're making now*) "I'm making a competitive salary here. But salary isn't the issue as far**

> as I'm concerned. I'm more interested in meeting with
> you and telling you some of the ideas I have for TNC."

If there's no way out of answering salary questions and you're asked to quote a dollar figure, you can offer a salary range, but never give a single figure. Then drop the subject quickly and move on to something new.

> **EXAMPLE:** "I'm looking at jobs that pay competitively—in the
> $50,000 to $60,000 range. Of course, I feel you can't mea-
> sure a job by salary alone. There are other factors that
> can be more important. For instance, I'm very impressed
> with TNC's new productivity incentive program . . ."
>
> *Note:* **This type of answer also shows that you've
> done your homework. It reaffirms your interest and sells
> you once again—four birds with one stone.**

## Step 3: The Close

Once you've made your presentation and the prospective employer has asked all the questions that he or she has, it's time to close the conversation. The close should be neat and simple: Restate your purpose, your interest, and your sales pitch, then zero in on getting that interview.

> **EXAMPLE:** "I'm looking forward to getting together with you to dis-
> cuss further the production control job at TNC. I'll be in
> town next week. Are you available next Thursday, or
> would earlier in the week be better?"
>
> *Note:* **By giving the person an option, you avoid a
> yes-no answer.**

If you're not coming across, and an interview doesn't seem to be forthcoming, stop pushing and close the conversation gracefully. A hard-sell technique won't work to get you an interview—at least, not during your first phone call. Instead of trying to break down a stone wall and get an interview from an unenthusiastic or downright cold prospective employer, thank the person for his or her time and get off the phone. But tell the person you'll send a resume, or find out when (and if) you can call again. That way, the phone call won't have been a total loss.

> **TIP:** *For the very aggressive, confident, and/or thick-skinned only:* **It's
> risky and hard to stomach at times, but sometimes being a pest**

**is a plus. If you can't get an interview or even the ear of a prospective employer, keep trying over and over and over again. People get so sick of hearing your voice on the phone or their secretary announcing your name that they capitulate and let you come in for an interview. It's a defense on their part—it gets you off their backs. But despite the negative way you landed the interview, it can work. Once you're in a prospective employer's office, you can show him or her how qualified you are and he or she will be glad you forced your way in.**

Your conversation should be short. Two to 10 minutes is usually more than enough time to introduce yourself, make your proposition, and wind up with an interview.

## Telephone Do's and Don't's

■ *Do* **dress professionally, even if you are calling from home and no one can see you.**

Professional clothes make you feel more polished—and that feeling will come across as you speak.

■ *Don't* **smoke during a phone call.**

While prospective employers can't see you, they can hear you.

■ *Do* **sit at the edge of your chair and keep your back straight.**

Good posture translates into a good speaking voice.

■ *Don't* **do all the talking.**

Just because this is a sales call doesn't mean you should rattle on endlessly. Ask questions. Listen.

# 6 Tactics: Landing an Interview

As your job hunt continues, you'll invariably get advice from friends, colleagues, books, and articles about the *only* surefire method of getting an interview. Everyone is an expert and knows the single tactic that works better than any other:

"Don't bother with resumes. Cold-call potential employers."

"Get as many headhunters as you can interested in you."

"Walk right into the company and tell the receptionist you won't leave until you've spoken to the person who can hire you."

The suggestions are endless, but these people are overcomplicating a simple issue. The truth of the matter is that *there is no one foolproof, success-guaranteed way to land an interview.* Anyone who tells you there is either has been very lucky or is lying.

There are a number of different methods that work. The trick is knowing when they work, whom they work best for, and how to get the most from each one you use.

Following are some brief explanations of the most common and most effective tactics. You will probably use at least three of them during your job search.

## WANT ADS

■ **Only about 15% of all job openings are advertised in newspapers as "help-wanted" ads. So they aren't the best way to find a job, but don't write them off.**

It's very common nowadays to hear and read that want ads are useless, that the only way to get a job is through contacts or friends, the "hidden job market." *Remember:* Companies *do* place ads looking for job candidates; job hunters *can* get interviews through classifieds; and it only takes a little time and effort. More important, you are probably reading the want ads anyway.

*A few tips that can improve your odds and save you time:*

- The first (and best) place to look for want ads is in the top trade publications in your field. The next best places are the Sunday classified section of the major daily newspaper in your area and *The Wall Street Journal* (or the *National Business Employment Weekly,* which compiles the *Journal*'s want ads—including those from the regional editions).

- In general, Mondays and Fridays have the smallest selection of help-wanted ads.

- Don't look only under your job title. Read through other related job headings and even unrelated headings. Sometimes a company (especially a newer or smaller company) lists more than one job in an ad. Also, by expanding your criteria you might stumble across something that you hadn't thought of but that looks interesting.

- Take note of ads for positions *above* yours, such as department heads, supervisors, or anyone who would be your boss. Staff members often are hired or replaced when a new manager comes on board.

### Answering Want Ads

■ **You'll answer most classifieds by letter. Make *your* letter stand out by mentioning your experience and qualifications immediately.**

But don't leave out the name and date of the newspaper, and remember to mention the job referred to in the ad.

Avoid opening your letter with the typical and dull "I am writing this in answer to your ad in the June 17 *Baltimore Sun*. . . ." The average employer receives hundreds of replies to newspaper advertisements, and the vast majority of them sound the same. It's better to sound different: more forceful and positive, and more to the point.

> **TIP: To make your letter more interesting, switch your sentence or paragraph around and put the "I" part last: "Your advertisement in the June 17 *Baltimore Sun* calls for a person with strong computer and communications skills. I have both. In my seven years . . ."**

■ **From the outset, set up a specific reason for the reader to read on and be interested.**

Read the ad very carefully. How the ad is worded will give you clues to how to sell yourself more effectively. Do they use words such as "stability," "integrity," "supportive environment"? Position yourself as a solid employee with a strong and stable work record who wants a career position. Show that you're a traditionalist with proven skills. On the other hand, if the company is described as "on the move," "a dynamic climate," and the position is described as "challenging," be prepared to come up with examples of your own *dynamic* employment history.

> **TIP: Some companies place ads with phone numbers to make it easier for them to screen applicants. Be wary when the first question you're asked is "What is your current salary?" or "What type of salary are you looking for?" This is usually a tip-off that the job is low-level or low-paying.**

As you read the ad, note the main requirements for the job. Be sure your letter addresses each one of them, preferably in the first or second paragraph.

> **TIP: To make your letter read better and look less like a copy of the ad, rephrase the ad. Strike the same notes, but make it sound different. For example, if the ad calls for "an experienced, innovative, achievement-oriented manager," then you're "a forward-thinking manager with a proven record who can produce results." Then give specific examples.**

■ **No matter how interested you are, don't answer an ad on the same day it appears.**

Most people who respond to an ad are sending in their letters and resumes on the same day and the prospective employer will be inundated with mail. Wait a few days before sending your reply. Your resume won't arrive along with that mass of applications—and the prospective employer will pay more attention to it.

> **TIP: The best day to answer an ad you saw in the Sunday paper is the *following* Sunday. This might sound risky, but it works. Your letter will stand out.**

> **TIP: If you come across an ad weeks after it has appeared, answer it anyway. You have nothing to lose. Chances are the company is still interviewing applicants (especially if it is a higher-level position or requires advanced technical skills). Or there may be another opening coming up.**

*One final note:* If you're thinking about placing a "position-wanted" ad—*don't*. Ads such as those draw little response and only waste your money.

## SAMPLE RESPONSE TO A WANT AD

*The ad reads:* Executive Administrative Assistant
Join an expanding, prestigious investment bank. Requirements include high flexibility to meet challenges with a personal approach, top-notch communications skills, ability to prioritize and work well under pressure. Interact with top bank officers. Office management experience and excellent computer skills essential. Box 1234

*The letter:*

123 West Paces Ferry Road
Atlanta, GA 30305

Box 1234
The Atlanta Constitution
555 Peachtree Road
Atlanta, GA 30303

The Executive Administrative Assistant position described in your ad in the April 21 *Atlanta Constitution* sounds like a job custom-made for me.

For the past four years, I have been executive assistant to the president of Harper-Blankenship, a small brokerage house. This position entails a wide range of responsibilities—including serving as liaison between the president and other officers, as office manager, and as administrative assistant. I have day-to-day contact with our clients, who are chiefly pension-fund managers for several large corporations, and handle all of my own correspondence, as well as that of the president.

Having final responsibility for all administrative duties—including overseeing a clerical staff of five and generally ensuring that the office runs smoothly—has taught me to make decisions quickly and efficiently. In addition, by working in a fast-paced environment, I have developed the ability to switch gears swiftly, matching my actions to the needs of the moment.

I have a bachelor's degree in Business Administration from the University of Georgia. My hands-on computer knowledge includes experience using WordPerfect and Microsoft Word for Windows as well as several spreadsheet and database programs.

Working as an executive assistant at Harper-Blankenship has been fulfilling, but it is time for a change and a move to a larger, and more stimulating, environment. This is what drew me to the position you described. Again, your ad was most interesting. I would like to interview with you for the Executive Administrative Assistant position and look forward to hearing from you soon.

Sincerely,

Angela Vezzetti

# TARGETED DIRECT MAIL CAMPAIGN

Direct mail—sending job inquiry letters to a series of companies —takes more time and effort on your part, but the chances of success are greater than with most other tactics in a job search.

*These are three basic steps:*

- First, put together a list of select companies; get the names and company addresses of people to contact from directories, colleagues, etc.

- Then, write a cover letter that is individually targeted to each company in which you express your interest and ask for an interview.

- Finally, follow up by telephone. Call the people several weeks later and ask for an interview.

## Compiling a Mailing List

■ **Making a *select* list is crucial.**

Don't confuse a targeted direct mail campaign with a mass mailing job search, where you may send a standardized letter to hundreds of companies. When you mass-mail resumes, you can't target yourself and your letters to the same degree. Sheer numbers prevent it. With a targeted direct mail campaign, on the other hand, you deliberately make your list short and select. The key strength is in having a narrow focus. You'll be selling yourself very specifically to each company you contact.

*Some tested ideas on how to proceed:*

- Your initial list should consist of 10 to 15 companies maximum. As you go along and get interviews (or rejections), add more companies to your list.

- If putting together a strong mailing list is difficult for you, consider buying a list from a trade publication that focuses on your specific needs. See page 175 for details.

- Research each company thoroughly. For this method to work, you should know what the company has been doing, any trends or recent developments, what they might be looking for.

- *Remember:* You are soliciting the company, not vice versa. There is absolutely no guarantee that any job openings exist. Keep track of industry trends. Which companies are hiring and which are cutting back? While you shouldn't base your list entirely on these factors, you should keep them in mind.

- Don't be overly idealistic when you select companies. Try to be practical about it, choosing the ones that both interest you *and* are reasonable goals. In other words, if you have only a little television experience, you're better off beginning with local affiliates rather than networks.

- Always address your letter to a specific individual, preferably the department head of the area in which you're interested. Get the right name by calling the company and asking. Say you're updating a mailing list. Don't send your letter to the president or CEO (unless you are aiming for a very high-level position). Letters directed too high get kicked down to personnel or tossed.

## SAMPLE TARGETED DIRECT MAIL LETTER

Richard Griffin
Sales Manager
Aldus Corporation
666 Bayshore Drive
Palo Alto, CA 94303

Dear Mr. Griffin:

This is an exciting time for Aldus, Inc. Under the leadership of the new management team, Aldus has seen unprecedented expansion and remarkable innovation. Now, with the introduction of the Vector System, Aldus is poised to dominate the computer systems universe. I am interested in joining the Aldus team—and helping you reach the market penetration I am sure you want.

For the past five years, I have been district manager for Zephyr Corporation. In this time period, sales in my district have jumped 27%—this, after a previous two-year slump. In addition, as district manager, I have:

- instituted a customer follow-up program that increased consumer confidence and improved market perception of Zephyr
- established new "core values" training for regional sales personnel, resulting in individual sales increases of up to 39%
- increased customer base from less than 4,000 to 17,000+

Before my promotion to district manager, I was a salesperson for three years. Among my chief accomplishments:

- won company "President's Award" given for exceeding sales quota by 100%—three years in a row
- took over flagging region and increased sales by 49%

I welcome the opportunity to deliver the same—or better—results for Aldus. I'll call you next Wednesday to set up a mutually convenient time to meet.

Sincerely,

Eric Sullivan

## Writing a Direct Mail Cover Letter

■ **Think like a salesperson when you write your letter.**

*Remember:* The person reading the letter might not have any jobs open, but you want that person to interview you anyway. How can you generate enough *immediate* interest?

■ **Use a tried-and-true selling technique and set up a *needs payoff*.**

Salespeople use this technique all the time. First they show the customer that he or she has a problem, then they show the customer that they have the solution, which of course happens to be the product they are selling.

The best way to begin is by identifying a problem or need the employer has, one that you can meet. Openly state the situation and how you fit in. In other words, show that you know what the company needs and then show that you have the solution: yourself.

> **EXAMPLE:** "In the May 18 issue of *Stores* magazine, I read that the Dawson-Pickett management wants to revamp the store's image and merchandising in an effort to attract a younger, more fashion-forward customer and turn around sales. Repositioning to capture the junior market is a challenge—and one that I've handled successfully in my 12 years in retail management. Most recently, I combined seasonal promotional activities with a heavy media presence to reposition a chain's established conservative image."
>
> *Note:* By referring to an article or a recent company trend, you also let the reader know this is a personalized letter, not a form letter.

> **TIP:** Career changers usually have a tougher time setting up a needs payoff. In today's tight job market, the tendency is for prospective employers to look only for people with backgrounds that fit perfectly. Take extra care to target yourself for the job. In the first paragraph of your letter, you must prove that you have the necessary qualifications and that your particular experience is what they need.

■ **Lead directly into a sales pitch, highlighting the experience and achievements you have to back up your claim.**

> **EXAMPLE:** "As fashion coordinator for Fashion Connection, a small chain of stores based in Florida, I designed a major pro-

motional campaign timed to coincide with college students' spring break. I arranged in-store fashion shows and special tie-ins with various swimwear manufacturers and ran advertisements on the Top-40-format radio stations. *Result:* Sales increased 37% for that period. In addition, store visibility went up and we reported a 24% rise in charge-card applications."

■ **Close on an upbeat note:** Restate both your ability to make a substantial contribution and the strength of your interest—then request an interview.

> **EXAMPLE:** "These are the kind of results I can produce for Dawson-Pickett. I would like to get together to discuss my plans with you. I will call you next Thursday to set up a mutually convenient time."
>
> *Note:* Because the letter is unsolicited, it's best to take charge of the followup immediately and say you'll call for an interview, rather than say "I look forward to hearing from you."

## Following Up by Telephone with a Direct Mail Campaign

■ **By following up with a phone call, you** *more than double* **your chances of getting an interview.**

Followup is the part of a direct mail campaign that many people forget or deliberately avoid. Few people want to pick up the phone, call prospective employers, and sell themselves cold. It can be difficult, it can be frightening. But there is a very compelling reason why you should steel yourself and take the time to follow up: If you don't follow up, you drastically cut down your chances of having your mail campaign work. You will have wasted a huge amount of time and effort.

■ **Have a rough idea of the key sales points you want to make before you call.**

Start by prepping yourself. Keep a copy of the letter in front of you so that you know what you wrote and when you sent it. Decide what you want to emphasize during your call.

■ **Give your name and ask for the prospective employer in a direct, authoritative tone.**

Your first major hurdle will be reaching the right person. Typically, you will speak with a secretary whose job it is to run interference. To get around him or her, don't let on that you are a job hunter. If pressed for a reason for your call, tell the truth but not the whole truth: "I told him I would call," or "He is expecting my call," is usually effective.

> **TIP:** One job hunter got around cautious secretaries by referring in a brisk, businesslike way to the key point of his letter: "I'm calling with the marketing plans for XYZ's new product line." This was the absolute truth: The job hunter *did* have some plans about how to market the new product line; he had referred to them in his letter. But this presentation made it sound a shade more official. It almost always got him through to the right person.

> **TIP:** Although it's important that you reach prospective employers, don't go overboard in your efforts. *A few ploys to avoid:* pulling people out of meetings; claiming you're calling on urgent, personal business; lying about who you are. You'll probably get the person on the line, but speaking to an irritated potential employer isn't your goal.

■ **Once you have reached the prospective employer, immediately refer to your letter.**

To make your call effective and to take advantage of limited time, don't merely say "I sent you a letter on such and such a date." Instead, refer to a specific aspect of the letter and resell yourself by repeating your strongest point.

> **EXAMPLE:** "Mr. Smith? This is Barbara Billings speaking. I wrote to you about my experience in updating images of fashion retail stores. In my letter of May 17 I mentioned how I increased sales for Fashion Connection. . . ."

■ **Briefly touch on the main points of your letter. Then get to your main objective: setting a date for an interview.**

> **TIP:** Don't quote your letter verbatim. You'll sound as though you're reading the letter or reciting from a prepared script. Instead, recap your letter with different wording.

> **EXAMPLE:** "Some of the plans I put into effect for Fashion Connection would work well for Dawson-Pickett. I think you'd be interested in seeing them, especially the ones that cap-

tured the youth market on a small budget. What would be a good time for us to meet—next Tuesday? Or would Wednesday be better? I'm free either day."

*Note:* **This tactic works especially well when you give yourself a *reason* for arranging an interview by offering to show something to the prospective employer (in this case, the promotion plans).**

■ **Be prepared for a hard sell.**

This prospective employer never asked you to call. You're the instigator. As such, you must continually prove that you are worth his or her time. Expect some employers to fend you off, and be ready with comebacks. Don't get antagonistic, whatever the temptation.

Following are three typical telephone put-offs, and how to handle them.

### 1. "I don't recall the letter."

Refresh the prospective employer's mind *briefly* by referring to one or two specific examples you mentioned in your letter. Don't rehash the entire letter. If you still don't strike a chord, judge the situation carefully. Either telemarket yourself into an interview or offer to send another letter (never a copy!) or (best) do both.

> **EXAMPLE: "I discussed the promotional campaign and tie-ins I put together when the store wanted to attract a different customer. One of them was a spring break promotion."**
>
> **[The employer still doesn't remember.]**
>
> **"I'll put another letter in the mail today that outlines my background and a few of my successful campaigns. I'm sure you'll be interested in hearing about the plans that attracted the teen- and college-aged customer you're after. Why don't I come in and show you the promotional package I developed? I'm free next Tuesday—or would Wednesday be more convenient?"**

### 2. "I haven't gotten to the letter yet."

Make sure he or she actually has the letter, then offer to call back at a later date.

> **EXAMPLE: "I'll give you a call when you've had a chance to read it. Would Wednesday be all right with you? Or would Thursday be more convenient?"**

**3. "We're not hiring right now" (or we're cutting back, laying off, etc.).**

This is difficult to handle. There's always the strong temptation to say, "Fine. Thanks for your time," and hang up quickly. If you can, fight it. Get something out of your efforts. Tell the person you don't want a job, you want an interview—even just an *informational* interview. Once you're in his or her office you might be able to turn it around into a job or a job referral.

But if you're *truly* aggressive and sales-oriented, push on with your phone call. You can brazen it out with "I have some ideas I'm sure you'll be interested in that will help your company save money," and the like. As one large employer said, "We always have jobs for the right people, even if officially we're not hiring."

- **No matter how well you sell yourself or how polished your techniques, you will still get rejections.**

While a targeted direct mail campaign is a strong tactic, it isn't failproof. If you do get rejections, work at not being bothered by them. *Remember:* With each rejection, you have a better idea of what employers want in a candidate; you are continually adding to your salesmanship. You are moving closer to getting an interview.

> TIP: If you consistently get rejections, rethink your strategy. Ask yourself: *Am I picking companies that are out of my league? Are my letters well targeted? Am I reaching the right person in each company, or should I redirect my letter? Am I proving my qualifications?*

## RESUME-BLITZING

- **Resume-blitzing is a widespread, shotgun approach to a direct mail campaign.**

With this method, you use an extensive mailing list consisting of hundreds of companies in your general field of interest and mail cover letters (usually called broadcast letters) along with resumes to all of them.

Many job hunters automatically think this method of papering the town with their resumes is the only logical way to land a job. The more resumes that go out to more companies, the better the odds, is the reasoning behind it. Consequently, it is one of the most common methods of job hunting. But you should think twice before you do this. Take into account the following:

- Fact #1: The typical Fortune 500 company receives over a quarter of a million *unsolicited* resumes a year. Yours will be just another one joining the slush pile.

- Fact #2: The average success rate of a mail campaign, i.e., getting a call for an interview, is 2%.

The success rate isn't as high as a targeted direct mail campaign for a very simple reason: *focus.* Because you are sending letters to hundreds of companies, by necessity, you are forced to send a form letter. You won't have time to write or send anything else. *Result:* You can't set up a specific needs payoff that grabs a prospective employer's interest.

Another disadvantage is that mass-mailing can cost quite a bit of money. Printing and mailing hundreds of resumes adds up. And if you purchase a mailing list, the cost mounts even higher. In addition, followup is difficult and time-consuming—when it's possible.

*Conclusion:* In most cases, launching a resume blitz isn't worth the time, cost, and effort. If you want to do a resume mailing, you're much better off with a targeted direct mail campaign.

*Consider resume-blitzing only if:*

- you're a recent college graduate seeking a management trainee or entry-level position

- you can sell yourself to a broad range of companies because your job target is so basic

- your job objective is so unique and your experience so well matched, you don't need to target yourself

If you fit into any one of these categories, if you don't have the time or energy to do a targeted mail campaign, and if you are prepared for a large number of rejections or no replies, a resume blitz can be worthwhile.

Blitzing does have one selling point for all of its drawbacks: It isn't a complicated method to master. You have to concern yourself with three steps: setting up a mailing list, writing a letter, and managing and tracking the campaign.

## Setting Up a Mailing List for a Resume Blitz

■ **To set up a mailing list you have two basic options: Put a mailing list together yourself or buy a preexisting list from a publication in your field, or from a mailing list company (see page 175).**

The mailing list is the heart of a resume blitz. To compile your own list, use the library as a start-off point. Your main sources will be reference directories and trade publications. If you are planning a job hunt that will focus mainly on Fortune 500 companies and the like, you can put together a list in the library with little trouble. (See Chapter 3, "Research," for specific information, techniques, and sources.)

> **TIP: Virtually every industry publication puts out a special issue that lists the top companies in the field. Check for those "roundup" or "top 500 companies" issues: They are excellent sources for addresses and often list the names of executives. For example, *Advertising Age* puts out a Top Media Companies issue.**

> **TIP: A best bet for free mailing lists is trade associations. Check the associations in your field. Most professional groups put out an annual membership directory or roster, listing member names, affiliations, addresses, and phone numbers. *Asset:* Because associations have a widespread membership mix, the chances are good you'll get the names of people you want to write to. *Drawback:* Lists are often arranged alphabetically by member name. You have to rely on the index to find the appropriate companies.**

*Anyone—from entry-level job hunters to job switchers to executives—can check the following annual book for lists of companies in a wide range of industries and career specialties:*

> *Jobs '95* ('96, '97, etc.)
> Fireside/ Simon & Schuster
> 1230 Avenue of the Americas
> New York, NY 10020
> —Available at most bookstores, this annual has leads to over 40 million jobs. A big plus: In addition to address listings of companies broken out by career specialty, industry, and state, it also includes listings of associations and research sources, and includes helpful information on trends in fifteen career specialties, twenty-seven industries, and the different regions of the U.S. It's an inexpensive source for a mailing list.

*Recent college graduates and MBAs should check the following publications, which are specifically designed to help them look for a job:*

**Peterson's Job Opportunities for Business and Liberal Arts Graduates**
Peterson's Guides, Inc.
Princeton, NJ 08540
—Lists employment opportunities at over 400 companies; listings include name, address, profile, contact name and phone number, starting salaries, requirements.

**Peterson's Job Opportunities for Engineering, Science, and Computer Graduates**
—Lists employment opportunities at over 1,000 manufacturing, research, consulting, and government organizations.

If you can afford the expense and *aren't* planning a general Fortune 500 type of company search, buy a preexisting mailing list. What you spend in money, you make up for in terms of time and effort saved.

Mailing lists are available from a number of sources: commercial mailing houses specializing in lists, newspapers and magazines, credit card companies, direct mail houses, and more. Compare prices and lists to find the best deal for you. At the end of this section we've included the names of the larger mailing list companies.

*Before you buy a list, be sure it meets the following criteria:*

- It is targeted to your area of interest. (Although you want an extensive list, a list that is too general is a waste of money.)

- It is current. (Lists over a year old often have outdated addresses, phone numbers, and executive names.)

- It includes the names and titles of the company executives who would hire you. (Many lists have only top corporate officers included, names that are useless for resume mailing purposes.)

- It is indexed for cross-referencing purposes. (You can arrange your list according to geographical location, company earnings, however you choose.)

■ **The best source for a preexisting mailing list that meets the necessary criteria is trade publications.**

Most trade publications sell their subscriber lists. These lists are ideal for a resume mailing because they are aimed directly at your targeted group of prospective employers. Usually the circulation department breaks out the lists into different classifications: job title, chief responsibilities, type of business, company products or services, geographical locations, company size, salary level, and more. Because of the numerous categories, you can make your mailing list as general or as specific as you want. For example, you can put together a list of marketing managers of midsized sporting goods manufacturers in the Midwest. Or you can make a general list of all managers in sporting goods companies across the country.

*For information on other mailing lists that are available to buy, check the following directories:*

> *Direct Mail List Rates and Data*
> Standard Rate & Data Service
> 3004 Glenview Rd.
> Wilmette, IL 60091
> 708/256-6067
> —Over 50,000 mailing lists of business people and companies, consumers, etc.
> —Title and description of lists, name, address, phone number, name of contact.
>
> *The Polk Mailing List Catalog*
> R. L. Polk & Company
> 521 Fifth Ave.
> New York, NY 10175
> 800/637-7635
> —Over 900 listings.

## Writing a Broadcast Letter for a Resume Blitz

■ **The letter you write for a resume blitz is called a broadcast letter because it broadcasts your availability to a large audience.**

While you cover the same ground in a broadcast letter that you do in any other job hunt letter (stating your job objective, highlighting your qualifications, requesting an interview), a broadcast letter has to be designed to appeal to the greatest number of prospective employers possible.

The best part about this method is that you only have to write the letter once. That one letter will be duplicated and sent to your entire mailing list. But you *don't* want this to be obvious. Employers, like everyone else, prefer letters that address their particular needs and desires, not some general "To whom it may concern" mailing. This is why you should know the tricks that will make your letter read as though it were written for an audience of one, not hundreds.

■ **Your opening paragraph is crucial in making your letter *appear* as personalized and specific as possible.**

*Remember:* Avoid overly canned openings, especially ones that read like advertising copy: *"No one thought I could do it—but I did. Generated profits in a business that had been losing money for 10 successive years, that is . . ."*

Openings like this are catchy, but they communicate one thing more than anything else: "This is my formula sales pitch letter that tells you how great I am, which I'm sending to everyone and anyone." Even if this might be true, don't let prospective employers know it.

Instead, try to personalize your letter by focusing it as much as possible. You won't be able to write about specific developments at each company on the list, but you can opt for the next best targeting mechanism: *industry* trends. Zero in on your job objective by discussing your area of interest and what's been happening in the field, and then state your qualifications.

> **EXAMPLE: "As corporate cutbacks become more and more common, the role of a human resources manager is becoming more and more challenging. Outplacement counseling, in particular, has become a vital function, and an area in which I have special expertise."**

## SAMPLE BROADCAST LETTER

542 Lowe St.
Ridgewood, NJ 07450

Mr. Oscar Gordon
Vice-President of Production
The Heinlein Company
100 Caltech Drive
Pasadena, CA 91106

Dear Mr. Gordon:

American companies need tight-fisted, cost-cutting professionals to streamline inventory procedures and compete more effectively.

As corporate budgets get tighter, the role of a cost-conscious scheduling supervisor becomes more and more vital. I know this from extensive experience. Over the past five years as a Supervisor for Production Control with a Fortune 500 company, I have slashed inventory budgets and streamlined operational procedures. More specifically, I have:
  · saved company over $100,000 by introducing and overseeing new obsolescence policy on local inventories.
  · introduced new inventory handling procedures reducing inventory costs by 5% per year.
  · been selected from management training team to be sole office representative for feasibility study of "Just in Time" inventory program review.
  · been awarded three Manager's Certificates of Outstanding Achievement.

I have a Bachelor's degree from Dulwich College, and am currently completing course work for my Master's in Business Administration at Fairleigh Dickinson University.

I'd like the opportunity to apply my skills in inventory management to a market leader such as your company and look forward to your call. I have many specific ideas on how to effectively cut inventory costs that I would like to discuss with you.

Sincerely,


John Lerner

■ **The remainder of your letter should be the same as any other cover letter you've written: a sales pitch and a close.**

## Managing and Tracking a Resume Blitz Mass Mailing

■ **Divide your list into workable units: an "A" list, "B" list, and "C" list.**

To make a large direct mail campaign work harder for you, roll it out in stages: in this case stages A, B, and C. This allows you to track the success of the mailing and modify your approach as you go along.

■ **Start by sending your letter and resume to the companies that are specialists in your area or those that particularly interest you: your "A" list.**

TIP: Don't concentrate only on large "name-brand" companies. Often smaller to midsized companies that are less well known turn up stronger responses because the competition for jobs is less. One job hunter did a resume blitz with two distinct letters and lists: one for well-known companies, the other for those that are less known.

TIP: Address your mailing to the people who would be your supervisors, not to the personnel, training, or employment department. If you aren't sure of the right name or title, call and ask the switchboard operator or receptionist for the name and title of the person who heads the appropriate department.

Because your "A" list consists of your primary targets, give it priority. After your first mailing, wait a week or two, then follow up. Don't wait for the companies to call you, call them.

TIP: Use your mailing list to keep track of your mailing. Beside each company name, note the date you sent out the letter, the date of your followup call, the date you received a response, and anything that happens. Even jot down the times when you've tried calling, but have spoken with a secretary and couldn't reach the addressee. This is especially handy when you speak with the people you've sent letters to—you can refer to specific dates and information.

■ **Make followup phone calls.**

You can bring your success rate up to 10%, which is far better than the normal low 2% rate.

In your followup call, refer to the date you sent the letter, briefly touch on the contents, and restate your job objective and desire for an interview. If you can't get an interview, ask for further information about the company or the names of other people to whom you should write. Don't let the phone call end your campaign. Use it for referrals to add to your list.

■ **Send out your "B" and "C" list mailings when you start getting responses from your original mailing.**

If you are having no luck getting interviews, consider changing your letter or adding to your list. Continue tracking responses and making additions to the list.

### Blitz Do's and Don't's

- *Don't* send photocopies or obvious form letters. Although this is a large mailing, you should be hiding that fact as much as possible.

- *Do* use a computer to run off your letters, instead of having them professionally set. A typeset letter looks better than a photocopy, but it's expensive and ends up saying the same thing: This isn't unique.

- *Don't* send more than one copy of your letter to the same company. You never know who will pass your letter around and who will wind up seeing it.

- *Do* match resume and letter stock. And use a simple, readable typeface and layout.

## TEMPORARY WORK

■ **If you have the time (if you are currently unemployed or have only a part-time job), seriously consider working as a temporary employee as a way of eventually getting a permanent job.**

"Temping" *isn't* what many people think it is. It can be one of the best ways to position yourself for a job—whatever your job objective. It isn't simply secretarial work and it isn't just interim employment that can help pay the bills while you're looking for a job. Temping (or free-lancing, consulting, contract work, or special project work) *is* a successful job hunting tactic—if you know how to make it work for you.

> **EXAMPLE: A systems analyst was laid off during a slump in the high-tech field. He sent his resume to several companies and was called back by one computer manufacturer. No full-time jobs were available, but they needed someone to work on a short-term, special project. A two-month job wasn't what he wanted, but he took the project anyway and did his best. When it was finished, he moved on, but his efficient work was remembered. A month later, he got a phone call and was offered a permanent job at the computer company.**

Because the number of temporary workers and the range of available jobs is growing at such a fast rate, you can find or create a temp job in virtually any field: not only in office staff positions, but also in technical and managerial positions. Financial consultants, accountants, engineers, computer systems specialists, publicists, lawyers, even doctors, are hired on a temporary basis.

*Temping is especially recommended if:*

- you have little or no experience in your targeted field
- you are seeking an entry-level job in a "glamour" profession, such as advertising, publishing, broadcasting, or film
- your target company isn't hiring
- you are a career changer, student, or recent graduate, or are reentering the labor market

*A few initial guidelines:*

- The simplest way to start temping is by going through an agency. Speak with a number of employment agencies to find out what types of companies they handle. Ask for specific company names: The more you know about an agency's clients, the better you can judge its potential to help you get a job.

> **TIP: Check to see if the agency is a member of the National Associa-
> tion of Temporary Services (NATS), which establishes guide-
> lines for the temporary services industry.**

- Pay particular attention to agencies with specialties: They work especially well for people seeking nonsecretarial work. For example, New York–based Accountemps specializes in placing accountants; Chicago-based LAW/temps places lawyers.

- Move beyond agencies once you've started temp work. Spread the word that you are available for free-lance work. Create your own temp network of clients. This is often the best way of getting temp positions that will lead to bigger and better things.

Following is a discussion of some of the best uses of temping.

## A "Back Door" Method of Landing a Job

This is the most valuable way to use temping. By getting inside a company and meeting prospective customers face-to-face, you avoid the problem of having to openly contact a company with the standard resume/letter. You can sell yourself in person rather than on paper.

It is ideal for people seeking entry-level positions, especially in the "glamour" industries. Since industries such as advertising, film, and broadcasting are continually flooded with resumes, your best bet for winning an interview is by getting inside the company *first*—in any capacity.

> **EXAMPLE: All three television networks were in the midst of a hir-
> ing freeze. A woman who wanted to work in casting took
> a job as a temporary secretary at one of the networks just
> to get her foot in the door. Her strategy worked. She
> impressed people with her skills, talked about her exten-
> sive experience in the film industry, and got offered a
> full-time job—*while the hiring freeze was still on.***

> **TIP: If you are offered a temp job at a company you want to work
> for, but in the wrong department—take it anyway. Once you're
> inside, you can learn more about the department you want to
> join.**

To make a temp position lead to an interview for a permanent job, *you must make sure that people know about you, your qualifications, and your ambitions.* No one at the company will be aware of your goals until you begin to tell them. Speak up, volunteer for extra assignments, and, in general, show that you are ambitious, dedicated, and focused on your goal. This is no time to be shy. Find out who can hire you and make certain you introduce yourself to those people.

It's important to remember that temp jobs are just that: *temporary.* You have to take advantage of whatever time you have.

> **TIP: A good, subtle way to impress prospective employers is by doing your work accurately and efficiently, no matter how low-level. Don't make the mistake of thinking temp work is beneath you or unimportant. Doing a good job on even the most minor task is often noticed.**
>
> ***Better yet:* Do a little extra work—and make sure the right people know about it. Stay at the office an extra five minutes to type a letter or finish a project. It will make you look like a committed, hardworking employee—the kind of employee a prospective employer would want to hire.**

## Learning Inside Information About a Company or Industry that Will Increase Your Salability

Temping gives you the opportunity to see *exactly* how to target yourself in a resume, letter, or interview. Instead of immediately setting yourself up as a potential job candidate, keep your eyes and ears open, and scout out a company or industry.

> **TIP: Don't be overly selective about the companies you work in, particularly at the beginning. Temping anywhere in your field can pay off: You'll still get information about the industry, discover the types of jobs available, and so on. In addition, sometimes working for a competitor is the best place to hear gossip about the company in which you're most interested.**

Listen to office talk for insights into what is happening at a company. Many times the grapevine is the best place to hear about upcoming events, what jobs may be opening, what managers are leaving the company, and so forth. Pick up clues about the corporate culture. Even small things can help you sell yourself: Is the atmosphere casual, informal? Does management expect people to work late hours or on weekends? Apply whatever you learn to your cover letter and interview techniques.

> **EXAMPLE:** When a young woman temped at a magazine, she learned that the company was very bullish on corporate sporting events. Later, when she sent them a targeted cover letter, she made sure to mention her involvement in different sports: specifically, how she coached a company softball team and ran in a city-wide corporate-challenge race. She got an interview, and a job offer. The interviewer commented on how well she would fit into the company.

## Adding to Your Skills and Qualifications

Temping is especially helpful for people reentering the work force, career changers, and those with little formal work experience.

In effect, let temping train you and make you more employable. Working as a temp allows you to fill out your background *before* and *during* your job hunt. Pinpoint the areas where you have gaps or trouble spots and look for temp positions that will help diminish them.

> **EXAMPLE:** A career changer was having no luck switching from government work to publishing because he had no experience in the new field except for a few college courses he had taken years before. After months of fruitless searching, many targeted mailings, and following leads through networking, he decided to take free-lance work as a proofreader and copyeditor. *Result:* His free-lance assignments gave him credibility. After listing publishers he had worked for in cover letters, and mentioning his work to contacts, he soon landed a full-time position at a large New York publishing house.

> **TIP:** If you are changing your career, reentering the work force, or have little experience, be sure to include temp jobs that relate to your job objective in your cover letter. You don't have to identify them as short-term jobs. Instead, emphasize functions, duties, and accomplishments.

## Increasing Your Network of Contacts

The people you meet through temping make excellent contacts, especially those people in upper- and middle-management positions.

Even if you don't get a job at one particular company, recognize that the people you meet there are potential sources of job leads and referrals.

Ask people about job opportunities at their company and in the industry in general, and if they can suggest other contacts or offer some general advice. Cultivate the people who are in jobs similar to your objective and those who directly supervise them. Both groups can give you the most insightful tips.

*For more information on temporary work and agencies:*

National Association of Temporary Services (NATS)
119 S. St. Asaph St.
Alexandria, VA 22314
703/549-6287
—Establishes guidelines for member agencies.
—Publishes an annual directory that lists member agencies, and other informational brochures and booklets about temporary work.

*Prominent agencies with offices nationwide:*

ADIA Personnel
100 Redwood Shore Pkwy.
Redwood City, CA 94065
415/610-1000

Kelly Services
999 W. Big Beaver Rd.
Troy, MI 48084
810/362-4444

Manpower
5301 N. Ironwood Rd.
Milwaukee, WI 53217
414/961-1000
*Mailing Address:* P.O. Box 2053
Milwaukee, WI 53201

Uniforce
1335 Jericho Turnpike
New Hyde Park, NY 11040
516/437-3300

Western Temporary Services, Inc.
301 Lennon Lane
Walnut Creek, CA 94598
510/930-5300

## EXECUTIVE RECRUITERS

■ **Executive recruiters (also called executive search firms or head-hunters) are hired by corporations to find them the "right person" for a *specific* job opening.**

Executive recruiters differ from regular employment agencies in that they usually handle higher-level positions requiring very specific experience: You don't just walk through the door and wind up with four interviews.

In addition, the positions that search firms handle are ones that aren't advertised in the media or broadcast throughout a company or industry. Often these positions are the top jobs in a field. Typically, they are in mid- to upper-level management, commanding a minimum salary of roughly $50,000. If you are seeking a job that pays less than that, odds are you should go to an employment agency (see page 191) rather than expect a call from a headhunter.

There are two different types of executive recruiters: general firms, which handle positions across a range of professions, and specialist firms, which focus on a specific field or industry.

■ **If you currently hold or are seeking a job in mid- to upper-level management, you should try to get your resume on file with several executive recruiters that specialize in your field.**

It is one of the best ways of landing interviews for jobs that you might never hear about in the so-called "hidden" job market. An added plus—you don't have to do the initial selling of yourself. It is the recruiter's job to sell you into an interview situation, then it's up to you to sell yourself in person.

■ **Your chief concern with executive recruiters is getting one interested in you.**

The top executive recruiters receive over 10,000 unsolicited resumes a year. Only a small percentage of these resumes stays in the firm's files. The rest are thrown away.

*Remember:* Executive recruiters are not in business to find people jobs. They are hired by corporations to find people to fill specific positions. That makes for a small, select pool of potential candidates that search firms will contact. *You* have to work to get yourself into that pool.

## Attracting Executive Recruiters

■ **The most foolproof method of being actively sought out and pro-moted by headhunters is the simplest: already having a job that is similar to the ones the recruiters are trying to fill.**

In light of that, it's a good idea to cultivate a relationship with a recruiter *before* you start an intensive job search. Most middle managers get about two to four calls a year from executive recruiters. The next time one calls you, talk to him or her even if you don't want the position offered. Find out what other openings the recruiter has or may have in the future; mention that you are interested in moving to another job; sound out the prospects.

One of the best moves you can make is to position yourself as an *information source*—give the recruiter names of potential candidates, tips about your company, possible openings, and other people to contact who might be interested in changing jobs.

> **TIP: To attract executive recruiters, join trade associations and professional organizations. Search firms often use them as resources and ask members for referrals. As an attention-grabber, write articles for trade journals or association newsletters.**

> **TIP: Recontact any recruiter who has previously called you. If he or she has been interested in you in the past, chances are you can get him or her interested again. Explain that you are now actively job hunting and suggest a brief meeting.**

■ **If the phone *doesn't* ring, or if you don't have the time or patience to wait for recruiters to contact you, it's time to take a more active role and directly solicit the recruiters themselves.**

Frankly, your success rate in attracting recruiters will depend a great deal on blind luck and good timing—for instance, whether a recruiter gets your letter the same day that he or she has a job opening requiring someone with your exact background. But you can create your own "luck" by knowing the right notes to hit with a recruiter.

*A few guidelines on choosing which executive recruiters to approach:*

• Ask people in your field to suggest recruiters to contact. Often they will be your best and most objective source.

- Have a friend or colleague who is regularly contacted by recruiters mention your name and suggest that the recruiter contact you. *Or:* Ask if you can use your friend's name as a reference when you call the recruiter. A personal reference can increase your chances of getting the attention you want.

- Recruiters are assigned to different specialties within a search firm—even if the firm is focused on only one industry. Always find out who is responsible for your specific area of interest at the firm and address your letter accordingly. There is less chance that your letter will be tossed aside.

- Be selective. Don't send a letter and resume to hundreds or even dozens of recruiters. It isn't worth your money or time.

## Selling Yourself to Recruiters

■ **Convince recruiters that you are worth their attention by sending them a targeted cover letter with your resume.**

A cover letter to executive recruiters should be similar to any other letter you write during your job hunt: as specifically targeted to the reader as possible, emphasizing your strongest points, and closing with a brief summary and request to meet.

However, unlike typical cover letters, this one isn't an attempt to "tease" a headhunter into wanting to know more about you. Instead, prove to a recruiter that you fit the firm's criteria, that you are the type of person the firm's clients would want to hire.

*To write a cover letter that will sell you to recruiters:*

- Spell out *why* you are the type of candidate they already recommend to clients. Leave little to the reader's imagination. Be clear, concise, focused, and thorough. Catchy openings and clever phrases are absolutely out. Explain what you're looking for, why you are interested in a new position, and what your qualifications are.

- Unlike other cover letters, a letter to a search firm *can* include your target salary range. Let the recruiter know you fit the firm's range.

- Let recruiters see how they can sell you to their clients. Give recruiters the ammunition they need by listing specific examples of your salable achievements in the second or third paragraph of your letter. Choose more examples than you would in a typical cover letter. Lift details from your resume. Bullet the examples to make them leap off the page.

- Keep in mind: Headhunters search for people to fit very specific jobs, so often your best chance of making a match is having a *unique* blend of qualities, abilities, and experiences. Make yourself stand out from other people in your field or position. Try to come up with *unusual* characteristics or abilities that will peg you as more of an individual.

> **EXAMPLE: A former government employee was having problems switching careers to finance. As a last-ditch effort, he sent to recruiters letters that mentioned his MBA but strongly highlighted his negotiating experience and his ability to speak two dialects of Chinese fluently. Three headhunters contacted him, each for financial sales positions that required fluency in Chinese.**

## Following Up with Recruiters

■ **Don't call recruiters to follow up on your mailing.**

This is one time when followup phone calls are just a waste of your time. The reason is simple: Recruiters can't help you unless they have a position that matches your qualifications. If no such position exists, you won't gain a thing by trying to push yourself into their office.

■ **If you've heard nothing four to six months after you've contacted a recruiter, try again.**

After a reasonable period of time, send out another letter and resume. This time the recruiter might have an opening you match.

## Interviewing with Recruiters

■ **Typically, your first encounter with an executive recruiter is on the phone. He or she calls to tell you about a job opening, and in doing so is *screening* you for a possible interview.**

Recruiters will first tell you a little about the job, check to see if you're interested and qualified, then ask you questions about your employment history, achievements, and objective. This is the time for you to ask questions as well. While you can't expect the recruiter to tell you the company's name, you *can* expect to find out other information that can help you determine if it's the right job for you.

> **TIP: If you get an unsolicited call from a recruiter, make certain the firm is legitimate and useful to you by asking what type of firm it is, where it got your name, and the kind of companies the recruiter handles. *Don't* agree to send in your resume until you are satisfied that the firm and offer are legitimate.**

> **TIP: Always doublecheck about confidentiality if you're currently employed.**

■ **If the screening interview goes well, you're on to the next step: a face-to-face meeting with the recruiter.**

The recruiter will want to go into more depth about your accomplishments when you see him or her in person. But you should also be prepared to answer more philosophical questions, ones that are designed to help the recruiter understand you and see if you'd mesh with the client company. Expect questions like: What kind of corporate culture do you prefer? In what work environment do you produce your best efforts? What has given you the most personal satisfaction—both in work and in your nonprofessional life?

*A few general tips:*

• You're better off being completely straightforward when you deal with recruiters. Lying about qualifications, or even your interest in a particular job opening, won't help you and, in fact, will probably hurt you in the long run.

• Be candid about *your* requirements for a job: from salary to corporate culture to responsibilities. This information will help recruiters decide if you're suitable for the opening they have in mind. The more guidance you can give them, the more accurately they can assess your needs.

• *Remember:* You want to cultivate a relationship with an executive recruiter. Even if you aren't asked to interview with a client, you've moved ahead in your job hunt by establishing ties with a recruiter. As suggested earlier, maintain these ties by becoming a valuable source: Offer inside information about your field, suggest candidates for openings, etc. Keep up the relationship even after you have found a job.

*To find names and addresses of executive recruiters, check the following:*

> *Directory of Executive Recruiters*
> Kennedy Publications
> Templeton Rd.
> Fitzwilliam, NH 03447
> 603/585-2200
> —This is the definitive directory, listing over 1,800 recruiters complete with addresses, principal names, specializations, and minimum salaries.
> —It also includes helpful information on how to use recruiters (from both the client and job hunter points of view).
>
> *Executive Employment Guide*
> American Management Association
> 135 W. 50th St.
> New York, NY 10020
> 212/586-8100
> —Lists executive search firms, employment agencies, job registers, and career counselors.
> —In addition to name, address, and phone number, entries include specializations, types of jobs handled and minimum salary ranges, policies on resumes and interviews.

## EMPLOYMENT AGENCIES

■ **Employment agencies, like executive recruiters, are contracted by companies to find candidates for job openings. Unlike recruiters, agencies usually deal with a wide variety of positions, from secretarial to middle management.**

There are basically two kinds of employment agencies: *general employment agencies,* which normally handle entry-level, secretarial, and nonmanagement or lower-management positions in the $25,000 to $30,000 salary range; and *specialist employment agencies,* which handle anything from entry-level up to and including middle-management positions. Specialist agencies are a better bet for anyone seeking a position above entry-level or secretarial slots, and cover a large number of fields from publishing to accounting to engineering.

■ **Unless you are aiming at an upper-level management position, it makes sense to sign up with at least two to four agencies.**

Because employment agencies generally don't handle the upper-management positions or the highly exclusive spots that executive recruiters do, they are easier to contact and use in a job hunt.

## Contacting Agencies

- Avoid general employment agencies if you have a lot of previous work experience. An agency that specializes in your field will probably have many more opportunities available to you than one that's more generalized.

- Ask friends and colleagues for recommendations of specific agencies, perhaps ones they have used for their own job hunt or ones they have used through their company. Be sure to get the names of individual counselors to contact.

- Call the personnel departments or office managers of companies in your field and ask them which agencies they have used. This will give you a good sense of which agencies work with which companies.

- Whenever possible, contact agencies directly by phone and save yourself some waiting time. If you don't have the name of a counselor, ask for the person who handles jobs in your specialty area.

- Avoid contacting agencies on Sunday, Monday, and Tuesday. Because of the number of ads that are run in the Sunday classifieds, agencies are busiest on those three days. Wait until Wednesday to call. You'll be given closer attention and won't be slotted as another desperate job seeker.

## When You Get to an Employment Agency

- Ask the counselor questions to be sure the agency will work well for you. Find out the names of the companies it works with;

whether it has successfully placed other candidates with backgrounds similar to yours; and the types of jobs it usually handles.

- Carefully read any contract you're given. You should expect to pay nothing for job-placement assistance: Agency fees are normally paid by the companies. Be on the lookout for hidden costs tacked on for extra services, such as resume writing and reviewing or job counseling. It's better to see an independent career counselor for those services.

- Beware of agencies that ask you to sign contracts immediately, demand money up front, guarantee placement, or boast of placement rates upward of 90%. There has been a recent increase in the number of fraudulent agencies that prey on desperate job seekers with such practices and stories; most reputable agencies report far lower success rates and don't push you into signing up.

- If you want a nonsecretarial position (entry-level or management trainee) but are still asked to take a typing test, think twice before working with that agency. The agency may be trying to pass off secretarial jobs or dead-end administrative assistant positions as trainee positions when they're not. *A major exception:* Entry-level positions in the communications area (television, radio, publishing, advertising, etc.) usually require typing skills. In addition, taking a low-level secretarial job may be the best way to break into these "glamour" professions.

## Once You've Signed Up with an Employment Agency

- Don't be intimidated by a counselor who tries to push you into having job interviews that don't fit in with your job objective. If you find yourself being pressured into them, consider switching agencies or asking for a different counselor.

- If a position comes up that isn't exactly what you want, but is in the right field or company, have the interview anyway. Use it to practice your techniques. Afterward, you can ask the counselor for feedback: What did the employer think of you, what problems arose, is there any one area of your presentation that needs work? You then can apply this information to more important interviews.

- Don't wait for the agency to contact you. Make it a habit to check in periodically and see what's happening. It refreshes the counselor's memory and increases your chances of being remembered when something suitable comes in.

- Consider switching agencies if you have no results after a few weeks. Counselors often start easing up on their efforts to place you if they haven't done so in a short time. If you sense this is the case (the counselor is unavailable to meet with you; no interviews are forthcoming; you rarely get through to speak with the counselor), you are better off starting fresh with a new agency than sticking with the old.

*For further information, check with:*

National Association of Personnel Consultants (NAPC)
1432 Duke St.
Alexandria, VA 22314
703/684-0180
—Publishes *Access,* a directory of member employment agencies that is organized by specialty and geographical location.

## ONLINE AND OFFLINE COMPUTER SERVICES

■ **Using a computer in job hunting is a growing trend.**

Now that the Information Superhighway is in the news every day, more and more people are using their computers to get a job.

Computerized job hunting is not really that different from other types of job hunting—the real difference is that it takes advantage of the speed and networking capabilities of computers to ease your job hunting task.

Depending on the specific method, computerized job hunting can offer you a number of advantages: It can let you access up-to-date openings from across the country that are specific to *your* needs; it can let thousands of employers scan your resume quickly; and finally, it can attract employers and give you employment targets and ideas you may have never considered otherwise.

That said, there are also problems. Using computer services can sometimes be expensive, time-consuming, and a waste of time. For all the hoopla, the fact remains that many times openings listed on the electronic highways are also listed in the newspapers—and therefore obtainable at a fraction of the cost and effort. Many times new electronic job banks are launched with a great deal of fanfare—only to fold a few months later. And often (although this is changing) there's a bias toward high-tech and unusual jobs.

Bottom line: Computers can be a fast and effective way of finding a job and they're getting better all the time. But don't overlook other less high-tech, less sexy methods.

■ **Here's how to get the most out of your computer by using computerized job banks in your job hunt.**

Most people focus on computerized job banks in their electronic job hunting. There are two basic types. They operate on very simple premises.

**The most commonly used are *resume banks*.** These are collections of resumes sent or modemed by job seekers and entered on the electronic database of a job bank firm. In effect, they're simply electronic resume files maintained by a firm or office that lets prospective employers take a look at them. For you, these are usually passive services. All you do is contact the resume bank company, pay the price (if any), send in your resume, and wait. You don't even need a computer for most of these services, since *they* maintain an electronic file, not you. Companies and executive recruiters that subscribe to the service key in criteria for positions they need to fill. If your resume meets the criteria, it is called up, and if it passes muster, you'll be called in for an interview.

Costs are fairly low—usually about $50 to keep your resume active for six months to a year. Some universities offer resume banks for free. Naturally, you can call or write many resume banks directly without a computer (see addresses on pages 197–198).

■ **The second basic type of job bank lists *job openings*.**

These tend to be more specialized, focusing on specific career areas, often governmental or high-tech, although increasingly, more general jobs are covered as well. In effect, these are electronic classifieds that you can speed through via your computer. They're usually *online* services. This means you must join a service that links your computer to computer service providers who control a computer network and many databases, including some job-related ones. Major computer online services like Prodigy, America Online, and CompuServe have job banks that you can see for a fee—you pay a monthly fee and use your computer with telephone modem to go online with their systems.

Or you might get onto Internet—a giant computer network that connects businesses, schools, and governments electronically, with thousands of databases and millions of computer users worldwide, including some job-related areas. You can get onto Internet via your company or university computer for free, or via a computer service company or a smaller "gateway company" that hooks you up for a fee.

The costs of going online vary—you must contact the sources listed below and ask. A rough rule with the giant computer network companies is to expect something like a $10–$20 monthly fee plus about $4 an hour after the first few hours of online use; you may also be charged extra to access specific databases or areas.

> **TIP: In addition to Internet, don't forget that many government employment centers, colleges, and libraries maintain computerized job banks that you can access by using *their* computers or by reading their printouts of the week or month.**

■ **You may also want to consider *computer bulletin boards (BBS)*, available through computer service companies and Internet.**

They sometimes have sections geared to careers—with areas to post your resume, get advice and information, and peruse lists of job openings. But first things first. What are computer bulletin boards (BBS)? BBS stands for *Bulletin Board Service.* A BBS or bulletin board is in effect a computer-based special interest group; a place within a computer network for you to chat with others interested in the same things as you. Simply put, they're the electronic equivalent of standing around the watercooler and talking with people interested in the same things as you. Computer networks and services set aside a certain area for their users to chat electronically, put up notes, comments, etc.—and increasingly, many include special areas for job hunters or those interested in certain careers. Prodigy has the *Careers Bulletin Board,* and America Online has the *Careers Board,* just to name two. Most are divided by career specialty and let job hunters post notes and resumes, look at openings posted by employers, and trade advice. But probably the best way to use bulletin boards is to play the online game—by dealing with others in the network regularly, showing your expertise by helping others and giving advice . . . and then putting out the word that you're looking for a job. In effect, you can treat it all as a networking exercise with people you know electronically.

Besides the biggies, smaller bulletin boards also exist—for example, *FedWorld* of Springfield, Virginia, is a bulletin board that lists federal government jobs. Many of these bulletin boards are free; they're usually specialized by either locality or career area.

One final note: Bulletin boards are open to all kinds, so exercise caution. You don't get the same kind of screening you might get with an employment agency or executive recruiter.

■ **Where can you contact job banks and other job-related computer services?**

The computer world is changing so rapidly that companies change overnight—and so do addresses. The sources we list below may have changed phone numbers, prices, and specialties by the time you read this, so you must do some checking on your own.

*America Online* (800/827-8364): Computer service that includes *Help Wanted USA,* a job-opening database for managers that tries to uncover job openings that aren't listed in the newspapers, as well as *Career Board,* a bulletin board divided by function on careers and career topics.

*CompuServe* (800/848-8199): Computer service with bulletin boards, has *E-Span* resume bank (see below) and many other services.

*E-Span* (800/682-2901): Resume bank that includes resumes of over 1.5 million professional, managerial, and technical candidates. Accessible via the Internet, Compuserve, and Genie.

*Help Wanted USA* (813/725-9600): Online listings of professional jobs available nationwide. Available on the Internet or America Online.

*Internet:* A huge "highway" of databases, people, businesses, universities, governments, etc., all interconnected electronically. It includes bulletin boards and databases useful to job hunters (as well as virtually everything else). Through Internet you can access the *Online Career Center* (317/293-6499), which lists professional jobs, and *Help Wanted USA* (listed above), which lists job openings nationwide. Other job-related services on the Internet include *Career Connections* (415/903-5800), which lists computer, engineering, manufacturing, and marketing jobs; *Academic Position Network* (612/853-0225), which lists academic openings, including faculty, staff, and administrative positions as well as graduate assistantships and fellowships; and *Federal Job Opportunity Board* (912/757-3030), which lists openings in the federal government. Get into Internet for free via your company or university, or sign up via CompuServe, America Online (phone numbers in this section), or national computer services like Delphi (800/695-4005) or local services in your area.

*Job Bank USA* (800/296-1USA): Resume bank covering all business levels, offers a quarterly newsletter, toll-free number for updates, discounts on career services and books.

*kiNexus* (800/828-0422): Found at many college career centers, where it may be free for students.

*National Resume Bank* (813/896-3694): Resume bank covering all business levels.

*Online Opportunities* (215/873-2168).

*Peterson's Connexion* (800/338-3282): Found at many college career centers where it can be free for students. This is international in scope. It's also accessible via CompuServe.

*Prodigy* (800/776-3449 or 914/993-8000): Computer service that offers an online resume bank and bulletin boards, as well as want ads from *USA Today* and the *National Business Employment Weekly.*

*ROC: Resumes on Computer* (317/363-1000): Resume service run by the Curtis Publishing Company.

*SkillSearch* (800/258-6641): Resume bank covering wide range; requires a college degree and at least two years of experience.

*The Ultimate Job Finder* (800/829-5220): Computer disks listing sources (professional magazines, etc.) that have job advertisements, including all sources listed in the *Professional's Private Job Finder, Non-Profit Job Finder,* and *Government Job Finder.* Very helpful; as with the books, a very comprehensive database of job sources. A new version should be released soon; call for details.

In addition, always be on the lookout for specialized resume banks and bulletin boards that deal only with specific locales or job areas. These are proliferating and can be the most useful for your job hunt.

Two sources may be useful:

*Harry's Job Search BBS Hot List,* compiled by Harold Lemon and updated periodically. (Send $2 to Harold Lemon, 3241 San Carlos Way, Union City, CA 94587.) It lists career BBS nationwide, many of them hard to find.

*The Electronic Job Search Revolution* (Joyce Lain Kennedy, New York: John Wiley & Sons, 1994). Role-playing and presentations: how to act your way into a job.

# 7 Interviews

## INTRODUCTION

Everything you've been doing in your job hunt—putting together the strongest possible resume, researching companies, setting up a network of contacts, writing cover letters, and trying out different selling tactics—has been leading to this point: the interview with a prospective employer that lands you the *job*.

The interview stage of your job search is the most crucial. You can make or break your chances of being hired in the short amount of time it takes to be interviewed. With so much at stake, many people lose their winning edge. They may have been successful up to now, but put them in a chair opposite a prospective employer and all is lost.

It doesn't have to be so difficult. *Anyone can learn to interview well.* Most mistakes that are made can be corrected, most techniques can be learned.

Interviewing effectively means commanding better interviewing skills; listening to suggestions that others may have; reading about interviewing; going back over past interviews in your head and analyzing what you did wrong, then thinking of ways to improve your performance; and, most important, *going out on as many interviews as you can to practice and refine your technique.* The more interviews you go on, the better your odds at getting the job offers you want. It may not be easy, but it's the best way to achieve interviewing success.

## GENERAL GUIDELINES

*Before we talk about how to interview, let's consider a few facts about interviewing itself:*

- You can get a job without a resume, but you can't get a job without an interview.
- The interviewer often makes the conclusive decision about you in the first three to five minutes of the interview. However "open-minded" he or she may try to be, the rest of the interview is often spent simply justifying that first impression.
- The interviewer is more influenced by your negatives than your positives. If the recruiter changes his or her mind about you during the interview, it's usually for the worse.
- Your interpersonal skills are more important than your background, experience, or education.
- Most people don't talk enough during an interview. Instead of taking charge of selling themselves, they allow the interviewer to ask all the questions, and content themselves with just answering them. They *respond*, they don't *initiate*.

*Before you create your own interviewing style, keep in mind what the following facts mean:*

1. *The best interviewees do it fast.* They set the tone of the interview in the first few minutes, then spend the rest of the time enhancing what they've said. This requires that you have a strong idea about what you're going to say before you say it, which can only be accomplished through preparation. You must practice your presentation and learn as much as you can about the company, interviewer, and position before the interview.

2. *An interview is in some ways unfair.* Who can figure you out in five minutes? Or even two hours? Instead of worrying about it, let it work for you. Don't let interviews intimidate you—at best they're an imperfect way of accepting or rejecting an *impression* of you, not who you really are. So you should create a strong, straightforward first impression. If you're shy and meek—no problem. Just try to make a less shy, less meek first impression. Work on gradually improving yourself—and you will succeed. Effort counts.

3. *Think about your negatives before the interview and have answers ready that will explain them sufficiently if they're discovered.* Unfortunately,

people pay more attention to negatives than to positives. The trick is to either keep them hidden or be able to explain them away.

4. *Recognize what an interview is and what it isn't.* It is not a rehashing of your resume, nor is it merely an opportunity to answer questions that an interviewer may pose: Interviewing is salesmanship. It is *selectively presenting the facts in an organized, confident manner* so that you can sell yourself into a job. This means that *you* must take control of your interview. The people who get job offers are the people who do the talking. Quiet, passive people *do* get job offers, but assertive people get more. They come across as effective and likable. And they can present the interviewer with clear and cogent reasons why they should be hired.

5. *The objective is always to be a brief, target-oriented interviewee.* Take interviews step by step. Step One is *preparation:* researching and preparing an effective presentation, planning what to wear, what to bring. Step Two is *practice:* going over what you're going to say and working on keeping a strong, positive attitude. Step Three is *the interview itself:* making certain to concentrate on the major aspects of yourself and your background that will sell you.

## STEP ONE: PREPARATION

■ **If you prepare for an interview, you'll be calmer, be more organized, and sound better during your actual presentation.**

Before you are interviewed, learn about the company and the position, and if possible, try to find out something about the interviewer as well. Read annual reports, trade magazine articles, and company literature in order to come up with questions to ask the interviewer. You should also prepare yourself for any possible questions that he or she may ask you. *Always* be on the lookout for information you can use to make yourself sound more knowledgeable, more interested, and *better* than the other applicants. (Reread Chapter 3, "Research," for suggestions on where to get the right literature.)

■ **Think of ways your background and experience might fit in with what you've read.**

For example, many companies today stress being "entrepreneurial," and their literature is full of references to their need for self-starting employees. If you are interviewing at such a company, start thinking *before* the interview of items to mention that will highlight your own entrepreneurial past.

> **TIP: For best results, review your research at least three times before the interview: a week before, the night before, and a few minutes before you go in. By the third time you should be able to remember the important facts you've accumulated, easily and without straining. When reviewing in order to memorize, the trick isn't how *long* you review, it's how *frequently* you do it. Information is more accurately recalled if you review it many times for a few minutes, instead of one time for an hour.**

> **TIP: Jot down key ideas, figures, or points you want to make on a 3 × 5 note card. Stick it in your pocket and review it right before the interview begins.**

> **TIP: Read the newspaper or watch the news before interviewing. Many companies, in a policy effort to hire "well-rounded" people, want applicants who can discuss current events. This is particularly true in publishing, public relations, advertising, television, and government.**

## What to Wear on an Interview

■ **Play it safe and dress on the conservative side.**

Even if you are interviewing for a highly creative position, you can't lose with a professional look. You are selling your professionalism—not your innovative fashion sense.

> **TIP:** *The rule of thumb:* **Wear the same type of clothing as you would expect your prospective boss to wear. People are automatically drawn to those who are like themselves. It's human nature. Take advantage of this fact whenever possible.**

■ **Dressing conservatively doesn't have to mean looking like a "corporate clone" who has internalized every dress-for-success rule.**

*Remember:* You want to come across as confident, successful, and professional. And you can do that by wearing something *other* than a pin-striped suit. In fact, if you ordinarily avoid conservative styles, you *shouldn't* dress too conservatively for an interview. You'll end up feeling uncomfortable, stiff, and unnatural. Instead, adapt a classic outfit to fit your personality

Don't use the day of your interview to try anything new.

Don't test a new hairstyle, break in new shoes, or wear a new outfit for the first time. You'll already have more than enough on your mind, so guard against having any distractions. The last thing you need is pinching shoes or petty concerns about your appearance. If you are intending to wear new clothes, try them on the day before. Get accustomed to the feel of them. If you have new shoes, break them in a week earlier.

> TIP: Little touches can make a difference: Shined shoes, manicured fingernails, a neat hairstyle, and a good leather attaché or brief-case will all add to your overall appearance and contribute to the first impression you create.

Before you leave for the interview, doublecheck yourself from head to toe in a full-length mirror. Be as critical as you can: This is your last chance to perfect your appearance. Are your shoes polished? Suit brushed? Do your socks match? Don't overlook even the smallest details.

## What to Bring on an Interview

■ **Bring along appropriate reading material; at the very least, it will refresh your mind and get you ready for the interview.**

Bring trade magazines or *The Wall Street Journal* to read while you wait in the reception area. Even better, bring specific newsletters or trade magazines that relate *specifically* to the position and the company. In this way, you can establish yourself as an expert before the interview, if the interviewer notices what you're reading.

> EXAMPLE: An applicant for a financial position at a limousine company took to his interview a photocopy of a newsletter about the limo business. The founder and president of the company, who had never read the newsletter, asked him about it before the interview had begun, and talked about the plans he had for expanding his business. The

applicant, in effect, got a job offer before the formal interview ever took place.

You should also bring the most important information you've gathered on the company, in case you quickly need to review it.

> TIP: Carry key points on a card in your purse or vest pocket. On unexpectedly tough interviews, where you find yourself being grilled on information that you know but can't remember, excuse yourself to go to the bathroom, and look over your notes. You've got nothing to lose.

*Always* bring extra copies of your resume. The interviewer may ask for another.

---

## STEP TWO: PRACTICE

■ **Practice can mean just going over what you plan to say, or it can mean actually going out and interviewing somewhere else *first* as a rehearsal for a more significant interview later.**

A practice interview is most useful if you haven't been job hunting for a while, and it's also a good way to work out flaws in your style. Apply for a job you don't really want, but plan to go on the interview anyway, as if it were just as important. Be aware of how you're doing and how the interviewer is responding to you. Do you sound confident? Are you organized? Does the interviewer seem interested—or is he or she falling asleep?

After the interview, think about what you did right, what you did wrong, and how to improve. Ask the interviewer for advice if you feel comfortable doing so. Then go on another interview and see if your improvements really help.

*One danger:* Some people do better on a "safety interview" just because they know it doesn't matter. Then they get nervous and do badly on the important one.

> TIP: Even if you don't think you need the practice, *arrange* your interview schedule so that you visit the least desirable jobs first, and thus can work out any problems with your interviewing technique *before* you see the best companies. Save the best for last.

■ **Never stop practicing, and never stop seeking and going out on interviews.**

Again, the more interviews you go on, the better you'll get. Don't make the mistake many job hunters make and hide out in the library or behind a typewriter banging out cover letters. It's an easy way out: "I can't go on interviews today because I'm too busy working. Besides, the job was too low-level. . . ." *Any* interview is a start. And as we stated in Chapter 4, "Networking," all interviews are good ways to meet people who are potentially valuable.

■ **Rehearse the interview yourself, or with a friend acting as an interviewer.**

This second form of practicing is essential. Plan in your head what you're going to say, how you'll answer tough questions, how you'll sell yourself. Be certain your friend acts as an interviewer, and not as a friend, and be certain you think of your friend in those terms. Have your friend critique you, and then try again.

> **TIP: Go over your interview in your mind while commuting to and from work, and during other "in-between" times. With almost no conscious effort, you'll have many answers on the tip of your tongue.**

■ **Work on developing an upbeat, positive attitude during your interviews.**

A common problem is the difficulty of projecting an optimistic attitude during the strain of an interview, or after a slew of job rejections.

> **TIP: Don't kid yourself into believing any false claims about how easy and fun interviewing can be. It's difficult for almost anybody: sitting in front of a stranger who is asking you personal questions about your background. If you accept that interviewing will be hard, it becomes easier to make it *less* stressful.**

■ ***Knowing* all you need to know beforehand makes interviewing easier and less nerve-wracking when it actually takes place.**

Research and practice are essential, but even with the right preparation, interviewing jitters and worries can crop up, particularly if you've been unemployed for a long time and really need a job.

*Five other key ideas to keep in mind:*

1. *Think of an interview as just a game.* If you win, you get the job. In this way, you can focus on the positive aspects and put off worrying until later.

2. *Think of all interviews as learning experiences.* If things go badly, you'll still be successful at having learned how *not* to interview and can concentrate on how to avoid similar problems in the future.

3. *Don't get intimidated by a single interview.* There will always be another.

4. *Try an old sales technique: Count rejections.* To avoid the sting of not being hired, tell yourself you'll probably get 15 or more turndowns before you get an offer. Try to find out the average number of turndowns for job hunts in your field. Think of each "no" as getting you closer to a "yes."

5. *Don't let fears clog your mind.* Turn your attention to thoughts of success. If you find yourself getting bogged down in "what if" scenarios, do something active or gently concentrate on positive things.

> **TIP: Read upbeat books and articles when not working or researching for the next interview. There is a definite link between this type of positive reinforcement and confidence during an interview. According to one bookstore owner, prominent businessmen are the primary buyers of Dale Carnegie and Norman Vincent Peale. Don't be embarrassed if you want or need encouragement.**

> **TIP: For a quick "psyche-up," just before the interview think back on the most successful interview or meeting of your life. Review it in your mind, and let that confident attitude flow into your interview. In fact, do this at *all* times when you're tempted to rehash your "failures."**

■ **Be honest about your interviewing style.**

One counselor noticed that every client who was coming to her for interviewing assistance was either too proud and arrogant, or too much of a shrinking violet. You should stay *between* what she calls the "twin pitfalls of arrogance and excessive humility." If you seem to have either of these characteristics, work hard with friends or coun-selors to change how you come across.

■ **Make certain you are interviewing for the right job and career.**

Sometimes the problem may be the job itself; poor interviewees for one job may blossom into confident, dynamic interviewees for another.

---

## STEP THREE: THE INTERVIEW

■ **Whether you're interviewing for a position as a banker, an astro-naut, or a sewer worker, interviewers want to know about three basic things: your experience, your interpersonal skills, and the reasons they should hire you.**

Whatever type of interview you're having, your strategy should be the same—to sell your way into a job. Only the formats and styles differ.

■ **There are only two parts to an interview: the first five minutes and the rest.**

In the first five minutes you should sell your *attitude* and person-ality. Show you're a winner by your stance, your confidence, and your demeanor. During the rest of the interview you should prove how the interviewer's first impression of you was correct. Highlight your skills and background and why you are right for this job.

### Just Before the Interview

■ **Always arrive early.**

Arrive at the office building at least ten minutes early. Give your-self at least that amount of time to avoid any last-minute mishaps. Wait in your car, or walk around the block, and arrive at the inter-viewer's receptionist a few minutes before the appointment.

**TIP: Go to the location of the interview the day before. The next day you'll be less worried about getting there and finding the place,**

and more able to concentrate on what you'll say during the interview.

> TIP: For nervous interviewees it's a good idea to arrive even earlier and get an orange juice or coffee near the office. It's a good way to relax. Even for anxious types, *one* cup of coffee or tea may cheer you and make you sound more confident. For smokers, it's a good time to stoke up on the last few cigarettes unobserved before going in.

■ **Have something pleasant to say to the secretary or receptionist when you arrive at the interviewer's office.**

Secretaries do as much work as executives, or more, whatever executives may say to the contrary. Don't overlook them. In all companies, a secretary has the power to mistype, misdirect, or forget your application. Many times a secretary can provide the little extra push that gets you hired.

> TIP: Don't confuse being friendly with being patronizing, or with pestering. One busy employment counselor's secretary complained of "nervously friendly applicants who try to joke with me while I'm typing or on the phone." A pleasant comment or two and a smile are usually enough.

In general, never ignore anybody on an interview. You never know who *really* makes the decisions.

■ **Try to get a *feel* for the office and the environment.**

While waiting to be called, look around the reception area and look at employees at work; this will give you an idea of what kind of organization it is, and whether you think you'd like to work there.

## Impressions: The First Five Minutes of the Interview

■ **Start the interview with a warm but professional tone and maintain it throughout.**

Be confident and businesslike, but also friendly and personable. The first five minutes are very important, but don't take that too literally and try to get everything over with quickly. The key is to create the right *impression* of yourself. It's not what you say, it's how you say it, and how you look.

*Concentrate on the following:*

- a firm handshake
- looking the interviewer directly in the eye
- a pleasant smile
- good grooming and dress
- upright posture
- a strong but not overbearing voice

> **TIP: Smokers and coffee drinkers: Don't forget you may have bad breath. Take a breath mint before going in. A surprising number of interviewers mention smoker's or coffee breath as a turnoff.**

■ **Smile warmly, offer your hand, and if it seems natural or appropriate, make a *light* joke or observation.**

Most of the time it's to your advantage to take charge of the conversation by saying something first. Show the interviewer that you're not going to be a passive dud during the next hour, that you're not going to just respond to his or her questions; that, in fact, you have something to offer. There's no need to get too creative in opening—just say something.

> **EXAMPLE: If it's raining badly, comment on how bad the traffic was because of the rain. It's not particularly fascinating (in fact it's dull), but it will get the interviewer chatting. Or, comment on the offices. Say something specific about them.**

### The Rest of the Interview: Selling Yourself as a Basic Strategy

*There are 11 basic attitudes and techniques for putting yourself across correctly in an interview.*

### 1. Sell Yourself

■ **Turn everything you do or say into a reason for or a means of getting yourself hired.**

Think of the interview as a sales call. Constantly ask yourself: *Is what I'm saying helping me to get a job?*

Tailor the interview to your job objective. Surprisingly, many people don't. Instead of selling themselves on specific points, many applicants get lost in defending their resumes, explaining their backgrounds, discussing their motives, or just chatting with the interviewer. Don't waste *your* valuable interview time on these things unless you feel that they're helping you; there's no reason to linger on topics or ideas that don't sell you. *Don't forget:* The only reason you're talking with an interviewer is to get a job.

> **EXAMPLE:** An interviewer mentions a bad gap in your resume, when you were unemployed for seven months. Don't get defensive and talk about the poor economy, rotten luck, problems in the industry, etc. Even though it'll make you feel better, it doesn't sell you. Interviewers hear excuses every day.
>
> *Instead:* Give a reason that exonerates and *sells* you at the same time. "Yes, I was job hunting for seven months after my position was eliminated when my company was taken over. As you can see, being unemployed gave me time to upgrade my financial skills: I took two courses at the local college and completed a degree. So I was able to put myself in a better position that used those skills as well, which is why I think this position suits me extremely well. . . ."

■ **You should be flexible and ready to *change* your approach, even if it means departing from a "normal" interviewing style.**

Don't get stuck in an interviewing rut just because you think you have to emphasize certain aspects of your resume. *Remember:* During the interview you're not only selling your skills and job background, you're selling yourself.

> **EXAMPLE:** An unemployed man who was interviewing for a plant manager's job had started explaining his resume, experience, and schooling when he noticed that the interviewer (and president of the small company) kept switching the topic to an upcoming football game. The applicant stopped and switched topics, highlighting his hobby of working as a high school referee and explaining how his experiences on the football field had helped him as a manager. He got an offer over more experienced applicants because he sold *himself.*

## 2. Link Yourself and Your Background to the Job

■ **Link what you're talking about with why you should be hired.**

When discussing your background, don't just state what you did, explain how it would be useful to the company. If your background doesn't exactly fit the job description, be creative. The best-qualified applicants don't always get the offers. Very often, it's the most confident and inspired individual who wins, the person who can *make* his or her background sound right.

> **EXAMPLE: In an unusual case of salesmanship, a secretary talked her way into a brokerage job: "Being a secretary for 10 years has been excellent preparation for this position as a stockbroker, better than being an analyst or an MBA. Brokers may rely on experts for the technical aspects of their job, but the crucial part is selling. As a secretary, I've learned how to get through to and talk with top executives and others with substantial assets."**
> *Note:* **She was hired over more seasoned brokers.**

■ **Don't make the mistake of merely reciting your job history or education.**

Amplify your past in a way that sells you to the interviewer. Extracurricular activities can be helpful.

Highlight your current job skills and duties that are applicable to the new job. Many people make the mistake of giving equal weight to *each* of their current job responsibilities. Don't waste your valuable selling time explaining things that don't matter: A brief mention of your more minor responsibilities is all the interviewer needs to know.

## 3. Emphasize Specific Accomplishments

■ **Don't just talk about what a good and loyal employee you are, give examples that *demonstrate* how you increased sales, improved staff morale, or recovered missing funds.**

Be specific. Interviewers want to hire people who can do things, not simply warm a seat and talk.

> **EXAMPLE: "In 1994 I was responsible for a sales staff of 10. My team increased sales by 35 percent, which was 15**

percent above the average storewide increase. I accomplished this by streamlining customer ordering procedures in my department, and top management has now adopted these for the company as a whole."

## 4. Be Professional

■ **Always maintain a professional posture and tone.**

Look directly at the interviewer while talking, just as you would when speaking to a friend, but don't overdo it. A common mistake many applicants make is to stare at the recruiter, which looks hostile and challenging.

> TIP: Pause intermittently as you speak to see if the interviewer is still paying attention. Before embarking on any long explanations, briefly sketch out the basics, then ask the interviewer if he or she wants more details.

Smile if appropriate, and avoid a monotonous style. A *light* sense of humor is almost always helpful.

> TIP: A career counselor advised her female clients who were going for "stuffy jobs" such as banking, big business, and accounting to avoid smiling too much when interviewing with men. Women have a tendency to smile more, and men interpret this—wrongly —as a passive gesture. Some women find this advice useful, others don't.

■ **Occasionally break into a topic that's slightly personal: Psychologically it's harder to reject and easier to hire someone who has a distinct personality that goes beyond a resume.**

Don't talk about dull generalities, talk about yourself and why *you*, personally, want the job. Political analysts all agree that President Reagan was a master of this technique, no matter what they thought of him otherwise.

> TIP: Talk positively of personalities you've encountered in the workplace: a particularly tough but always fair and supportive boss, top-notch coworkers, etc. Speak of your past and try to help the interviewer *picture* it. Don't use jargon.

> **EXAMPLE:** "I particularly enjoyed working as an operations clerk at Merrill Lynch—the toughest job I ever had. I was in at 6:00 A.M. and out at 10:00 P.M., but I learned how to process stock transactions better than anyone."
>
> *Avoid:* "I worked as an analyst at Merrill Lynch, which was a challenging position that expanded my career horizons." Sentences like this make you sound like a robot. Or worse, a boring robot.

## 5. Pick Up Cues from Your Interviewer

■ **Tailor your style to fit the interviewer.**

Be yourself during the interview, but don't overdo it. If the interviewer is a joker, tell a few jokes and laugh along with him or her. If the recruiter is a serious type, *don't* tell a few jokes. Keep the conversation straight and professional.

■ **A quick glance around the office and a few minutes of discussion can give you an indication of what the interviewer is like.**

The best job applicants are sensitive in reading signs that reveal the interviewer's personality. Look for personal items to give you a clue. Again, be careful of overdoing it; for example, avoid praising photos of children: It sounds fake.

> **TIP:** Often the interviewer is as shy or as nervous as you are. Putting the recruiter at ease is an effective way of getting hired. Try to see through gruff or impersonal interviewers. Very often, they are new and awkward in the role.

■ *Listen* **to the interviewer and pick up on cues for subjects to discuss.**

If the interviewer talks about the stresses of work in general, you should emphasize your ability to handle stress.

> **TIP:** Try to read how the interviewer is reacting to what you say. If he or she looks bored, stop and ask if you've covered the topic adequately. *React* to the interviewer. Many overly arrogant applicants ignore subtle cues and blithely keep on talking their way through the interview and out of a job.

## 6. Believe in Your Own Myths

■ **Being the ideal candidate means acting and thinking about yourself as you are at your best.**

Talk about your triumphs; don't weaken yourself by mentioning your failures. If your failures come up, acknowledge them, refer to them as what they are, and explain how you learned from them. Then turn the conversation back to what you have to offer. Remember, you're selling yourself, not telling your life story.

> **EXAMPLE:** "In 1994, I was the top salesman in my office—and I could do even better at a firm like yours. . . ."
>
> *Not:* "Although I did pretty badly last year, I'm sure I could perform a lot better at your firm."

> **EXAMPLE:** If asked about a failure directly, answer in the following manner: "Yes, I was laid off in 1994. I was low in seniority. It was unfortunate, because I feel I had a lot to contribute, and I got along very well with my fellow employees. But there was one advantage to having that hiatus: I had the time to develop a career game plan, which is why I've applied for this job. It *fully* meets my skills and career expectations."

■ **Even though estimates are that up to one-third of job applicants lie during interviews, it's usually a mistake to lie or hide mistakes or failures from prospective employers.**

If you're ever found out during or after the interview, you definitely won't get the job. Admitting to failures won't necessarily hurt your chances as much as you may think. Surveys consistently show that most failures, such as being fired or failing in a private enterprise, don't matter much to interviewers. In today's erratic business climate, being laid off or losing at a new business venture no longer carries the weight it once did. What *does* matter is how you've dealt with it and how confidently you've taken things in stride.

## 7. Don't Apologize

■ **Interviewing apologetically is a common mistake, made most often by people who feel they're too young, too old, or over- or** underqualified for the job they're seeking—which covers just about everyone.

People often get negative ideas about their qualifications from reading or hearing about the average age or experience levels in the positions they seek. So they start the interview with an apology: "I know you normally hire younger [or older, or more qualified, etc.] applicants but . . ."

*No but's.* Say why you're good and stick to it. If it seems that the interviewer has some objections, figure out what they are and communicate the *advantages* of hiring someone your age and with your level of experience.

> **EXAMPLE: "My 35 years of on-the-job experience would be a real advantage in this job, because I know how to publish this type of local paper with my eyes closed. I don't need a lot of supervision. . . ."**

> **EXAMPLE: One man in his sixties brought a magazine article to the interview that reported that senior citizens have better attendance, less sick time, and greater productivity than younger men. He was hired.**

None of this is to say that overcoming such obstacles is easy. But it's always better to face a problem squarely and confidently than to apologize for what you are. (Even though there are age discrimination laws, it's better to convince an employer of your worth, rather than threaten legal action.)

## 8. Never Say "Maybe"

■ **Always sound positive during the interview.**

Never let weak and mealy-mouthed words such as "maybe," "kind of," or "hopefully" clog your speech. Lukewarm words make you sound lukewarm, and make it less likely you'll be hired. Be direct.

> **TIP: If asked whether you plan to stay in this career, say "Yes!" instead of "I think so," even if you aren't certain. You can always change your mind later and, in the meantime, you sound positive rather than weak and vacillating.**

■ **Don't worry about seeming more arrogant or pushy than you usually are.**

Unless you've been told you're too arrogant, the odds are that you're not firm *enough*. Many interviewers criticize applicants for being too shy and reticent. An interview is no time to be demure and polite about your accomplishments.

## 9. Summarize

■ **Summarize your main points periodically.**

After each "section" of the interview, or after each long question, briefly summarize what you feel is important for the interviewer to remember, and how it fits in with the position you're applying for. The objective is to keep impressing upon the interviewer's mind the factors that make *you* the right person for the job.

> **EXAMPLE:** After describing your last job for a few minutes, summarize and repeat your most significant accomplishments: "So I feel my biggest accomplishment during this period was supervising 100 employees in the largest company warehouse construction project, which is why I was so interested in your ad. . . ."

When it becomes obvious to you that the interview is winding down, start summarizing the main points you've been making. Do this only if the interviewer gives you the chance—not if he or she wants to chat about something else. But if the interviewer asks whether you'd like to add anything, you should always answer "yes," and then quickly relist your accomplishments.

> **EXAMPLE:** "So, all in all, my background points to a strong interest in publishing as a career. As we discussed, because of my college degree in Transylvanian literature and my internship with a literary magazine, I feel . . ."

> **TIP:** A good trick to sounding professional is to *number* your accomplishments: "There are three major reasons why I feel this job is right for me. One . . ." Statements like this make you sound organized and intelligent. This advice is frequently given by career, media, and political consultants. Henry Kissinger often

does this during interviews on television—"There are three elements to a coherent foreign policy: one . . ."

## 10. Close the Interview

■ **Closing an interview can mean asking for the job, especially if you're applying for a sales or sales-related position.**

In these cases, treat the end of an interview as you would if you were closing a sale. If it seems as if the recruiter has settled on you as his or her first choice, end the interview by affirming that you have been hired. If it's a first interview or it's obvious that the interviewer can't or won't hire you, then close by highlighting your attributes and establishing an exact date for your next meeting.

> **EXAMPLE:** **Salespeople at the Xerox corporation advise sales force applicants to ask questions toward the *end* of the interview ("Is there any reason you wouldn't hire me?"). If there are objections, you have a chance to rebut them and then *close* with a confirmation you're hired or an agreement to meet again.**

■ **In most cases, it's better to wait for the interviewer to indicate he or she is ready to end the interview.**

If you're applying for a nonsales job, you don't need to close the interview with a hard sell. Instead, thank the interviewer for the meeting, and repeat how much you are interested in the job and how well qualified you think you are for it. People often forget to do this or are too embarrassed. Do it anyway—it definitely helps. It brings home the message that you are a person who firmly believes that he or she is right for the job.

> **EXAMPLE:** **"Thanks, Mr. Jones. I appreciated this opportunity to talk about my qualifications. I'm looking forward to talking with you further about the job; as I've said, I'm very enthusiastic about it and know I could make a significant contribution to your company's new marketing drive."**

## 11. Be Yourself

■ **If you interview with a false front, you may lose by *getting* the job.**

Create your own interviewing style, but don't confuse selling yourself with being fake. You could end up mismatched, working at a job that genuinely doesn't suit you.

> **EXAMPLE: A woman imitated a friend's bold interviewing style at an interview with an entrepreneurial computer company. She got the job, but was laid off several months later: She couldn't maintain the tough, streetwise act she had put on during the interview.**

The key to successful interviewing is interviewing at *your* best, not someone else's.

## TYPES OF INTERVIEWS AND ASSESSMENT

No one interview is ever like another, of course, but there are certain types of interviews that share particular characteristics and that should be treated accordingly. In what follows we've sketched out the most common of these, ranging from group interviews to in-basket tests. Expect to face at least one of these during your job search; the days of having only one-on-one interviews are long gone.

### Group Interviews: If You Are Interviewed *with* a Group

■ **If you are interviewed with a group of other applicants, your objective is to show that you're a team player who can effectively lead as well as work with others.**

Group interviews are usually organized with five or so job applicants seated around a table. There are various types of group interviews, but all are designed to test your interpersonal and negotiating skills.

Sometimes each applicant is given a separate handout outlining a company program, and he or she is expected to defend this program to the group. Since all programs can't be accepted, the group must then decide which ones should be used and work together to arrive at a consensus. This method is popular with the Foreign Service of the U.S. Department of State, among others.

In other variations, the group as a whole is given a problem to solve and is expected to arrive at a joint conclusion. Several major retailers like to use this interview technique. In some cases, a group interview can turn into a full-fledged simulation of a business, in which applicants are asked to come to an agreement on production schedules and budgets. Sometimes an interviewer will announce in midsession a complete change of agenda; in this case your ability to cope with spontaneous decision-making is being tested as well. In every instance the applicants talk, while several evaluators are sitting on the sidelines, taking notes.

■ **Group interviews can be very tough: You have to interact with five or more people you've never met and withstand having several people watching and evaluating you.**

The very nature of this test is stressful. You have to show that you are a leader, but so must everyone else. Somehow, you've got to compete with these people without appearing to be overbearing and prove that you're the true leader in the group, or at least one of a few true leaders. Many people suffer from a modified form of stage fright in these circumstances.

■ **The longer you wait to take a major role, the greater your anxiety, and the harder it will be to participate.**

The key is to jump in early. Assume the role of *moderator* as soon as you can. Open the discussion, suggest an order of presentation, *ask* the others what they think. Instead of arguing your points, try to mediate between the others. *Remember:* You are being evaluated for leadership, and effective leadership often comes from not being too aggressive. You must act as a team player, one who is capable of getting along with others and leading them to *one* objective. It doesn't have to be *your* objective as long as it is obvious that you've been instrumental in getting the group to agree on one or more major issues.

■ **Show yourself to be a patient, persistent, people-oriented leader with enough flexibility to negotiate among many kinds of people.**

Offer creative solutions to problems. *Don't* jump to conclusions, browbeat others, or speak only when spoken to. Don't flaunt your knowledge. Instead, demonstrate your ability to get people to work well together.

TIP: Inevitably, there will be a loud talker who tries to monopolize the conversation. You can win supporters by calling on other people to speak.

*For example:* "That's a good point, Mr. Loudmouth. How do you think that will affect the plan, Mr. Quiet?" This will quickly gain you gratitude from the quiet ones, who will then turn to you for leadership. This technique has been used successfully by a number of candidates during the U.S. Foreign Service exam.

■ Take responsibility for *closing* the meeting.

Summarize what the group has decided, mention the opposing viewpoints, and announce conclusions.

EXAMPLE: "Well, we've established that programs one and five will be adopted, and part of program four. Are we all in agreement? [Look to see if there's a response.] We're all in agreement then. . . ." (Turn to the evaluators and tell them your team has finished.)

TIP: In some of the more aggressive retail chains, take a correspondingly more aggressive tack. Here, you may be better off firmly taking charge and not letting up. A woman in New York retailing was told after her group interview: "We hired you because you didn't shut up or give up. In this business, you've got to deal with salespeople the same way."

TIP: In some cases you will be asked to evaluate yourself after the session. Be realistic. Your evaluation will be matched against those of the assessors, and if it differs significantly you will lose points for not judging yourself accurately.

## Group Interviews: If You Are Interviewed *by* a Group

■ Being interviewed by a group tests how well you can deal with the public and customers in a stressful setting.

This type of interview has become increasingly common and is almost always tough. Group interviews are used most often by government employers, universities, banks, and consulting firms, and for higher-level private industry positions.

The best way to do well is to be calm, organized, and relatively brief. There are too many people involved for you to be giving long-winded answers.

■ **The chief difficulty is having to confront three or more people, all of whom are firing questions at you before you have the chance to catch your breath.**

One trick is to rephrase the questions after they are asked to give yourself more time to think of an answer. Don't be afraid to pause and think before speaking, or openly ask for more time.

> **EXAMPLE: "How would I handle the marketing of Nutsy Nuts in Albania? First . . ." OR: "That's an interesting question. Let me think about it for a minute. . . ." Taking a moment shows that you're not intimidated by the group-interview process and are able to take charge of the situation.**

■ **Having more interviewers usually means facing more technical questions.**

You must be well prepared. Typically, each interviewer will have a specialty or concern that he or she feels is essential. One danger is in thinking that you have to answer all their questions. If you don't know an answer, say so! *Remember:* These interviewers are testing how you'd interact with the general public, so attempting to bluff your way out of something is far worse than just admitting your ignorance.

■ **Don't worry about the "feel" of the interview.**

Because more people are involved, a natural flow is lost and you may think that things are worse or more awkward than they are. Keep in mind that many of the people present are untrained as interviewers and can be extremely uncomfortable with the entire interviewing process.

> **TIP: Don't ignore *anyone*. One applicant to a company that had a reputation for being tough and hard-driven treated a question asked by a young, frail-looking observer sitting in the corner very lightly. He wasn't hired. That observer was the very quiet, very studious, very delicate personnel director.**

■ **Most important, don't hesitate to make the points *you* want to make.**

Many people go through group interviews passively: They just respond, they don't initiate. Be brief, but don't make the mistake of letting the interview proceed as though it were an interrogation in which you simply allow the interviewers to grill you. Instead, treat the group interview as if it were a regular interview. Don't be intimidated because there are so many interviewers: Ask questions, make your points, and sell yourself.

## All-Day Interviewing or Multiple Interviews

■ **Particularly at large companies, an all-day assessment is a formal process, used for entry-level and midlevel applicants.**

All-day interviewing usually occurs after an initial screening interview with one interviewer. If you pass this first hurdle, you are called back a week or so later for a series of six to eight individual interviews with managers of various ranks.

The day starts with a meeting with the original interviewer, who sells you on the company and goes on to explain whom you will be meeting. Lunch is spent with a manager who is usually closest to you in rank, and the day often ends with an interview with a high-level manager, quite possibly your projected boss.

Within the week following your all-day assessment, all the people you've seen will arrive at a consensus about whether or not they want to invite you back. If so, you are called for a final interview with your direct line manager. Sometimes you're being considered for more than one position, in which case you will meet with two or more line managers.

■ **Part of the screening process is to see how well you react to the rigors of an all-day interview.**

A whole day of interviewing can be very grueling. Don't worry about being repetitive. Each interviewer will want to know the same things about you, so tell him or her the same things you've been saying to everyone. Varying your format occasionally will help to reduce your fatigue. Don't overdo it—by the end of the day some applicants have talked about so many different things that their interviewing style begins to suffer, and they forget to include the major points. Keep reminding yourself to sound fresh and somewhat spontaneous. Interviewers often turn down applicants who sound overly rehearsed with their presentations: This was frequently mentioned as the biggest turnoff by interviewers at a large package-goods corporation. The problem is that, as the day goes on, it becomes harder and harder to sound spontaneous and unrehearsed, particularly when someone asks you for the third, or worse, the sixth time, "What are your strengths?"

> **TIP: Keep your ears open for unusual or difficult questions in the first set of interviews, and start formulating good answers. They will usually crop up again.**

> **TIP: Use what you've discussed in earlier interviews during your later ones. *For example:* "In the last interview, Tom Goetz said that he's set up quality-control circles in his division with excellent results. He said that he got the procedures from you. How has this idea worked in your division?" Supplementing your interviews with insights from other employees keeps the conversation going and implies that you and the previous interviewers got along well.**

> **TIP: One successful applicant at a Fortune 500 firm suggests that new applicants should have some tough *questions* about the firm and its business in reserve. By the end of the day, when you're tired and can't think anymore, ask the interviewer these questions. This will establish your intelligence, and while the interviewer is busy formulating answers, you can get some rest and time to reformulate your own answers.**

> **TIP: One interviewer at another Fortune 500 firm says that an applicant should be ready for a nonbusiness-oriented interview: "I like to throw off candidates at the end of the day by discussing hobbies, politics, cultural events, and other nonresume items. It tests their ability to deal with the unexpected and allows me to see how easily they can handle the public and their coworkers."**

■ **Bring at least 10 resumes.**

Inevitably, someone will want an extra copy. Also, you may have to supply a copy of your resume to people who are called in to interview you at the last minute.

## Luncheon Interviews

■ **The purpose of a luncheon interview is to assess how well you can handle yourself in a social situation.**

Almost no one *likes* lunch interviews; almost everyone feels nervous and unnatural during them. But, for some reason, many interviewers insist that they are a good way of judging candidates.

■ *Rule of thumb:* **Stick to the middle ground during a luncheon interview.**

When ordering, choose middle-priced dishes; if asked to select a wine, pick a middle-priced brand. Steer away from controversial topics, difficult-to-eat food (lobster, spaghetti, chicken), and heavy drinking. In conversation, follow Benjamin Franklin's old credo: "Never contradict anyone."

> **TIP: Don't assume the interviewer is psychoanalyzing every move you make. Some career counselors go so far as to advise applicants to taste food before putting salt or pepper on it—otherwise the interviewer will assume you are impulsive. Most important, try to *relax*. If you're too self-conscious, it will be an awkward and difficult lunch.**

> **TIP: Common advice is to *avoid* drinking alcohol, even if the interviewer drinks. The reasoning is that it's better to look good, and to keep your mind fresh. Better advice from an interviewer who drinks: If you drink, go ahead and have *one*. Sometimes one drink establishes you as "one of them" and not a prude.**

■ **When it comes to conversation, let the interviewers take the lead.**

Luncheon interviews are primarily social events, so a hard sell can look unprofessional. But *do* sell yourself. Bring up hobbies and special interests that reflect your character and show you're the right type of applicant.

> **TIP: Even if you hate sports, it's a good idea to scan the sports pages a few weeks before the interview. Often the conversation will turn to sports, and it's helpful to be able to at least *mention* a key player or two, before trying to change the subject. If you don't follow sports at all, don't make the mistake of thinking you can wing it through an entire discussion without getting caught.**

■ **Avoid politics.**

If asked your opinion on a controversial topic, make a minor point that won't offend anybody. If at all possible, link your answer to what concerns you most: the industry you work in and the job you want. More forceful people can say the truth: They don't like to discuss politics in social situations or at work.

> **EXAMPLE:** *Interviewer:* **"That senator is a complete incompetent. I blame him for the mess we're in in Asia. What do you think?"** *Applicant (for a grain-trading company):* **"What interests me most about the whole affair is the economics. I'm concerned over the precedent an embargo might set in relation to our business. Did the senator suggest an embargo?"**
>
> **This turns the question back to the interviewer and keeps things technical, noncontroversial, and boring, thus avoiding any personal conflicts.**

> **TIP:** If you want to be sneaky, try to turn the question around so you can find out the interviewer's opinion before expressing your own. *Danger:* The interviewer may just be testing you, or others at the table may disagree with your opinions.

## Job and Performance Assessment Interviews

■ **Some companies want to see how you handle the job *before* they even offer it to you.**

Increasingly, many corporations (and some government and nonprofit agencies) put you in simulated job situations. They may ask you to make believe you're the boss, they may ask you to make a sales presentation, they may put you in with five other applicants and ask you to come up with a solution to a corporate problem. All the while, they're watching and assessing your performance. You'd better do well: This may be the most important part of your interview.

The corporate rationale: Some applicants are better at giving good interviews than at delivering top-notch job performance. So why not cut through the interviewing hype by testing how they'd actually do on the job?

This type of interview can be to your advantage, particularly if you're the type who *doesn't* interview all that well. You can make the interviewers rethink their earlier assessment of you. And if you've already done well on the interview, this is your chance to really clinch a job.

Below we'll deal with the general aspects of these interviews, and after that, we'll go into detail about two specific subtypes of these exercises that are slightly different: telephone sales interviews and in-basket testing. Also, recheck the section on group interviewing on page 219.

■ **The key is to *always* remember what is being tested: your leadership and people skills, communications skills, and problem-solving ability, or more simply: *What can you do for the company?***

That's the key to *all* these exercises. Think about what the company wants—and during these exercises, show how you've got what it takes. How? Easy question, more difficult answer. Take it step by step.

### Step 1. Do Some Scouting

First of all, find out if your target organization conducts interview exercises, and if so (if possible), what type. Call the corporate recruiter (or your recruiter or employment agency) and ask what the interviewing process will be. Or do a little snooping at the library. Check out recent articles—sometimes they will highlight new interviewing trends and mention specific companies. And even if it seems that your interview will be a "standard" one, be ready anyway. You never know. By being prepared, you'll be ahead of virtually any other candidate.

### Step 2. Do Some Research

Research the company, the field or industry, the problems they've been having, the corporate "personality." Jot down key points, memorize key facts, *know* the industry or field. Take some time at this: Think about the company and industry on the way to work, during lunch; mull over solutions to problems, potential ways to expand, etc. By taking some time, you'll put your subconscious creative brain to work, and arrive at strong, well-thought-out answers.

### Step 3. Practice

Even if you don't know what type of interview you'll be having, practice various scenarios. At worst, you'll be the most prepared applicant they'll ever meet; at best, you'll be ready for anything. Make believe you'll be selling the company product; *visualize* how you'll sell it; practice in front of a friend or spouse.

### Step 4. Think About What Type of Person the Company Is Looking For

Companies want (or think they want) people who interact well with others, can lead a team, are assertive but not aggressive, can solve problems creatively, can communicate well, etc.

You know the buzzwords, now work on conveying the picture of an ideal candidate. Before the assessment, assess your own faults and strengths and work toward improving them. If you're too aggressive, plan *now* to act less aggressive and more assertive at home and work. *Practice* improving your interpersonal skills by dealing with people in a more ideal way. Hone your communications skills by preparing beforehand as well. Write down key phrases about the company and its products, sales ideas, industry directions, etc. If you *know* all this beforehand, during your interview the right words will trip off your tongue almost effortlessly. While others are struggling to think of a new direction for Product X, you'll let loose with a closely reasoned analysis. Who needs to know that you thought of it all on the way to work a few weeks ago?

Finally, to show how well you interact and lead others, see page 219.

### Telephone Sales Interviews

■ **Telephone sales interviews are sometimes given to applicants who are obviously expected to do a large amount of telephone selling.**

These test situations are supposed to simulate the "real" work as much as possible. They are often conducted by outside testing firms, but are given at your prospective employer's office. Stockbrokers, magazine advertising salespeople, and financial salespeople are typically asked by large firms to come in for this type of assessment after a successful first interview.

The test begins when you are seated at a desk with a telephone and given memos, some phone numbers, and a paper detailing your duties for the next hour or two. At a stockbrokerage, for instance, you may be given four different, partially incomplete call sheets with the names of investors or potential investors. You will have to cold-call the potential investors and try to sell them on the firm's investments. The people you call are actually employed by the testing firm and will later evaluate your performance. Often, you'll be asked to make a call to a supposedly irate customer, and you will have to inform him that an investment you recommended lost money. In all cases your job is to fill in the blanks on the call sheets and try to get the people interested in making new investments that the firm is selling.

■ **Be a little more aggressive and persistent than you would be on a real sales call.**

Be ready beforehand with your best sales attitudes. Use your creativity. In a test interview, you've only got an hour to demonstrate what a dynamic salesperson you are, while in an actual job you could always call back or try again the next day.

## In-Basket Tests

■ **In-basket tests are usually given by large bureaucratic firms as a way of determining your managerial aptitude.**

In-basket tests are corporate games of make-believe. They're not interviews, since they only involve you and a stack of paper. But they usually occur after an interview, or as part of an all-day assessment.

Generally, you're given a desk for an hour or two and told to act as if you were a manager temporarily replacing someone else, who has left an in-basket full of memos, notes, and files requiring action. You may also be given some reference material such as an office manual or a job description, but basically you're given a minimal amount of information about the job and its priorities. You've got to figure things out on your own and take appropriate action in the next one to two hours.

■ **The best (and only) way to take the test is to act as a good manager would and go through everything in the basket first.**

The tried-and-true trick that most companies use in these tests is to put memos at the bottom of the in-basket that supposedly were written later and therefore contradict earlier memos. One meticulous person didn't understand this and did things in order; he wasted a half hour writing a detailed memo on a project only to find a later memo that said the project had been shelved. He panicked and didn't finish the test. These tests can get like that—the tension builds up as the time limit approaches.

■ **Beat the time problem by going through the in-basket and making "to do" lists; put memos and papers in a prioritized order.**

There's often not enough time to do everything, and it will go against you if you don't get the important things done first. As time winds down, go through as much as possible of the low-priority material and quickly jot down notes so a secretary or assistant can take action later. This shows that you can delegate authority and that you have a handle on most of the work.

■ *Remember:* **The in-basket tests show how well you behave as a manager.**

You'll have to write brief letters, write followup instructions for a secretary or administrative assistant, and answer letters. Judgment decisions will crop up as well: Do you take action yourself, or do you wait and talk to the division head? Do you answer a complaint from an important client who demands an immediate answer, or do you wait and write an action memo to the company lawyer, who's out of town and won't be back for a week?

## SPECIAL SITUATIONS DURING INTERVIEWS

The unexpected always comes when you least need it or want it —which means during your most important interview. Below are some of the most common surprises and problems that can occur, ranging from arriving late to facing down an interviewer who is making more than the usual fuss over your spotty employment record. You may also be asked to undergo preinterview testing. These tests are becoming increasingly common, and more and more people are unpleasantly surprised when their interviewing day begins with a multiple-choice personality test. The rest of this section is designed to reduce the shock of these rude awakenings as much as possible.

### If You Are Late to the Interview

■ **Don't let being late blow your chance for a job—here's what to do.**

If you are late, apologize briefly but sincerely for causing a problem and express the hope that you can go on with the interview anyway. Virtually every interviewer will still want to see you, and it probably won't affect your job prospects. If you are very late, call ahead and explain the situation. Have a reasonable excuse: Your car broke down, the train was late, etc. *Don't* give an excuse that makes you sound irresponsible, such as saying you overslept. Whatever you do, don't panic or get flustered. Don't let being late set a negative tone for the entire interview.

## If You Are Asked to Take an Intelligence or Personality Test

■ **Companies that offer these tests most often *require* them as a part of their assessment process: If you don't take the test you won't be considered further.**

In general you're best off taking these tests, even if you disagree with the notion philosophically. If you don't pass them with flying colors, you can always explain during the interview that you do badly on standardized tests and go on to highlight your qualifications. A good interview and your personal attributes could outweigh any test results. You may get the job over someone else who tests well but makes a bad impression in person.

*Intelligence* tests vary with the company and the testing service they use. Many are simply IQ tests, with questions designed to test reasoning skills. These include word analogies, number or letter patterns (What is the next letter in the series s m t __ ?), and mathematical reasoning questions.

■ **Review the basics of the business before going in.**

Some firms offer *aptitude* tests based on their business. One nationwide investment firm, for example, gives an assessment test that lasts one to two hours and covers 25 reading comprehension questions and 25 mathematical questions. Both sections deal primarily with investment. The reading comprehension test has a passage dealing with a merger, and questions relating to the passage deal with the ramifications of the merger. The mathematical section focuses on your reasoning ability, with reference to investment specifics. Questions may describe a hypothetical portfolio, with investments in bonds at a certain percentage, or monies in certificates of deposit paying at another percentage, and income at another specified level. The applicant may be asked to calculate the total income, or evaluate the present value of the investor's portfolio. These questions tend to be algebraic, often requiring you to solve for two variables. Those who pass this test are called in for interviews and further assessment.

The major problem with these tests for most people is that you often can't use a calculator. People accustomed to pushing a button to add a column of figures or to compute the present value of an investment must now use pencil and paper.

> **TIP: Before taking a test, practice your basic mathematical skills. Most people find themselves surprisingly rusty even with simple multiplication.**

*Personality* tests are more difficult to assess. Some companies offer multiple-choice tests that examine personality in a seemingly facile way. ("How would you rather spend a Friday afternoon: watching TV, reading Shakespeare, or playing tennis with a friend? Do you agree or disagree with this statement: 'I enjoy going to parties and meeting new people'?")

The best way to answer these questions is to ask yourself: *What kind of person does the firm want to hire?* Think about the particular industry and the sort of people who are successful in it. In general, your answers should show that you are an energetic, outgoing team player. Obviously, if the position is detail-oriented, play up your liking for detail; if you're interviewing for a service position, choose answers that indicate you enjoy helping people.

In a similar vein, psychologically oriented firms may have candidates draw pictures and explain them. Successful applicants have reported doing simple line drawings quickly and decisively, and interpreting them briefly and in a light tone.

## ■ Be ready for tests that judge your honesty.

Here you'll probably face a lie-detector test or a series of true-false questions that ask some very basic questions about attitudes. Over 25% of major U.S. corporations use lie-detector tests for some employees; half of all supermarket chains require them. A few firms require handwriting (graphology) tests; these are especially common in Europe, as one shocked upper-level manager learned when he was told that his interviews had all gone well but that he had to submit to handwriting analysis before he could be hired.

## ■ And now there is another test that is becoming increasingly common: the drug test.

Many large firms now routinely administer drug tests (usually urine tests), despite the public controversy over whether they're legal. A recent Gallup poll reported that 28% of large corporations (5,000 or more employees) screen applicants for drugs. The percentage is expected to increase, particularly for jobs where safety is a prime factor.

A word of advice: Don't take drugs before an interview, of course, but also refrain from taking cough syrup, drinking gin, or eating poppy seeds (such as you would get on a bagel, for example). In some sensitive tests, the chemicals in these foods may show you as having used illegal drugs. Not a great way to open an interview: "No, I don't use drugs, but I just *love* poppy-seed bagels. . . ."

## If the Interviewer Is Hostile

■ **Sometimes "stress interviews" are given by companies in highly competitive industries that want to test how tough you are.**

Occasionally you may come across an interviewer who is out for blood. The first consideration you must face is that this person represents the company; so, do you still want to work for it? *Remember:* There is no rule that says you *must* sit through an abusive interview. But if you choose to stay, *don't* lose your temper and don't argue with the interviewer.

■ **Stay cool and respond to your interviewer's criticisms with calm, rational statements that highlight why you are well qualified for the job.**

The purpose of hostile interviews is to see how well you handle stress. Don't take things personally and don't react negatively—don't let them fluster you.

> **EXAMPLE:** After the interviewer says that, in his opinion, your academic credentials aren't worth a damn, say: "Some people think that practical experience counts for more. If you look carefully at my experience, you'll see that I learned as much on the job as I did at school, and in fact, my last promotion was due to my success at . . ."
>
> *Note:* The applicant acknowledged the objections, but explained that she also had useful hands-on experience. She didn't bother arguing with the interviewer about the value of her degree, but neither did she agree that it was worthless.

- **Ignore any hostile remarks and concentrate on what the interviewer is looking for in a candidate.**

As with all interviews, concentrate on selling yourself. If the interview gets too hard to take, or the interviewer seems against you personally, quickly wind down the session and leave on a calm, upbeat note.


## If You Get Trapped in a Lie

- **Telling the truth is not only morally better, it's *easier*.**

Lying is a bad tactic: Most applicants get caught in the contradictions of a lie, or sound so nervous while they're trying to lie that any possible advantage is lost. Still, many people will lie during interviews, usually on the spur of the moment, in response to an awkward or difficult question about their past.

> **EXAMPLE:** *Interviewer:* "So, you've only changed jobs twice in the last five years?"
> *Nervous applicant, who actually changed jobs three times:* "Yes, only twice."

In cases like this, don't give the interviewer a chance to catch you in a lie. Correct yourself briefly. But don't make an issue of it; just go back to your main discussion.

> **EXAMPLE:** "Excuse me, I meant to say I changed jobs three times. And, as we were discussing, all those jobs gave me skills that I can put to work immediately. . . ."

If the interviewer catches *you*, correct yourself and keep on going. Treat it as a minor mistake, one that you made because you were so absorbed in the discussion at hand.

> **EXAMPLE:** "Oh, yes, you're right, I changed jobs three times. I meant to correct myself earlier. But the point I'm trying to stress is that my experience . . ."

One note: With age discrimination (and other forms of discrimination) rampant, sometimes you may feel impelled to lie. If you do lie about your age, or something else, just make certain to be consistent and rehearse—so that you can sound convincing.

## If the Interviewer Makes Suggestive Comments

■ **If the interviewer is making sexually suggestive comments, the normal and usually correct approach is to look the person in the eye and say that you expect to be treated as a professional.**

Usually the person is too embarrassed to persist, or will say he or she was only joking. If the person continues to offend you, walk out. If, however, the interviewer asks more vague, "personal" questions that seem inappropriate, politely remind him or her that you are here to discuss business-related topics. If you feel strongly about the situation you may want to notify the individual's superior at the company, and/or the appropriate civic or government group.

## If the Interviewer Harps on Your "Spotty Resume"

■ **Most people have gaps, false starts, periods of unemployment, and new career directions in their pasts.** *Problem:* **The more changes you've been through, the worse you look to a prospective employer.**

Layoffs, career changing, and an uncertain economy have all made "normal" career paths obsolete. Almost no one can say he or she started in one career, advanced steadily in one firm, and now is looking for the same type of job at a different company.

There's no easy way to get around this problem, but there are some good strategies. Earlier, we explained how to tailor your resume, when to avoid mentioning unemployment gaps, and when to *explain* unemployment periods and different careers. Use the same approach during your interviews—show how all the jobs in your past have led you to this career and this interview. *Remember the key concern of an interviewer:* Will you stay with this job if you're hired?

■ **Stress that your job hopping has given you experience and the knowledge that you needed to have to be absolutely certain about what you want to do now.**

Refer to this job or career as the capstone of your career, as a permanent move for you. Be as strong and determined as possible. The interviewer will be suspicious of your motives if you're a proven job hopper; you must forcefully convince him or her that you are sincerely interested in the job. Talk about what you have learned. But don't dwell on the past. Direct the conversation toward the job and the future.

> **TIP: Try to anticipate this problem *before* the interview. Successful job hoppers rely on better preparation, personal introductions, and good planning.**

> **EXAMPLE: One man in his mid-thirties applied to a large trading firm, after having had brief stints as a paralegal, newspaper manager, and graduate student. The interviewer looked at his record with mild disgust: "Who asked you to interview here with *your* record?" he asked. "The senior vice-president," the applicant replied, much to the interviewer's surprise.**
>
> **The applicant had made a point of anticipating the problem by networking with employees first, *before* the formal interview process. Armed with the "unofficial" backing of the SVP, he was hired.**

## If the Interviewer Asks About Chronological Gaps in Your Resume

- **If your resume shows that you had periods of unemployment, or the interviewer discovers it, explain how even during those periods you were involved productively in other activities.**

Talk about fund-raising groups, clubs, volunteer work—anything you did that shows you are a hard-working person who always keeps active. Try to show how these activities will make you a better employee *now* and link your activities to your goal of selling yourself into this job.

> **EXAMPLE: "Yes, I was unemployed for six months. Rather than sit back, make phone calls, and send out resumes, I organized my time so that I could work part-time as a clerk to pay the bills and still volunteer to help my town's fund-raising efforts to get a new school built. I actively campaigned door to door and received a record response— which is why I know I could be very effective in your**

sales department. Even during my own unemployment, I achieved a sales record. . . ."

## If You Had Low Grades in School

■ **Don't worry about grades after your first job; worry even less if you have an MBA. Employment surveys show that having good grades is among the *least* important factors in getting hired.**

Employers look at grades in only one context: How will this affect the employee's job performance? Don't volunteer that you had low grades, but if asked, tell the truth. The odds are that a firm won't check, but if they do, you can be fired for something that doesn't make much difference anyway. Make certain to show how your other skills will make you a valuable employee.

■ **Stress *reasons* for having had low grades that explain how other vital activities took away study time.**

For example, you could explain that earning your way through college or having to attend night school prevented you from getting high grades. Play up extracurricular activities in which you had a *leadership* role. Never sound upset or apologetic. You're not stupid or lazy, you just didn't have enough time to study. You were too busy supporting your mother, raising children, etc.

> **EXAMPLE: "My GPA was 2.0—but as you can see from my resume, I had one part-time job and one full-time job during college. These jobs taught me quite a bit, particularly about how to juggle responsibilities and handle high amounts of stress. That's why I'm interested in this job. . . ."**

# 8 The Most Common Questions Interviewers Ask

## INTRODUCTION

Behind every question an interviewer asks is one other: "How well can you do the job for me?" Or, more bluntly, "Why should I hire you?"

When you sit across the desk from an interviewer, he or she already has a mental checklist of skills, personality, and experience that together adds up to the right employee, the right person for the job. Interviewers know whom they want to hire. You have to demonstrate that *you* are that person.

This is where preparation and anticipation come into play. If you already know (or have an idea of) what you're going to be asked, you can make certain that every answer you give adds to your sales pitch.

- **One important point to keep in mind: Interviewers today are more savvy than ever. They assume you've read books and articles, gone on other interviews, and rehearsed neat, pat answers. So they try to throw you a curve ball.**

Their job is to get *behind* the answers you've committed to memory. So most of them are avoiding the general obvious questions. Instead, they've developed new methods of interviewing and variations on the tried-and-true questions. You may have faced some of these different types of questions and situations already. If you haven't you probably will run across one or more of the following:

- *Open questions:* "How do you feel about . . ." This gets you talking and reveals how you think and formulate answers. Key: Be organized. Take a minute before answering to organize a coherent answer.

- *"Show me" questions:* "Give me a specific example of how you reprimanded an employee, and tell me what happened afterward. Was your reprimand in keeping with company policy, or did it differ?" In other words, the interviewer is going beyond the general to real-life incidents. Key idea: It's easier for applicants to lie (or fudge) generically. The closer you get to things that actually happened, the easier it is for the interviewer to assess your *true* personality and work style.

- *Leading questions:* "So you think XYZ Corporation is well positioned overseas?" This type of question makes the weak-willed agree—and may lose them the job. Don't let the interviewer think you've agreed for the sake of agreeing. If you agree (or think you should agree), give reasons *why*.

- *Probing questions:* Followups allow the interviewer to control the interview and determine the depth of your knowledge and communication ability.

- *Mirror probes:* "So you say XYZ Corporation is well poised to expand overseas. Why?" Be careful—this kind of question can catch you if you've made an unsupported statement.

- *Transition questions:* These center on the main transforming events of your life—and seek to detect the "real" person beneath the practiced interviewee. Expect probing questions about why you switched schools, careers, job objectives, etc. Emphasize positive movement in your answers—for example, if asked about career changing, say you made such changes to better your career, and explain why.

Whatever the questions, interviewers today are more apt to take notes, weigh your deficiencies and your pluses on forms, and try to make a decision in an objective manner.

- ■ **But keep in mind that *behind* the more sophisticated questions of the 1990s are the same old questions.**

No matter how interviewers ask the questions and what specific questions they ask, they still need to know the same things as always

—they want to know your strengths and weaknesses, your personality type, your skills, and how they fit the needs of the company and the job.

*The bottom line:* Most "new" questions and "new interviewing techniques" are merely rephrased versions of the old tried-and-true ones. The trick for you as a job hunter, then, is to:

- recognize "new" questions for what they are

- prepare mental answers *before* you're asked, so you won't be fazed and waste time stumbling around

To help you with this, the following pages list the 14 general interview questions and several situations you'll be faced with—so you can identify what the interviewer is after and be able to respond with the kind of answer that gets you the job. You should tailor the answers to fit your personality and specific job requirements, but in each case you can and should be *selling yourself.*

### 1. Do You Have Any Questions? (When Asked at the Beginning of the Interview)

This is a favorite of so-called "behavioral" interviewers who want to avoid canned responses by getting you to take the initiative at the very beginning of the interview.

Of course, you should always have something to ask. But don't be typical and ask just anything. Instead, take advantage of the hidden sales opportunity and ask questions that immediately position you as a strong job candidate—questions that highlight your potential role *with* the company and show how knowledgeable you already are about the business.

To sound informed and up-to-date, concentrate on current news you've picked up in trade magazines or professional journals, not the basic run-of-the-mill information every other applicant usually uses. And, whenever possible, incorporate an example of your own expertise into your question.

> **EXAMPLE: "I was interested to read in last week's *Widget Age* that your company captured 50 percent of the widget market last quarter. It reminded me of *my* work with widgets at XYZ, Inc. We were trying to expand our market share, so I launched a campaign specifically targeted to the teen**

> **market. We didn't have a large budget, so I concentrated on local print and some radio. What were the key elements to your success?"**

Be sure not to ask anything about benefits, salaries, or personnel policies. You want to show how knowledgeable and achievement-oriented you are, not how greedy you are.

> **TIP: Do *not* make suggestions on how to manage the interviewer's company or ask leading questions that end up with you explaining how you would run things. Some people make this mistake, particularly MBAs, as a way of indicating how useful they would be to the company. Maybe they would be—if they got an offer. Most interviewers cite this as a major turnoff.**

If you have no experience in a relevant area, ask questions about planned expansions or operations in the department or area where you want to work, making sure to show off your knowledge of the company at large.

In other words, if you can't talk about yourself, show off your knowledge about the company. Then ask how the company's proposed changes will affect your department. This way your questions won't look frivolous, and they will communicate to the interviewer that you've done your homework.

This approach works particularly well when interviewing with line managers (versus professional human resources people). Managers tend to be uncomfortable during interviews anyway. This type of question gives them the opportunity to discuss what they know best: their own work in their own department.

> **EXAMPLE: "I was impressed with the way the firm has kept its strong service record in the face of rising labor and parts costs. What measures have you taken to maintain your record?"**
>
> ***Added bonus:* Questions like this keep interviewers talking and make you sound smart at the same time. A young officer once interviewed with General Douglas MacArthur and asked him one slightly flattering question. MacArthur kept talking for an hour, never giving the officer a chance to say a thing. Later, he praised the officer as a "fascinating conversationalist"—rare praise from the general.**

## 2. Could You Tell Me a Little About Yourself?

This is the open-ended question that scares the most people. It shouldn't. Use it as a low-key way of selling yourself into the job and overcoming anything that may seem to be a problem on your resume.

Remember that the interviewer doesn't care about *you*, but what it is about you that can solve his problems and fill an open position. In light of this, avoid launching into a life history. Instead, give only the information that supports your credentials for the job. *Briefly* outline your background—job history, goals, schooling, even hobbies or memberships—always relating it to the position you're interviewing for.

For example, point up parallels between your work experience and the requirements for this job; mention courses you've taken that make you more qualified; touch on outside interests (in most cases, virtually any sport is ideal) and link them to your leadership qualities and ability to get along with people.

Don't be afraid to stretch things a bit, but don't lie. Just present the jobs and experiences in your past so that they form a coherent pattern—even if you didn't have the foggiest notion at the time that you were building a foundation for your career.

> **EXAMPLE: A recent college graduate in history, interviewing at a bank, highlighted his after-school job and the one or two economics courses he had taken. He explained how his interest in banking had developed during his job, where he learned how to keep books and manage a small enterprise. He discussed how this led him to realize that banking would be the right career choice, *enhanced* by his liberal arts degree, "since banks require people who are generalists with perspective, who are able to deal with many kinds of people and situations." His reasoning convinced the interviewer and he got the job.**
>
> ***Note:* The real reason he wanted to go into banking was that he couldn't think of anything else he could do. But it's unlikely he would have gotten the job offer if that's what he had told the interviewer.**

Everything you say about yourself should fit together to form one cohesive message: I have unique qualities that make me the right person to fill this particular position.

> **EXAMPLE: A laid-off marketing manager from a large firm, who interviewed with a smaller company, emphasized her past**

work responsibilities in a way that showed they could easily be applied to a smaller company: broad control over a single campaign, tight budgeting procedures, leadership of a small team. Who cared that she'd be coming from a larger company? She demonstrated how everything she did there would help her do an even better job at a *smaller* firm.

TIP: According to a GE engineer, "Even if you are interviewing for a purely technical position, strongly stress your interpersonal skills. Few scientists or engineers work alone; unless you are unquestionably brilliant, interpersonal skills are important. Always talk about wanting to be a team player."

### 3. Why Did You Pick That Job (or That Company, or That College)?

This is another open-ended behavioral question that floors some applicants. The key to answering it: Consider the factors that led you to past choices *before* the interview. In all cases, show that whatever you've done, you chose to do for practical, responsible reasons. Avoid the most common beginning response to such questions: a long, drawn-out "Uhhh . . ." Have your reasons ready, so you can be direct and to the point during the interview.

EXAMPLE: "I worked at that firm because it offered me the best opportunities for growth. I began the job as an account manager, and ended by supervising the entire Southwest region. It was an excellent experience."

EXAMPLE: "I picked State College for two reasons. It had a strong economics program and, frankly, it was less expensive than Private University."
*Note:* No one can fault you for being frugal.

If the company or career decision you made was obviously a bad choice, don't waste time discussing it. Briefly state why you made your decision, stressing the rationale for doing it at the time.

EXAMPLE: "I accepted the offer because the company was poised for substantial growth, which was substantiated by articles in *The Wall Street Journal* and the trade magazines. The market collapsed a year later, of course, and things changed. But given what I knew and what the experts were saying at the time, it was the right decision. As it happened, I learned quite a bit while I was there that is applicable now. For example . . .”

## 4. Have You Received Any Other Offers?

If you have other job offers, it's usually best to say so. It shows that someone else thinks you're good enough to hire, which ups your chances at the current interview. Add, of course, that this is the job you're most interested in—even if it's not.

## 5. Are You Interviewing Anywhere Else?

There's usually no harm in saying that you are. Just don't say where. To do so might hurt your chances for an offer, particularly if the other firms are more prestigious or pay higher salaries. If asked, just say you'd prefer not to say.

If this is not your first-choice company, *don't* tell the interviewer this. Interviewing is like proposing marriage: No one wants to be told that he or she is the number-two choice. According to job counselors and recruiters, a surprising number of applicants do admit to this. For example, commercial bank recruiters in the 1980s reported being told by many MBAs that their first choices were investment banks, and that they were interviewing at commercial banks "just in case." Even when they didn't say so openly, they clearly implied it by talking about investment banks the whole time. Needless to say, these people were not offered positions.

Never admit to interviewing for jobs in another field—even if you are. If you're asked, say no or avoid the question entirely. Who wants to hire someone who is not even sure what he or she wants as a career?

## 6. Is There Anything About Your Personal Life that May Affect Your Performance in This High-Travel, Demanding Position?

Employers are prohibited by law from asking anyone if their family will interfere with their job. This, then, is the "legal" way around an illegal question, usually addressed to women.

The answer is "no."

TIP: In general, interviewers cannot ask about your personal life: sexual habits, children (their ages, your plans regarding them, and how you take care of them), religion, age, weight, whether you own or rent a home, possible criminal record, military background. Divulging such information is subject to certain restricted limitations depending on the sensitivity of the position. The Pentagon, for example, very often goes into all aspects of a candidate's personal life for security-related jobs; expect the same from all jobs that require security clearances. Even with private firms, these questions will often be hinted at, and the more you can ease the interviewer's mind, the better off you'll be.

## 7. What Are Your Strengths?

This question is nowadays often asked a bit differently, since interviewers are aware that job hunters are getting more sophisticated. Here are some new versions of what is essentially the same question:

- How do your customers (or bosses, or subordinates, or coworkers) describe you?

- What do you think accounted for your rapid rise in XYZ Corporation (or your great record at school, etc.)?

Mention *specific* attributes that you have, which your employer *needs* in the job. If you're a detail nut and you're applying for an auditing job—great. Talk about it. But give examples: Explain how you found the missing million in the Billings account. Interviewers, like all people, remember specifics, not generalities.

> **EXAMPLE:** *For a managerial position:* "My greatest strengths are my ability to supervise and my interpersonal skills. Last year I won the company's supervisor award, but more important, I think, was an employee poll that voted me the best supervisor of the year. I believe that good operating results come first and foremost from good employee relations."

Avoid being dull or using clichés. Don't say that your greatest strength is your attention to goals, that you are "motivated by challenges" and are a "perfectionist"—unless you have memorable examples to prove it. Do you realize how many "goal-oriented perfectionists" walk through employment office doors every week?

## 8. What Are Your Weaknesses?

Today more than ever, interviewers are rephrasing this question to catch you unawares. If you hear any of the questions below, the odds are the interviewer is trying to get you to reveal your weaknesses:

- What areas have you developed the most in the past year?

- If you were offered a free self-improvement course, which one would you take?

- In your last evaluation, where did you rank the lowest? (There's an implied threat here—they may call and ask for your references directly or indirectly. The tendency is for the interviewee to give an honest answer. But remember, most employers will *not* reveal very much, so you might be able to get away with fudging.)

- What do friends criticize about your personality?

- What would your boss (or subordinates, or teachers, etc.) say you need to improve?

How should you answer? Pick weaknesses that are not weaknesses in terms of the job you want. Pick a strength carried a bit (and only a bit) too far. Try to make your answer sound *real* and not rehearsed—don't jump in with a hurried and obviously memorized spiel. Interviewers hear pat, rehearsed answers every day and are ready to probe further: "Let's go into that weak point you mentioned. . . ." Keep things brief and try to turn things around to examples that can even sell you.

> **EXAMPLE: Almost every dedicated employee worries too much about work, and overworks. So . . . "My biggest weakness is that I can't relax when I'm working on a big project. During our last public relations campaign, my friends [or husband, wife] complained that they barely saw me. Since then, I've set aside at least two hours a day, and one full weekend day, to spend with them. Unless, of course, something major comes up. . . ."**

To repeat a point: Be sure to give examples that *sell you.* Your objective isn't to discuss your weaknesses as much as it is to discuss how and why even your weaknesses make you an ideal candidate.

Whatever weakness you bring up, briefly stress how you've taken steps to overcome it. Self-improvement shows that you can not only see a flaw, but also act on it. Be careful not to mention any faults that could in any way impinge on your position. Don't mention nervousness, sloppiness, carelessness, poor organizing skills, or anything else that might make you seem like less than an ideal employee.

### 9. Why Do You Want This Job? or, Why Should We Hire You?

This is the best opportunity you'll have to sell yourself. Use it.

Explain why this is a logical position for you: Sum up your work history and reemphasize your strongest qualities and achievements. Most important, let the interviewer know that you will be an asset to the company.

Many interviewers report that candidates *don't sell themselves strongly enough*—at all levels. Avoid the problem by stating flatly and openly why you want the job: because you're convinced that you have the right skills and background to make you the right candidate. Then move into your sales pitch, explaining why and how you can contribute to the company. Give specific examples.

> **EXAMPLE:** **"I know this business, and I know your company's excellent record. I started as a clerk with a smaller company in production control, and I worked my way up. This position as supervisor in one of the largest and best-run firms in the business is the culmination of my accomplishments. My background, experience, and enthusiasm make me certain that I'm the right person for the job. For example, you've stated that you need someone with strong managerial skills. My years of experience, and recent success . . . ."**

> **EXAMPLE:** **"This position combines my talents and skills and uses them very effectively. As we discussed, before my current job I was a copywriter. Soon after, I had overall creative responsibility for a small account. This position puts both experiences to work in a product category I know well and have many ideas about. I've already explained how I turned around a flagging product line. I know I can accomplish even more here with your already successful line. For example, I have extensive experience in broadcasting. We could put together a new television campaign. . . ."**
>
> *Note:* **Saying "we" strikes a positive note and implies that you already envision yourself as part of the team.**

### 10. Why Did You Leave Your Previous Job?

The best answer is usually the easiest: You left your previous job for more responsibility and a substantially higher salary. Avoid any suspicion on the interviewer's part that you had problems with your former employer. Often, that *is* the case, but if at all possible, stress the reasons that make you look like a responsible but somewhat ambitious employee. You left because you were seeking better growth potential, a unique business challenge, and a higher salary.

If the interviewer knows you had problems with your previous employer, don't lie or struggle to change the subject. This often occurs in small towns or close-knit industries where everyone knows what everyone else is doing or can easily find out that information. Acknowledge your previous difficulties at work, stress that they were unique to that situation, then talk about the *positive* aspects of the job, what you learned, and how that experience can be helpful in this job.

Whatever the temptation, don't bad-mouth your previous employer. Don't forget that the interviewer looks at things from a different angle. You may someday leave this job, too. If you did, what would you say about them? Negative gossip makes you look unprofessional.

Be careful. Some interviewers may lure you into making negative judgments about ex-employers. Even if the interviewer genuinely seems to feel the same way you do about your previous employer, avoid being conspiratorial about your opinions.

> **EXAMPLE: Several people have reported that interviewers encourage them to make negative statements. One interviewer started by being very sympathetic: "That company is a real pressure cooker." The applicant agreed, and the interviewer made a more negative judgment, to which the applicant also agreed, and so on until the applicant was telling all.**
>
> *Note:* **This is a common pitfall with younger or less-experienced applicants.**

> **TIP: Don't lie or defend your previous employer either. If your previous employer was tough or unfair, try to concentrate on what was good about the job (you learned freight-forwarding procedures, etc.) and how you can apply that experience to *this* job.**

The same principle applies if you've switched careers. It's always best to take the positive approach: Your previous career was fine, but

THE MOST COMMON QUESTIONS INTERVIEWERS ASK

you've always wanted to work in this field. Avoid the temptation of talking about how bad it was being a paralegal, etc. Save that discussion to have with your friends. You never know what background experience may be of interest to an interviewer, and what you might lose by downgrading it.

> **EXAMPLE:** **A would-be refugee from "big-city" life applied to a "down-home" mail-order house specializing in camping gear. The interview was excellent until the applicant began criticizing his current employer for its rigid, corporate, urban way of retailing. The interviewer's face dropped, and the interview was soon over without an offer. It turned out that the interviewer was looking for a candidate who could update ordering and handling procedures. By expressing his dislike for his competitor's ways, the candidate talked himself out of a job in a small town.**

## 11. Where Do You See Yourself in Five Years? In Ten Years?

When interviewers ask you to project your career into the future, give a bland reply. Say you see yourself at the same company in a position of greater responsibility. Talk about the *job,* not the title, unless the company is an openly aggressive up-or-out organization. By concentrating on the position itself, you establish your commitment to the work, as opposed to being overly ambitious and fixated on money or title.

Be brief. Talking about the future isn't as productive as talking about the present and why you're a good candidate for the job. Moreover, since you don't know the company's plans for the future, you might say something that could disqualify you.

> **EXAMPLE:** **"I expect to still be involved in financial services, with a solid client base that I'd develop with you at XYZ brokers."**

> **TIP:** **Avoid making an overly glib and ambitious statement such as "I see myself in your job" or "I see myself as president of the company." Although it may make you seem like a go-getter, in today's uncertain economy it also sounds threatening—or foolish. Who wants to hire someone who's openly gunning for his or her job?**

> **TIP: Sometimes honesty works best of all. Several employers in extremely high turnover industries such as stock trading have _preferred_ applicants who answered "I don't know"—at least they were being honest and weren't trying to snow them.**

## 12. What Salary Range Did You Have in Mind?

Don't say. If the numbers you pick are too high or too low, it may put you out of the running even before the interview is over.

Almost always, people will respect you if you say that you'd prefer to discuss salary later. In some cases, however, the interviewer will insist on discussing it then. First, try to get the interviewer to set the range. Turn the question around: "What salary range has the firm been considering?"

If you still have to give your price first, think back on your research and come up with a figure that meets the standards within the industry and is reasonable in light of your background. Choose a figure that's a little on the high side: It's better to look valuable than cut-rate. But stress to the interviewer that it's the _job_, not the potential salary, that particularly interests you.

Especially with entry-level positions, but also in fields where competition is tough and applicants are many, you may be told a salary and asked if it is suitable. If it falls within a reasonable range, it is best to say yes, but beyond that be as noncommittal as possible. Chances are the job is an easy one to fill. If you say no, you'll be out of the running. By saying yes and curtailing further discussion, you keep them interested in you, but you also reserve the opportunity to negotiate a better benefits package, or vacation arrangement, after an offer is made.

## 13. How Would You Sell Me on My Company or Product?

Asking you to give a spontaneous sales presentation is a quick way for interviewers to weed out applicants. This tough task is commonly presented to people who are applying for sales jobs, and is increasingly used by banks and brokerage houses. Most people aren't prepared for it and answer by stumbling and stammering their way through a very amateurish monologue that is embarrassing to them and painful (or amusing) for the interviewer to hear.

Be ready beforehand. Before any interview, go over the product or services and practice being on a sales call. Be thorough in your research, but don't worry too much about it: The fact that you are prepared to give a measured and coherent answer is what's important.

Make a point of saying you welcome this opportunity. After all, that's why you're interviewing here: to get the chance to represent the company and its product. Then proceed as if you were on a sales call, highlighting the advantages of the product or service.

> **EXAMPLE:** "Yes, I'd like the chance to show how I'd sell your product. After all, that's why I chose to interview here, because I believe in the company and what it sells. I'll begin with the top-of-the line product, which is the best of its kind. . . ."

> **TIP:** Use props to underscore your salesmanship. One young bank applicant photocopied an advertising article on the bank's new cash-management service and used it during his sales presentation. Don't be afraid to copy this technique: It shows resourcefulness and a strong sales mentality.

### 14. Can You Think of Anything Else that You'd Like to Add?

The answer to this question is always yes.

If the interviewer neglected one critical area that further qualifies you, mention it now. Even if nothing critical was omitted, use this opportunity to resell yourself. Combine points from your resume into a logical, understandable reason for hiring you.

> **EXAMPLE:** "Yes, we were talking about your inventory control system. I understand that it's not a principal function of the job, but I'd like to add that I've had several months of experience as an inventory control clerk. So, together with my experience as a manager, I feel that I've got a uniquely appropriate background for this job; I could quickly and effectively take charge. . . ."

If the interview has gone badly, use this time to counter all the negatives that the interviewer may have mentioned. *Don't* bring up your weak points unless you feel fairly certain that the interviewer is going to make a negative decision: Repeating the negatives can be counterproductive. You may wind up, at the very end of the interview, *reminding* the interviewer of reasons not to hire you. But if you have had a bad interview, a forthright stand on the relevant issues can sometimes turn the interview around. You have nothing to lose.

**EXAMPLE:** "I can understand your objections to a candidate who has switched careers three times in 10 years. But I'd like to add that by hiring me you'd be employing a man who is now *determined* to make this one work. I've demonstrated my firm dedication to this career by taking the night courses I mentioned and working very hard. My references will all corroborate how excellent my skills are, and what a real advantage they'd be in this job. You'd be getting all my experience and ability at a far lower cost than you'd normally have to spend. And you won't find such dedication in anyone else. . . ."

# 9  *Followup*

## INTRODUCTION

After you've finished an interview, you can't just relax and wait for a job offer. The minute the interview is over—sometimes even *during* the interview—you should start thinking about followup. What can you do to further convince the interviewer that you are right for the job? The answer is the all-too-often-forgotten followup letter, or, in some cases, phone call.

Don't make the mistake many job hunters do and dismiss the idea of followup as a time-consuming nicety, something that makes you look polite but doesn't accomplish much else. Followup is too important to be pushed aside.

## FOLLOWUP LETTERS

■ **While thanking the interviewer is technically the reason for a followup letter, what you actually are doing is taking advantage of a sales opportunity.**

A followup letter is often your *last chance* to convince a prospective employer that you are the right person for the job. Writing one effectively often can make the difference between a job offer and a polite "We regret to inform you that the position has been filled. . . ."

■ **The sooner you write a followup letter and send it, the better.**

You will come across as interested, aggressive, and courteous—all positive signals when it comes to landing a job.

> **TIP:** To make the best impression, write and send a thank-you note on the same day as your interview; or send it the following day but date it the same day as your interview.

## How to Write an Effective Followup Letter

■ **Since this is ostensibly a brief thank you, keep your letter short: one page or less.**

This is more than enough space to (1) remind the prospective employer of your interview, (2) sell yourself one more time, and (3) recap—which are the three essential sections of a strong, well-organized followup letter.

## Section #1: The Basic Reminder

■ **Start simply. Unlike any other type of letter you send during your job hunt, a followup letter *doesn't* have to grab the reader's attention from the outset.**

All you want to do in the opening of your letter is remind the interviewer that you were interviewed for the job and that you're very interested in it. A basic, no-frills "Thanks for your time today. I enjoyed discussing the position" is fine to begin with.

> **TIP:** The letter's tone should match the intended audience—the interviewer. If he or she was casual, make your letter a bit looser and more informal. If the interviewer was very traditional, stick with a formal business letter.

Next, restate your interest in the job, being sure to mention the exact position you discussed. If possible, give your "interest" statement a double value: Write it as a mini sales pitch that introduces your strongest qualifications and thus leads directly to the next section.

## Section #2: The Sales Message

■ **To back up your qualifications for the job and remind the prospective employer of your interest, repeat the highlights of the interview.**

In this portion of the letter, you should continue the sales pitch you began during your interview. Refer directly to specific points you discussed. Be sure to mention several examples of your qualifications, ideally those which the interviewer appeared most interested in. *Remember:* Your aim *isn't* to come up with a new way of presenting yourself. Instead, you should be building on the foundation you already established during the interview.

This is a good place to give the interviewer additional information that will strengthen your case. If you've learned more about the position or the company and realize you should expand upon your qualifications, do it here.

*Note:* If any misconceptions arose during your interview, or if the interview went poorly in general, this is where you should straighten things out. One important exception to this rule: If a problem came up during the interview (your qualifications weren't right; you didn't have enough experience, etc.), and you dealt with it successfully then, *don't* bring it up again in a thank-you letter. Leave well enough alone.

Whichever tactic you focus on, you should be constantly hammering home one point: "I am the person you should hire."

## Section #3: The Recap

■ **Close your letter as concisely as you opened it.**

The last paragraph in the letter should be essentially a repeat of your opening: Thank the interviewer again for his or her time; restate how interested you are in the position and why you are qualified.

> **TIP:** *For aggressive types:* Set up a reason to have another interview and say you'll call to arrange a definite time.
>
> *Example:* "Based upon our discussion, I have outlined a series of training programs that should work well for AMB Enterprises. I will give you a call early next week to set up a time in which you and I can go over them."
>
> *Note:* This approach can either force the interviewer to make a quicker decision *or* strengthen a weak interview.

## SAMPLE THANK-YOU LETTER

Mr. Mark Conrad
Executive Vice-President, Human Resources
MegaBux Incorporated
666 Sixth Avenue
New York, NY 10022

Dear Mr. Conrad:

Thank you for meeting with me today to discuss the Director of Training position. I was especially interested in your comments about the need for expanded employee education in light of MegaBux's rapid growth and latest acquisitions.

**[A basic opening; nothing flashy, but the writer has hit all the right notes. By referring to a specific aspect of the conversation, he nudges the interviewer's memory and makes himself stand out. Even better, he leads smoothly into his sales pitch in the next paragraph.]**

As I mentioned during our conversation, I have a proven track record in the development and implementation of training programs. Most recently, I designed and oversaw a series of intensive sales training seminars for Alta Industries. The proof of their effectiveness was dramatic: Sales increased 23% and the sales staff reported better understanding and higher morale.

**[He immediately repeats his strongest selling point—one that matches the job opening. Again, nothing flashy, but it works.]**

Again, many thanks for your time and attention. There is no doubt in my mind that developing a corporate-wide system of interactive employee education programs for MegaBux would be a rewarding challenge—the type of challenge I know I can meet successfully. I look forward to hearing from you in the near future.

**[A utilitarian close; he thanks the interviewer again at the bottom, repeats how interested he is in the job, how confident he is that he can do it, and gets out of the letter gracefully.]**

Sincerely,


Lawrence Putnam

## FOLLOWUP TELEPHONE CALLS

■ **One hard-and-fast rule applies to using the phone:** *Don't* **use a phone for followup if it makes you uncomfortable.**

But there is a major exception to this rule. If your interview was a few weeks ago, you've already sent a followup letter, and you still haven't heard back, swallow your discomfort and pick up the phone. If the worst is true and the prospective employer has hired someone else or decided you weren't right for the job, you have absolutely nothing to lose.

On the other hand, you may also discover that your fears were unfounded. In that case, your phone call should turn into a small sales pitch.

*Consider using the phone for followup if:*

- your interview went badly and you want to aim for a second interview

- you've gotten another job offer and you need to know where you stand at this company before you make a decision

- you have new, important information to share with the interviewer—and you want to be sure he or she gets it immediately

### How to Make Followup Phone Calls

■ **As you would with a followup letter, keep it short and to the point.**

As with other phone calls you may make during your job hunt, you should answer any questions the person on the other end of the line might pose *before* he or she has to ask them. Explain who you are, why you are calling, when you were interviewed, and for what position.

> **EXAMPLE: "Mr. Brown? This is Sandra Kinney. We met two weeks ago, May 17, to discuss the marketing assistant position that's available at Magitech. . . ."**

Be straightforward when you ask about the status of your application. You want to know if you're still in the running. Again, it's up to you to bring up the subject. Depending upon the exact circumstances, you might mention having other job offers, give the employer new information, or try to close in on a job offer.

> **EXAMPLE:** "I wanted to know if you've reached a decision yet. I've received another job offer, but before I make a decision, I need to know about the position at Magitech. . . ."
>
> *OR:* "As I'm sure you realize, I'm very interested in the position. Since we met, I've taken the time to draw up several sample marketing plans to show what I have in mind for Magitech. When could I come in to show them to you?"
>
> *OR:* "Is there anything else you need to know about me before you reach a final decision? I'd be glad to stop by. . . ."
>
> *OR (for the confident, aggressive sales personality only):* "I'm looking forward to working at Magitech. I think I can contribute a great deal to the marketing team. Could we meet to finalize your decision?"

Another method that works, especially if you're calling because you've heard nothing, is to be honest and direct. Ask what is happening—no tricks, no gimmicks, nothing but curiosity. "I was hoping to hear from you and decided to call to see if you've made a decision yet." Follow *that* up with a reminder of your interest and top qualifications: "I'm enthusiastic about working for Magitech. As I mentioned during our interview, my five years' experience in marketing widgets . . ."

■ **When you call an employer to follow up, you must be prepared for rejection.**

An employer may tell you flatly that you weren't right for the job; someone else has already been hired. Hearing even the most polite rejection, the "I'm sorry, but . . . ," isn't easy, and it certainly isn't pleasant, but it also isn't the end of the world. If you have the temperament, ask the employer what the problem was—it's possible that you may be able to overcome his or her objection. At the least, you can find out what (if anything) you can improve upon in future interviews.

■ **Recognize that many rejections aren't your fault and can't be avoided.**

Keep reminding yourself that there are other positions out there, other interviews you'll be having, and other followups. Stay optimistic. Each day—and each rejection—brings you closer to a job.

# 10 Assessing a Job Offer

## INTRODUCTION

You've been offered a job; now comes the hard part. Do you accept it immediately or do you wait? Do you start negotiating for better terms or do you accept the total package as is? Is the salary competitive? What about benefits? How do you assess the job you've been offered and decide if you need it or want it?

As with the rest of your job hunt, the best way to handle these questions is in a step-by-step manner: methodically and carefully looking at each question and problem. In most cases, try to resist the temptation to accept an offer immediately and throw the consequences to the winds. This is especially hard if you are unemployed, but you'll be far better off in the long run if you look before you leap.

Before accepting a position, break the offer down and analyze it.

*The three basic steps to take are:*

1. assessing the company

2. assessing the position

3. assessing the salary and benefits package

If everything looks good, accept the job. If certain aspects look bad, consider *negotiating* a better package. If all aspects look bad, ask yourself: *"Why in the world did I interview for this job in the first place?"*

## GENERAL CONSIDERATIONS

■ **As a rule, don't accept an offer on the spot.**

In the first flush of success, particularly if you've been unemployed for a while, your natural inclination will be to accept and forget the potential consequences. But you should realize that the consequences can be severe, ranging from a lower than normal salary to a slow career track to bad working conditions. In other words, you might not know what you're getting into.

Tell the interviewer you need a week to think about and assess the offer. This will give you time to analyze the company, the position, the salary, and the benefits package. Most companies *expect* you to take at least a week.

> **TIP:** *First warning flag of a bad job offer:* **When the interviewer presses you to make a decision immediately. This suggests a problem with the quality of the company or the offer. The position may be one that the company is having difficulty filling, or the company itself may be having problems that the interviewer doesn't want you to find out about.** *Ask* **the interviewer why he or she needs a quick decision, and look at those reasons suspiciously.**

There are a few exceptions. Sometimes, you'll have to make a fast decision for all the *right* reasons. Entrepreneurial companies, which pride themselves on being fast-moving, may want someone who can make a decision on the spot. This is particularly true when the founder of the firm makes an offer. He or she is used to gutsy, seat-of-the-pants decision-making and expects such behavior from subordinates. If you want the job, you may have to say yes quickly.

With lower-level positions in highly competitive industries, an immediate acceptance or reply in a few days is also sometimes the norm. In the words of one interviewer: "They need us more than we need them. If they can't decide quickly, they can walk out without a job." It's usually easy to tell if your firm and/or offer falls into this category. The salaries in such firms are low, benefits are standardized, and employment officers, rather than line managers, are the principal decision-makers. Even in this case, you usually can negotiate for an overnight delay or a delay of a few days.

## STEP ONE: ASSESSING THE COMPANY

### Business Record and Finances

- **After holding back from accepting the offer, start your next day by analyzing the company and its business.**

It may take only a few hours to research and analyze a company or institution, but the benefits of doing this can affect the rest of your career.

Ask yourself: *Where is the company going? Is it gaining or losing market share? Would I be working in a strong division? If not, would the rewards be worth it?* Analyze nonprofit institutions and government positions in the same manner. Is the area or function receiving adequate and increasing funding? Are the functions of the position well supported and respected by the profession or the rest of the institution? In other words: *Is this company a good place for my career?*

> **TIP:** *Advice from an older but wiser middle manager:* **If you are offered a high-paying, high-visibility position in a division that needs to be "turned around," think twice before you get enticed by challenges, above-average salaries, bonuses, and visions of yourself on the cover of *Forbes* magazine as "The Turn-around King." In today's cost-cutting atmosphere, entire divisions can be sold off, and managers as quickly dumped, by the new owners. Or the "turn-around" division may be impossible to turn around, leaving you looking like an ineffective manager who has wasted several years. Know what kind of risk-taker you are before accepting high-risk positions.**

- **Check library references and personal contacts for a reading on the company and its future.**

Read between the lines and make certain to go beyond surface impressions, particularly with smaller, less-known firms. Don't rely merely on credit reports from *Dun & Bradstreet*. Many disreputable or even failing businesses maintain strong credit ratings to the very end. Instead, ask if you can speak to your potential coworkers in the firm. Get a reading from what they say—or *don't* say—about the company. Speak with friends or acquaintances in competing corporations and read the trade magazines to get a feel for the company and its place in the industry.

**EXAMPLE:** *A worst-case scenario of a newly minted MBA who accepted a job with a trading firm that had plush offices and an impeccable credit rating:* The interviewer explained that the company traded "consumer electronics goods and other items" to certain nations. The MBA didn't press to find out what the "other items" were when he accepted the very generous offer. He did check a credit source that rated the firm A+. He found out a lot more after a few weeks on the job, when FBI agents knocked on the door. They were investigating shipments of arms to the Middle East. The MBA quickly applied to another firm, offering a unique reason for having left his previous job: "I didn't find gun-running compatible with my long-term career plans."

**TIP:** For major firms and industries, check *Value Line* or other sources to get a quick fix on your potential employer. See Chapter 3, "Research," for other ideas on how to find out more about your company.

## Company Culture

■ **Check if you are compatible with the firm.**

Are you and the corporation compatible in terms of working and social styles? If you prefer bureaucratic management, you might be very unhappy in a small, hard-charging, entrepreneurial company. Or vice versa. Pick up clues from the interview itself: How did they treat you? Did you feel comfortable during the interview? Did you like the people?

Compatibility with your new firm isn't a minor consideration. Never presume that "I'll just get used to it." Maybe you won't. Besides, unhappiness with your work often means a slower career track and less money or advancement down the road. Job satisfaction pays practical career dividends, while *you* pay for your career dissatisfaction.

**EXAMPLE:** One woman made a "successful" job switch to another firm in the same business. She got more money, but lost on everything else. Her first firm was entrepreneurial, friendly, and casual. And she was on the fast track. Her new firm was a giant in the field, slow-moving and bureaucratic, with employees seated quietly in their cubicles all day. For a few thousand extra dollars she traded away her happy and productive work environment—and suffered from depression and problems on her new job. Was it worth it? Only if $3,000 extra for *one* year was the only factor in her decision.

■ **Compare your prospective employer's management style with that of the rest of the company.**

Openings often occur when a manager is in trouble with senior management: The manager's employees may be leaving so as not to be part of a losing team. Make certain you're not *joining* that team.

■ **See how well the combination of your style and your employer's style would mesh with the company as a whole.**

Managers hire people who either match or complement their style. However, if your employer is a very different type of person from the company norm and he or she leaves, you might be forced to leave as well, even if you're just *perceived* to be similar.

> **EXAMPLE: This happened to a man employed in the materials-processing center of a large fragrance manufacturer and marketer. His immediate supervisor was a nontraditional, seat-of-the-pants administrator with a messy desk and sloppy procedures who was also bright, fun to work with, and somehow got the job done brilliantly. But he was completely at odds with the conservative, slow-but-steady style of upper management. Shortly after the man was hired his supervisor was forced to leave, and the employee had a problem. He was associated with the old manager and was viewed suspiciously by the new, tough, no-nonsense manager, who quickly brought in his own people from his old division to shake things up.**

## STEP TWO: ASSESSING THE POSITION

■ **Ask for a job description and do some other checking; don't just *assume* you understand the position.**

The most important part of assessing your offer is the most obvious and, for that reason, the most overlooked: the position itself. See where the normal career track lies and estimate how long you are expected to stay in the position. What are the job responsibilities, and are they clearly spelled out? Again, talking to your predecessor can be very valuable and can give you a good sense of what you're accepting if you take the job.

> **TIP: If you have nagging doubts about the management, get a *written* job and responsibilities description.**

■ **Review the history of the position.**

What happened to the person before you? One man thought his position looked very attractive until a brief investigation showed that the average tenure in the job was one year. Three previous employees had each held the position for one year and then were fired. This doesn't necessarily mean that the firm is disreputable or the position is wrong for you. Many sales-oriented companies and stockbrokerages maintain strict "up-or-out" policies; if you can't sell or make money, you're fired. But you should *know* this in advance, and be prepared.

It's the same case at lower levels with large "management trainee" classes—where many aspiring Fortune 500 banking and financial people get their start. Find out how many management trainees are kept on after the year or so of classes is over, and what happens to the average trainee after training.

> **EXAMPLE: Certain larger banks use the trainee position as a way of observing a candidate's performance, so they can later "weed out" the lower-than-average performers. Others, like the Morgan Bank, maintain a strong commitment to *all* trainees and expect them to remain. Don't make the error of assuming that all large corporations treat entry-level employees the same.**

■ **Another major consideration: How does the position you've been offered fit in with your short- and long-term career plans?**

A low-paying, high-stress job actually may be better than any alternative if it is the only way to break into a new business or industry. For example, "glamour fields" such as television or entertainment typically offer anyone who is not experienced or well connected low-paying, unprestigious jobs. If you accept this as the cost of getting your foot in the door, then you can work your way up.

> **EXAMPLE: One midlevel, former government employee who wanted to break into television news learned this the hard way: He was offered a low-paying network news job, but he**

> arrogantly turned it down, figuring that with his experience he should be earning far more. He realized later that he had made a mistake. His job hunt was still in progress when one network froze its positions and others started having major layoffs, so he found himself without any news job at all.

This approach should also be considered by career changers and unemployed middle managers who are forced to switch fields. Sometimes the only way to get the right job is by taking the *wrong* job first and accepting low level, low pay, and low prestige. In many cases it's better to take a step backward *now* rather than suffer the consequences of long-term unemployment. But always look carefully at career paths: Does the position offer opportunities for career growth? Or is it a dead-end administrative assistant job?

> TIP: Unemployed managers and recent college graduates should be particularly careful when going to employment agencies. Less reputable firms may offer "high-growth administrative assistant" positions that, in reality, are dead-end jobs.

## STEP THREE: ASSESSING THE SALARY AND BENEFITS PACKAGE

■ **This is the point when it all comes down to the brass tacks stage: Is the offer what you want or what you deserve?**

Assessing a salary and benefits package really boils down to one simple question: Is the offer fair?

The easiest way to answer this question for you—find a way of comparing what you're being offered with what you've gotten in the past, or with what others in your field at your level are getting.

■ **The basic rule of thumb: To decide whether the job offer is right for you, analyze the offer in terms of what your current (or most recent) job provided you.**

In other words, you want to be sure you aren't losing by accepting the new job.

The simplest way to compare is to list your current (or most recent) salary and benefits. Be sure to include whichever of the following apply:

- salary

- bonuses (if any)

- pension plan (including SERPs)

- company contributions to a 401(k), if any. (*Note:* Don't factor in your own contributions to a 401(k). While these help you save taxes, it's still your money, not the company's. Count only matching contributions made by your employer.)

- approximate annualized value of stock options (the average stock value for the past three years or an estimate of future value based on earnings per share), if any

- company-paid car and car allowance

- any special insurance coverage (coverage for your or a family member's special medical condition that goes beyond the usual coverage)

- life insurance

- company-paid health programs

- company-paid memberships (country clubs, etc.)

By matching the total of the above against what you're being offered by your new employer, you can quickly see if the new package equals—or, ideally, exceeds—the old one.

> **TIP: This is also the time to determine what perks and benefits *aren't* important to you—such niceties as club memberships, perhaps —and which are must-haves and, as such, potential deal-breakers.**

> **TIP: When you're comparing the past and the present, be sure to keep in mind that economic times have been tough in the recent past. As a result, companies may still be less generous than you'd like. Call it a continuing fallout from the restructuring and downsizing companies were forced into because of the poor economic climate. More companies have cut back on medical coverage, retirement plans, and the like. Similarly, there has been an increased emphasis on bonuses and other incentives to replace the old annual merit raise. When you're considering a job offer, it's vital to know what salary and benefits are normal for the industry, what company policy is, and the like.**

■ **If you're a recent graduate, haven't held a full-time job before, or are switching careers into a completely different field, you have to take a different tack.**

If you fit into any of the above categories, you have no personal basis of comparison by which to judge your job offer. But that doesn't mean you have to go on intuition or sheer luck alone. What you have to do is judge the offer based upon what *others* get in the same position at the same level of skill. And this will take research on your part. Read trade papers and scan the want ads to get a feel for what other companies are offering in terms of salary and benefits for a position like yours. Ask your networking contacts.

■ **Finally, do remember that, to a great degree, a good salary and benefits package depends on a number of factors.**

A good salary and benefits package depends on industry and professional standards, the position you're going for, your background and experience, your goals, and more. Salary and benefits packages vary widely between different industries—and between different companies *within* the same industry.

The bottom line, then? Yes, the best way to assess a salary and benefits package is to determine if it meets or exceeds what others are getting for the same position at the same level of skill. But it also matters that *you* feel comfortable with both your salary and benefits.

■ **To help you better understand your job offer and how to asses it, the following pages run through the basics of a salary and benefits package.**

In the following pages, you can read about the different elements that you may find in a salary and benefits package—from salaries and other financial compensation such as bonuses to pension plans to insurance. You'll be able to learn about the benefits that are commonly offered, less common features that you may want to ask for or that may be included in your particular offer, and so forth. All of this should help you better evaluate the offer you receive.

> TIP: Yes, the salary and benefits package is an important part of the job offer, but don't let it outweigh the opportunities afforded you by the position itself. In general, the older and more experienced you are, the more important your benefits are—and vice versa. If you are young, consider the *experience* and *exposure* the job will give you well ahead of any benefits package.

## Salary and Other Financial Compensation

■ **The salary you're being offered is probably the easiest aspect of the job offer to assess.**

You probably already have a good idea of whether the salary offered is a fair one. The basic (and obvious) rule of thumb: It should meet industry standards for the position. As mentioned before, if you're at all unsure what these standards should be, because you've changed careers or industries, check it against want ads and articles in trade publications, annual salary surveys published in magazines and newspapers or available through trade and professional organizations, and word of mouth from friends and acquaintances in the field.

■ **Be on the alert if you're offered a salary much higher or lower than your last job or than the norm in the industry.**

If the salary you're offered is much *higher* than your last job or than industry standards, it may be a tipoff to hidden problems with the position, the company, or both. It may mean the company is trying too hard to get you to take the job. Maybe no one else would take the job and they're trying to make it more appealing to you (which means something is clearly wrong). Or possibly they're trying to compensate for poor working conditions. Do some background digging to be sure of the situation. And do keep in mind that, if the salary is much higher than anything you've received in the past, it could just mean you've been underpaid in the past.

If the salary you're offered is much *lower* than your past jobs or the industry norm, it may be a tipoff to problems with *you*. Have you been underselling yourself? Is your presentation of yourself and your skills undermining you?

> **TIP:** If you think the salary you're being offered is too low, be sure to doublecheck on what others in the industry are being paid. Maybe your expectations are unrealistic and you're pricing yourself out of the market. And do remember that there are instances when a lower salary is almost a given—you're changing careers, for example, and thus can't get what you've been getting.

> **TIP:** Don't just look at the hard salary figures when determining whether the salary works for you or not. Remember to factor in benefits and other compensation (bonuses, etc.). They may make

**up the difference between what you think you should be getting paid and what you really would be getting paid.**

■ **In addition to base salary, your offer may include other forms of financial compensation—bonuses, stock options, and the like.**

These other forms of financial compensation are becoming more common in job offer packages. Some replace the traditional annual raise; others are given to keep base salary lower.

If you're offered any of these alternative forms of compensation, be sure to keep them in perspective. Remember: A base salary is *guaranteed*—you'll get it no matter what. But other forms of compensation are usually incentive-based and *aren't* guaranteed. So if the economy or the company hits hard times, or simply when the company doesn't meet the expectations laid out in its strategic plan, you don't get the bonus or incentive or whatever form the compensation is taking.

That said, it's probable that at some point or another, you'll run across one or more of the following types of compensation, especially for those of you in the executive ranks.

• *Bonuses:* These used to be limited to upper management but are being offered down the line nowadays, especially to middle managers and supervisors. Bonus amounts vary widely, as do the conditions under which they're given. Usually bonuses are given annually and are tied to how well you (or the department or other area you are responsible for) perform(s). Often they're also tied to how well the company has performed—although it you're a top achiever, even in lean times, bonuses can be quite generous. At the upper level, bonuses typically equal 30% to 40% of base pay (although a number of industries and companies pay more —bringing bonuses up to astronomical amounts). At the middle level, it's roughly 20% to 30% of base pay.

> **TIP: If you have the negotiating leverage (you have related job experience under your belt and are going for a middle- to upper-level job, you know the company is eager to hire you, etc.), try to lock in a guaranteed first-year bonus. The reason? Most bonuses are performance-based and, because you won't have been at the company long, your new employer won't have much chance to see you perform.**

• *Sign-on bonuses* (also called "one-time" or "special" bonuses): These are given, obviously, upon your accepting the job, and they are becoming more and more common, especially to replace other, more expensive perks. Often they're offered to offset relocation costs. The amount of the bonus can vary widely—but they are rarely extremely high.

> **TIP: In some cases, you can negotiate a fairly generous sign-on bonus as a replacement for other perks (company car, country club, etc.) that would be paid for over a period of time. The reason? One-time, up-front costs are cheaper for the company. This tactic makes sense if you need the up-front money: For example, if you've been unemployed for a long time and need cash to meet immediate payments or to pay off high credit debts.**

- *Stock options/grants:* This type of financial compensation is very popular, offered to employees by nearly one-third of all U.S. companies. Most common are stock options, in which you have the option to purchase company stock at a set price. These usually cannot be exercised for a set time period. There are a number of different stock options arrangements; some companies may offer more than one type. With stock grants, you are given shares of company stock. One variation of a stock grant is a restricted stock grant, under which you receive stock only after a certain period has passed or upon meeting certain goals.

- *Stock purchase plans:* These allow you to buy company stock (up to a preset amount) at book value or at a discount. One variation on this—you buy an amount of stock at market price, then the company matches your purchase either dollar for dollar or a percentage thereof and buys you more stock.

- *Gain-sharing:* This is a type of group bonus plan, in which employees receive a percentage (usually 50%) of a company gain in productivity or savings. It's most common in manufacturing companies, although its use has spread to other areas as well. This type of group bonus plan can also apply to smaller groups —for example, to a small team working on one specific project as a reward for getting the project off the ground.

- *Pay-for-quality arrangements:* Again, reward is tied to company performance. Under pay-for-quality arrangements, management rewards employees for doing better than in the past, for meeting quality goals, etc. The payment may be a bonus or a portion of the base salary and may be paid on an individual basis or to a group.

> **TIP: You may also hear about "lightning strike" or "instant" incentives, since they're in use by nearly one-third of all U.S. companies. These incentives, though, shouldn't really be factored into your salary and benefits package, because of their unpredictability. This type of incentive—ranging from cash (a percentage of your salary) to other awards (trips, televisions, etc.)—is given, as the name denotes, out of the blue, for special performance.**

## Severance Agreements

■ **If you're on the middle or upper level, your job offer may also include a severance agreement or package (also called exit terms).**

These used to be for the upper levels only, but with the ups and downs in the economy in the recent past and with the resulting corporate downsizings, they've become a common option for middle managers as well.

Severance agreements are designed to make sure that you won't be left in the lurch if you lose your job. They can be a valuable part of your package, particularly if you work in an industry that's prone to fluctuations depending on the condition of the economy or if you are thinking about working for a company that has a history of downsizing. In many cases, your job offer will include a set severance agreement. If you aren't offered one, it's something you should strongly consider asking for.

What should you look for in a severance package?

• *Salary or severance payment:* Ideally paid for a year or more if you are fired. Obviously you can negotiate for a compromise—one year plus stock options, or the like. You usually can receive your payment as a lump sum or as a weekly or monthly payment.

> **TIP: Opt for a lump sum if you're worried about the company's long-term financial stability or if you want to invest the lump sum to ensure covering financial outlays if you are laid off or fired. More often, however, you are better off trying for receiving your severance pay as regular salary. Why? Because usually receiving continuing salary payments means you'll also still be participating in company retirement plans and will continue contributing to a 401(k) or the like. In addition, often receiving severance as a salary means you'll also receive continued insurance coverage for the duration of the severance pay.**

- *Continued medical coverage:* Again, coverage for a year or more is best.

- *Continued life insurance coverage:* Not as important as the previous two options, this still can save you money in the long run.

> **TIP: If you are negotiating a severance agreement, try for a longer period of severance pay, but agree to have benefits coverage drop upon your taking a new job.**

- *Relocation expenses:* Applies if you have to relocate to take the job. In this case, the company agrees to pay for your move back should you be fired.

> **TIP: A good negotiating stance, if your company bases its severance packages on length of service with the company, is to ask for terms that match those of an employee of your age or one at your job level.**

There are other items that may be part of your severance package, but they aren't as crucial as the above. These include such features as continued employee discounts on company products (if applicable), continued free use of the company's product/services for a set period (one to five years, typically), and school tuition for your children.

## Benefits

■ **Benefits packages are a very important part of any job offer. In fact, benefits packages (including retirement plans, company-sponsored health and life insurance, and disability) usually can be worth 20% to 40% of your salary.**

In simple English, this means you would have to earn 20% to 40% *more* to afford similar health coverage, retirement benefits, and the rest . . . which can translate into a lot of money.

Given this, it's clear that you have to carefully weigh the value of the benefits you're being offered. Although it is difficult to give dollar values to certain benefits, try to determine their worth by reading through the company's printed material on the subject. Many people don't even glance at the written plan because it's too technical and boring, or they're intimidated by the accounting terms and "legalese."

Don't make this mistake. Remember—it all adds up to money . . . in *your* pocket.

> **TIP: Keep in mind that many companies are scaling back benefits to save money. In other words, you may not be offered as much as you might have been in the past. However, you still should expect the basics—medical, disability, and pension—at the very least.**

When you read through the basics of a benefits package, look for omissions and signs of bad management. If you see problems or discrepancies, take your concerns to a qualified accountant or lawyer. Typically, the larger the company, the lower the odds of there being anything unseemly about your plan. It also works the other way: With smaller firms, it pays to look carefully at the full range of benefits.

■ **You may have to compare and choose between different benefits packages offered by the same company.**

Often you'll be faced with a variety of choices in terms of the benefits you want or can get. It may be tough to wade through the material and the terms, but it's well worth your time. There are two general types of benefits packages:

• *Standardized packages,* in which the employer offers you a package —specific health insurance, disability, pension, and so forth. You may have some choice, but in general what they offer is what you get. There's minimal flexibility and negotiability.

• *Cafeteria-style packages* that allow you to design your own package from a variety of options. In this case, you can custom-tailor a package. You usually are required to sign up for some form of medical, life, and disability insurance, but can select among varying coverage levels and deductibles. You then can shop among other options, which may include supplemental insurance coverage for family members, elect such special perks as legal services and childcare, decide *against* a certain form of insurance and *for* higher amounts of another, and the like. Such packages are usually more popular among employees than the standardized package.

You may have to choose whether you want the standardized or the cafeteria-style package. Or, if you opt for the cafeteria style, you will have to choose exactly what benefits you do want from those available to you.

But whichever type of benefits package you are confronted with, you must take the time to think carefully about the worth of the package you're getting and whether it meets your needs.

Following are some specifics about the different types of benefits you may be offered, the features to look for, and what to look out for.

## Pensions and Retirement Savings Plans

■ **There are a number of different types of pensions and company-sponsored savings and retirement plans that are part of a typical benefits package.**

The old days when there was only one type of pension plan are long gone. Today, companies may not offer a traditional pension plan at all, or they may require that you choose among pensions and retirement plans.

It can get a little confusing. Again, the key is knowing the different types of plans so you can better assess the job offer and the relative worth of the benefits package.

Here, then, to help you sort out the different plans, is a brief rundown of the various common retirement and company savings plans.

■ **First, *pension plans*. These are plans that your employer sets up and pays into—designed to give you money for your retirement.**

Pension plans used to be a mainstay in benefits packages, but nowadays, many employers (especially smaller employers) aren't offering them at all. But they're still fairly common—and they're a definite plus as part of your benefits package.

Briefly, here's how they work: The employer contributes money in your name to a pension fund, which is invested. You receive your pension money when you retire or leave the company—provided, of course, you are vested. The most common vesting schedule is the simplest: You are fully vested after five years with the company; if you leave the company in fewer than five years, you forfeit your claim to the pension money. Some companies, however, institute a partial vesting schedule: After three years of service, you get 20% vesting; four years, 40%; five years, 60%; six years, 80%; seven years, 100%.

There are three specific types of employer-provided pension plans: defined benefit plans, defined contribution plans, and, less common, cash balance pension plans. In addition, small companies may offer their employees a special type of pension plan called a Simplified Employee Pension (SEP).

■ A *defined benefit plan* is the old-fashioned company pension plan that used to be the norm, but is fast fading.

With this type of plan you receive a *guaranteed* amount of money upon retirement based upon your years of service, salary level, and other factors. This amount is predetermined and is not affected by how the company pension fund is performing, how much the company has contributed, and so forth. The amount of money the company contributes to the pension fund in your name can vary—the only set figure is your benefits.

The good aspect of this type of pension plan? You can track the amount you'll receive upon retirement. In addition, these plans are federally insured, so no matter what happens to your company or the economy, you'll get a fixed payment from the plan.

But there's also a downside, namely, that you usually have no input in this type of plan. Your money is invested by professionals; you can't choose investment vehicles. In addition, these plans are typically not portable—if you change jobs, you usually can't switch your pension over to your new company. Finally, while federal insurance does guarantee you payment, it only guarantees a set amount (only up to $2,250 a month of promised benefits for plans ending in 1991—or $27,000 a year at age 65—not exactly a fortune).

> TIP: There has been a good deal of concern about the state of a number of pension plans—and about the stability of the pension system in general. If you are at all concerned about the safety of the pension fund, *check it out now!* Not later, when you've accepted the offer. Check the company's annual report or the financial section of the 10k report that is filed with the Securities and Exchange Commission with larger public companies. Or ask for a copy of government form 5500, which will tell you about the plan's investments, how many investment managers there have been, and so forth. Check what the fund has been invested in and how well the investments have performed relative to the book value of the fund. Better yet, get an outside pension expert to review the management of the plan.

■ The other common type of pension plan is a *defined contribution plan.*

This type of pension also deals with a fixed amount of money— but the fixed amount isn't what you'll get from the plan. Instead, the company contributes a set amount (usually a percentage of your salary) to the company pension fund in your name.

With a defined contribution plan, you often have a degree of control over you money. In most cases, you can choose what the money will be invested in. Usually you can choose from such options as company stock, other stocks or stock funds, and fixed income securities. But, of course, there's a greater element of risk. Unlike a defined benefit plan, a defined contribution plan does *not* guarantee the amount you'll receive upon retirement. It depends upon a number of variables: how well the fund was invested, the state of the economy, the current value of the investments, etc.

The big plus is that most defined contribution plans are portable. In other words, if you leave the company, you can take the money with you (not literally—if you did you would pay a 10% early withdrawal fee). You can roll your account into your new employer's similar plan if you change jobs or into your own IRA.

There are a number of different types of defined contribution plans. The most common ones are 401(k)s, profit-sharing plans, Employee Stock Ownership Plans (ESOPs), and thrift plans. All of these plans are described later in this section.

■ **A less common and newer kind of pension plan combines aspects of the other two: It's called a *cash balance pension plan*.**

With a cash balance pension plan, each employee has his or her own individual account. The amount in each pension grows over time based on percentage of pay plus annual interest credits. This type of pension plan actually combines the strengths of both the defined benefit and the defined contribution plans. As in a defined contribution plan, benefits can build up earlier than with defined benefit plans. But at the same time, as in a defined benefit plan, the amount remains trackable. You know what's in your account at any time.

■ **Finally, there's a special type of pension for employees of smaller companies—a *Simplified Employee Pension*, or *SEP*.**

A SEP is a pension specifically designed for small companies. Briefly, here's how it works: Your employer can make annual contributions to the account equaling 15% of your annual salary or $30,000, whichever is less. The employer can deduct this from its taxes, and you don't owe taxes on it either, as it is not considered taxable income. One big plus with these plans: Often you can also contribute by deferring a portion of your salary—up to a set maximum. If you're also participating in a 401(k) (see below), this maximum applies to the total contributions you make to the two plans. In some cases, employers offer SEPs in addition to defined benefit pension plans. If this is the case and you're also participating in another pension plan, employer contributions for all plans together are limited to 25% of the total amount in the plans of the minimum-funding standard of the defined benefit plans. If your total plans have excess contributions, you'll face an excess contribution penalty of 10% unless you withdraw the excess before filing your tax return and report the excess as income (although you'll probably face the 10% early withdrawal penalty in this case).

■ **There are other retirement savings plans that also may be part of your benefits package. In some cases, these will be offered as pensions; in others, in addition to pensions.**

Nowadays, it's not enough to only know about pensions. Companies offer a number of other plans that may actually *be* your pension, or plans that you can use to raise money for your eventual retirement. Among them are 401(k)s, profit-sharing plans, ESOPs, and more.

■ *401(k)s,* **a type of company-sponsored savings and retirement plan, have become increasingly common—and they're a great benefit.**

Most experts agree that 401(k)s are one of the best ways to save money for retirement. It's a big plus if a 401(k) is part of your benefits package. With one, you can save money on company time—and reap the benefits of tax-deferred growth.

In some cases, the job offer may include a 401(k) as your *straight company pension plan*. In this case, the employer will contribute an amount to a trust account in your name. The employer contribution is not considered part of your annual income, so you are not taxed on it.

In other cases, you may be offered a 401(k) as a *salary reduction plan*. Under this type of setup, you make the contributions yourself. Usually you agree to take a reduction in your salary (or agree to go without a salary increase) and the amount by which your salary is reduced (or not increased) is put into a trust account. You can contribute as much as you want up to a set yearly maximum, which changes each year to keep up with inflation. Under some plans, the employer matches all or part of your contribution. The most common matching amount is 50% of your contribution. (One bad note: More employers are cutting back on matching contributions and, in many cases, completely eliminating them.) Again, you don't pay taxes on the contributions—neither on the salary you save in the account nor on the employer's matching contribution—until you withdraw the money (usually at age 59½ or upon retirement).

Whichever type of 401(k) you are offered, in most cases you can choose where you want the money in it invested. Most commonly, you'll pick from stock funds, bond funds, or Guaranteed Investment Contracts (GICs).

The big plus of 401(k)s: The income earned on the account also grows tax-free, until you withdraw it, typically upon retirement or at age 59½. If you withdraw the money before retirement or age 59½, you must pay a 10% penalty on the taxable portion of your 401(k), along with the tax. There are very few exceptions to this rule. The same goes for the interest you've earned on your investment: It cannot be withdrawn without paying a penalty in addition to the tax. But on the positive side, many companies permit *borrowing* against the money in the plan—something you normally can't do with pension plans or IRAs. This is a good thing to check out when assessing your benefits package.

These are a great addition to your benefits package for some very simple reasons: You save in taxes, your employer is usually matching all or part of your contribution, which further increases your nest egg, and you have portability—if you leave this position, you can roll the money into another employer's 401(k) or into an IRA.

■ **_Profit-sharing plans_ are one of the most commonly offered company plans—and they're a nice addition to your benefits package.**

With profit-sharing plans, your company annually puts a percentage of its profits into a fund for employees, which is invested in one of a number of ways. Typically you can choose how you want your profit-sharing money invested. Common options are company stock, a diversified stock account, or a fixed-income account. The amount the company contributes each year in your name can vary— from absolutely nothing (if it was a bad year) to a maximum amount of $30,000 or 15% of your salary. You're fully vested in a company profit-sharing plan after three to seven years with a company, or between your third and seventh years, and can receive your profit sharing at any point after that should you quit, retire, or be fired— or you can get the money if you're disabled.

Usually profit-sharing plans are offered in addition to other pension and retirement plans. And in these cases, they're a welcome part of your entire benefits package. You don't have to do anything—no personal contributions, no deferments from your salary, nothing—just sit back and eventually collect the money.

*But* sometimes profit-sharing plans are offered as your only pension plan. And, in this case, they're not quite as good. Be aware that they're not the best possible pension plan. First of all, it would be a defined contribution plan, so you won't be able to estimate eventual retirement savings. But more important, since the plan is completely based on the company's profits, you're heading into risky territory. You have absolutely no control over the amount you receive—if the company falters, you lose a good portion of or all of your retirement nest egg.

■ *Employee Stock Ownership Plans (ESOPs)* **are another type of retirement investment program.**

ESOPs are similar to profit-sharing plans, but instead of receiving a share of company profits, you receive shares of stock in the company, the number of which is based upon your salary. The normal range—shares equaling from 5% to 25% of your annual salary, up to a maximum of $60,000. You usually don't pay taxes on the stock you own until you leave the company or sell it. When you reach age 55, the company must offer you a choice of other investments for a portion of your account balance.

The plus side of ESOPs—depending on the worth of the company stock, you may get a healthy amount of money for doing nothing but working in the company. Of course, you may lose everything if the stock plummets. The bottom line? In general, ESOPs are a nice thing to have as part of your benefits package, but they are not to be counted on for future retirement planning and therefore are not a crucial element.

■ *Thrift plans* **(also called savings plans) combine aspects of profit-sharing plans and 401(k)s.**

Thrift plans are related to profit-sharing plans, but their setup is similar to 401(k)s in that your employer can match your contribution to the plan. Unlike 401(k)s, in thrift plans you contribute a percentage of *after-tax* pay—usually between 2% and 6%. The company can contribute a matching amount, usually one-fourth to one-half of your contribution, but sometimes up to the full amount. The money in the thrift fund is invested, usually in stock mutual funds, sometimes in individual blue-chip stocks or company stock. Your contributions to the plan aren't tax-deductible, but as with other company plans, earnings on the investment are tax-deferred, allowing you yet again to reap the benefits of compound growth.

As with other plans, you receive your money when you retire, resign, or are fired—in this case, as with profit-sharing plans, in a lump sum. The positive point: Because the amount you contributed was from after-tax pay, you *pay no taxes on that amount,* but will owe taxes on the remainder—the earned income and any employer contributions. Similarly, as with other plans, you will face a 10% penalty for early withdrawals from the plan but only on the earned income and employer contributions, not on your savings in the plan.

Like 401(k)s, these are a nice addition to a benefits package because you can make a decent amount, especially if the company matches a healthy percentage. In addition, because earnings are tax-deferred, you can avoid a tax bite as you save. In addition, you often can borrow from your vested benefits penalty-free.

■ **There are other types of retirement plans as well, such as those designed for high-paid employees.**

Depending upon the type of job you're going for and the level of salary you've reached, you may run across other retirement plans, such as *Supplementary Employee Retirement Plans (SERPs),* which are retirement plans designed to supplement the retirement benefits of employees typically earning over $200,000. Unlike a regular pension, in which the company pays pension benefits from a specific pension fund to which it has been contributing pension money in your name, with a SERP, the company pays your benefits out of its general operating profits. There is no prefunding. In addition, because a SERP isn't a standard qualified pension plan, you don't get the guarantees you get under other plans—you could lose the entire amount funded by the SERP if the company goes bankrupt, or if you leave the company. *Excess retirement plans,* or *restoration plans,* are similar to SERPs in that benefits paid upon retirement can exceed the federal tax law limits. But unlike a SERP, in an excess retirement plan the money is provided under the qualified plan formula.

## Medical Benefits

■ **Another crucial part of your benefits package is the medical benefits you'll receive. Problem is, this is a difficult area to assess given the proposed changes for health insurance.**

As of this writing, health-care reform wasn't passed but remained a long-term objective of the federal government. If and when health-care reform goes into effect, the type of medical benefits an employer offers you may be drastically affected. For example, some employers might well entirely cut out cafeteria-style benefits packages (those in which an employee can choose benefits from a range of options, including extra health-care coverage . . . or choose no coverage at all in favor of other benefits, such as extra retirement savings plans). Many cafeteria plans provide less coverage than the basics proposed by the government. When employers wind up paying more to meet the standards, they may want to drop other benefits entirely to keep costs down.

■ **Whatever the outcome of health-care legislation, chances are you'll receive some sort of health insurance in your benefits package. The big question is what type?**

Already employers are changing the type of medical coverage they offer, in response to possible reform and the rising prices of health care. In fact, the tried-and-true, old-fashioned medical insurance job holders used to be able to count on is no longer as common as it used to be. More employers are cutting back. Some have scaled back their coverage, increasing the cost of dependent coverage and cutting retiree coverage. Others are offering new alternatives to standard health insurance. Still others are instituting cost-sharing programs, in which you are given a choice of coverage and share the costs of your health insurance with the employer.

The bottom line? There are a number of employer-provided health benefits now being offered (if health-care reform passes, some of these may still be in effect; others may fall by the wayside). As with other elements of a benefits package, it's vital that you know the different types of coverage so you can more accurately judge the job offer you receive.

Following is a quick rundown of the most common health-coverage arrangements and specific features to be on the lookout for.

■ **A standard *"fee-for-service"* group health plan is the traditional form of employer-provided health insurance.**

This type of plan is growing a bit less common, but it's still one of the most popular forms of medical benefits. In fact, as of 1990, on average three of every five insured employees chose this type of insurance plan. With this type of plan, you have a deductible—an amount of medical fees you must pay yourself (usually ranging from $100 to $300, but in some cases a deductible is instead a percentage of your salary). Once you've met this deductible, the insurance kicks in. Usually it covers at least 80% of your expenses up to another limit (usually between $2,000 and $7,000), after which the plan covers 100% of further medical expenses up to a lifetime cap.

These plans usually cover hospitalization and major medical expenses. The *better* plans also cover dental and eye-care expenses. The *best* add in orthodontic and substance-abuse treatment coverage. Some plans offer dependent coverage for no fee; others require you to pay extra for this. Some do not cover your spouse unless you, the employee, are the primary wage earner in the family.

■ *A standard health plan restricted by board approval* **is the newest variation on the standard health insurance coverage.**

Essentially everything remains the same as in the past—at least 80% to 85% of your medical expenses are covered once you've reached the deductible, but with one crucial difference: Medical recommendations that you receive are reviewed by a utilization review board. If the board considers any recommendation (from medication to other treatment to hospital stays) unnecessary, you will be covered either minimally or not at all.

■ *HMOs (Health Maintenance Organizations)* **are another form of medical coverage that is growing in popularity.**

An HMO is a network of doctors and hospitals that provides medical services to company employees for one set per-patient fee—which is paid by the employer. Services covered can range from office visits to hospitalization to surgery. In addition, with some HMOs, you'll also be covered for prescriptions, eyeglasses, and other special health services. Usually, regardless of the type of care you need, your employer will pay the same set fee (which is why these plans are usually cheaper to employers than standard health coverage—as long as the greater percentage of their employees are healthy). However, in some cases, particularly if you opt for more extensive coverage, you may have to kick in part of a fee, or may be required to pick up expenses after a certain set amount that the employer will pay.

■ **Another health-care option, which is not strictly an HMO but is similar, is a** *PPO (Preferred Provider Organization)*.

These combine certain aspects of standard insurance coverage with HMOs. Like an HMO, a PPO is a network of doctors and hospitals. But instead of receiving a set per-patient fee, they provide *discounted* health-care services to PPO members. You often have to pay a deductible or copayment—usually 10% of costs. If you go to doctors or hospitals outside the network, you pay a higher percentage, usually 20% to 30%.

■ **A newer form of health coverage, and one that may increase in popularity if health-care reform passes, is *corporate medical centers*.**

These are just what they sound like: medical treatment centers set up and staffed by a company. Usually these centers are onsite at the workplace. They're growing in popularity because they enable employers to cut costs while still offering medical coverage to employees. Usually under this type of medical coverage, your health-care costs are completely paid for by the employer . . . but *only* if you seek treatment at the company clinic. Go elsewhere, and you'll have to pick up the tab.

■ **Finally, you may be offered *catastrophic coverage*—a limited form of coverage.**

As the name denotes, catastrophic coverage is designed to pay medical expenses in the event of a major illness or catastrophic accident. Deductibles are usually very high (over $1,000) and often must be met only through payments made for treatment of a single illness or accident. In other words, you often can't pay down your deductible with regular office visits or unrelated treatments. Because it's such a limited plan, most companies don't offer only this option. In fact, this type of plan is so limited that it is a good choice only for the young and healthy or those covered under a spouse's health plan. The major plus, though, is that these plans are often offered *free* to employees.

■ **There are other health-related benefits that a company may offer —not typical coverage, but other ways of keeping your medical expenses down.**

One form of health-related benefit that some companies offer is a *medical spending account* or a *flexible compensation plan*. With these, you contribute part of your salary to a company-run account. From this, you can pay for premiums and out-of-pocket medical costs with pretax dollars. These aren't crucial to a good benefits package, but if they are offered, be aware that they can be real money-savers. The one drawback: You can't deduct any reimbursement under this type of plan from your taxes.

*Wellness programs* are another health-related benefit that is growing in popularity with employers and employees alike. In effect, they're designed to attack potential problems before you have to resort to a doctor or hospital. The specific programs can vary widely depending upon the employer. Some companies offer onsite health club facilities; others will pay memberships to health clubs. Many offer stress-reduction programs and additional programs as well. Don't underestimate the value of these programs: Certain large corporations estimate that 10% of their employees use the counseling program annually.

Finally, some companies offer *health incentives*. Again, this is a way of keeping you healthy while they keep costs down. Usually, the company will offer an insurance discount to healthy employees. To qualify for lower out-of-pocket costs, you usually have to be a nonsmoker with acceptable weight, cholesterol, and blood-pressure levels. Some companies offer variations on the theme—charging you extra if you smoke, drink, or don't use a seatbelt.

■ **Usually you'll be given a choice among forms of health coverage from the list above.**

Or you'll be able to determine specific features in your coverage —whether you want dependent coverage or family coverage, for example. You may even be able to decide just how much coverage you want—from nothing at all to a complete plan.

Here are some guidelines that can help you get the most out of your employer-provided health insurance:

- The most important rule of all: If you are given a choice between different plans, *don't let your employer make the choice for you.* It's too important a decision to pass along. And your employer will probably choose the more expensive standard plan—which will cost you more.

- *Be sure to check exactly what the plan you opt for will cover.* Among the things to check for: Does the plan cover psychiatric expenses? Many don't. Are dental, orthodontic, and eye-care coverage offered? Eye-care plans are increasingly common, but many firms still limit their coverage. If the plan includes dental coverage, check also for orthodontic. If you plan on having children, check for pregnancy and dependent coverage. Many plans have no pregnancy coverage, while others require you to pay extra for dependent coverage.

> **TIP: Where dental insurance is concerned, the rule of thumb is simple: If you get it for free, great. If you have to pay extra for it, it's usually not worth the money. Yes, there are exceptions to the rule, but generally it's that simple.**

- *Find out if current medical problems will be covered by your new employer's plan.* This is especially important when dealing with smaller companies. Some plans won't cover existing conditions, so you'll be left having to pay your own medical expenses even if you're theoretically covered by your employer's health plan.

- *If you're a two-income family, doublecheck how benefits are coordinated.* Dependent coverage is an area that employers are trying to cut back on, especially because so many families are two-income families with two different employer-provided health policies. Be sure you're familiar with the "coordination of benefits" (or COB) rules. These lay out which plan will be the primary one—that is, the first to pay—and which the secondary one. In addition, they determine how much each plan pays. In the past, once the primary plan paid up to its limit, the secondary plan kicked in and paid the remaining amount. But this is no longer a given. Why can't you count on 100% coverage between two policies any longer? "Nonduplication of benefits." Under this rule, the secondary policy won't duplicate benefits paid by the primary plan. In plain English, this means that often you won't get any coverage on the secondary policy even after the primary policy has paid up to its limit.

  It gets more complicated if you have children. In the past, companies used the "gender rule"—the father's plan was the primary plan and covered the children. But recently more companies have switched to the "birthday rule." With this, the person whose birthday comes first in the year has the primary plan.

- *Something else to be on the lookout for where dependent coverage is concerned is a dependent premium or family premium*—you pay a higher premium rate to carry your spouse or children on the policy.

**TIP:** Here is an idea for two-income couples with no children. If your company charges a *family premium* or *dependent premium*—that is, a higher premium to cover both you and your dependent spouse regardless of whether you have children or not—don't opt for dependent coverage. Instead, each of you can get insurance coverage from your employer as a single. The outcome? Savings of up to 25%.

- *When both spouses are covered, one of you can decide to be carried on your spouse's policy and drop your own.* Some companies are so eager to cut back on health-care costs that they even offer buyout benefits—such as a bonus or extra vacation time—for dropping out of company health plans. No, it's not common, but it is a sign of the times. In this sort of situation, or when you are charged a dependent premium, and the like, dropping out of one policy may make sense. Before you do so, though, be sure to weigh the policies carefully to decide which is best. Does one charge a dependent premium while the other doesn't? Which has the best benefits? Deductible? And check what happens if you drop the policy, then decide later to go back to it—many plans will allow you to resign, but then won't cover you for preexisting conditions.

**TIP:** A word of warning—even if you opt not to get health insurance and decide to be covered by your spouse's policy, you may be hit with a horrible surprise called "phantom COB." In this situation, the employer who is providing the health coverage coordinates benefits with the health coverage you *could have* gotten at your company. In effect, the plan you decided not to take is still treated as the primary policy. And the outcome of this? You wind up with no coverage when you thought you had it. The one way around this possibility—keep both spouses' policies if the one of you who was going to opt out has the first birthday.

**TIP:** Don't assume you *must* get health insurance. If you're offered a *cafeteria-style benefits plan*, you can choose to forgo health insurance entirely, and instead opt for a higher contribution to your 401(k) plan or other company savings plan. In some cases, you can even apply the savings in benefits directly to your salary. This, deciding against health coverage altogether, is becoming a popular option, especially as more people opt to be covered on their spouses' insurance. If you have the opportunity to do this, be sure to weigh the cost benefits and compare features of both

**health policies. Depending upon the specifics, this may be a good idea.**

## Disability Insurance

■ **Disability insurance—which guarantees you a certain income should you become disabled and unable to work—is another typical part of a benefits package.**

Most disability plans are pretty straightforward. A typical disability plan pays a percentage of your salary—up to about 60%, up to a set monthly limit of $5,000 to $10,000. Some plans allow you to augment the employer-covered amount—for a set contribution, your coverage is increased, but even these plans usually cap at about 70% to 80% of total salary.

The variables to be aware of: waiting period before payments start; length of benefits coverage (the two most common are coverage until age 65 and lifetime coverage). The better disability plans include a residual benefits clause, which gives you partial benefits for partial injuries, and an inflation protection (or cost-of-living adjustment) clause, which adjusts your benefit to keep in sync with inflation. Also be sure to check how the policy defines disability. Some will pay only if you are completely unable to work, others will pay if you can't work in your regular field. Most coverage falls between these two extremes.

Also find out if *short-term* disability insurance is offered. At many large companies, it's part of the standard plan, but elsewhere it can be a valuable option benefit.

## Long-Term Care Insurance

■ **Long-term care insurance is not commonly offered by employers, but it's a potentially valuable benefit that you should check for.**

Nursing home care and extended home care are not well covered by Medicare, and the costs for such care can be astronomical—reaching well over $50,000 a year in some cases. Given this, it's a good idea to see if your employer offers this type of coverage. More often than not, an employer will not pick up the price of this coverage, but will allow you to contribute personally for coverage. In this way, you'll be covered on a group plan—which means the premiums will be much lower than if you bought long-term care insurance on your own.

## Life Insurance

■ **Life insurance is a common part of a benefits package, but it's actually not that important.**

In fact, life insurance shouldn't be a major factor in your evaluation. The reason? Life insurance coverage provided by an employer is generally on the low side. But you generally *do* have the option to contribute to the insurance and so augment coverage. The typical arrangement: The employer-covered cost of basic life insurance is computed as a percentage of your base salary up to a low maximum. If you choose to buy supplemental coverage, you pay an additional rate, generally a very small percentage of your base salary as well.

The bottom line where life insurance coverage is concerned? It's a fine benefit, but not one that should make or break the job offer.

## Vacation, Sick Leave, and Personal Days

■ **Another area of your benefits and perks package that's usually standard: You'll probably be offered the norm—one to two weeks of vacation per full year of employment and one to two weeks of sick days and personal days.**

Vacation policy is fairly standard among most corporations. About 75% of all U.S. corporations provide two weeks of vacation per year after one full year of employment. And over 50% give employees 10 or more paid holidays as well. Long-term employees often get up to four weeks off. In some cases, you can carry unused vacation, sick, or personal days over to the next year. This isn't common, but if it's available it's a nice perk. In this way, you can stockpile time and wind up with a longer vacation than you'd otherwise get.

## Childcare, Family Leave, and Other Family-Related Benefits

■ **Childcare benefits (also called dependent-care benefits) are increasingly common: Over 3,000 U.S. companies offer some type of childcare benefit.**

This development makes sense. Since it has become more common for both parents to work, it has also become more common for companies to try to help out these working parents. But the type of childcare benefits offered can cover a great range. Some companies offer onsite day care. Others pick up the tab if you send your child to a day-care center selected by the company. Still others offer direct reimbursement for childcare costs (up to a set limit, of course) that you arrange on your own.

■ **Another popular type of family benefit: a dependent-care spending account.**

According to recent articles, this type of benefit is offered by about 90% of large U.S. employers and by 47% of all U.S. employers. And it's a great benefit to get.

With a dependent-care spending account, you can pay dependent-care expenses with pretax dollars (in 1992, up to $2,500 could be placed in the program if an individual tax return was filed; up to $5,000 if a joint return). Expenses can be for a day-care center, a nanny, day camp, after-school programs for children, or programs or home assistance for disabled parents or spouses.

■ **Family leave, also called parental leave, is another common benefit offered.**

This used to be simply maternity leave, but a growing number of companies offer leave to the father as well. Family leave gives the father or mother paid or unpaid leave upon birth or adoption of a child. According to a recent survey by the Washington, D.C.–based Bureau of National Affairs and *HR Magazine*, 83% of the corporations surveyed offer this.

■ **There are a number of other family-related benefits that may crop up in your benefits package.**

Other family benefits to be on the lookout for include:

• *Adoption benefits*—financial assistance to help defray the costs of adopting a child. Among the different arrangements offered (in order of frequency): reimbursement of legal fees, reimbursement of medical costs for birth mother, reimbursement of agency/placement fees, reimbursements on medical expenses of the child. In most cases, there is a maximum limit on the amount reimbursed (typically ranging from $1,000 to $3,000).

• *Elder-care benefits*—services and financial assistance to help those taking care of elderly parents. Benefits vary widely, covering a range including referral services, senior citizen care centers, unpaid job leave to care for elderly parents, seminars. Most commonly offered are information and referral services.

## Educational Benefits

- **Many larger corporations—90% of the Fortune 500 companies —maintain educational programs where the cost of job-related courses or degrees is refunded.**

The scope of educational programs can vary widely, even within the same industry. Some firms offer complete tuition reimbursement, others pay on a sliding scale according to grades: 100% for an A, 90% for a B, and so on. Some companies can be very strict when it comes to defining what constitutes a job-related course, others can be very lax. An extreme example of this came from an employee who somehow managed to be reimbursed for a graduate course in Egyptology—which probably had little to do with his job as a financial analyst.

- **Look also at in-house training programs and technical or managerial development programs at major universities, where companies sponsor month-long (or longer) employee-training workshops.**

Particularly with larger, well-known firms such as IBM or General Electric, the technical or managerial training offered can be very worthwhile and can translate into higher salaries if you leave. As one senior executive put it, "The only thing better on a resume than a Harvard MBA is a General Electric management job. Half of America is run by GE grads." Don't underestimate this type of hidden benefit.

## Other Benefits/Perks

- **There are other benefits and perks that aren't crucial at all, but are icing on the cake. In other words, these shouldn't make or break your job offer, but they can make the offer more appealing.**

Here's a quick rundown of some of the more popular benefits not otherwise covered. The list is by no means complete or comprehensive. It is merely intended to give you ideas of what companies today have offered—and ideas on what you may want to ask for. Remember, even the smallest perk can add measurably to the value of the job offer or to your overall satisfaction with the job. Given this, the following benefits may be ones you want to try for:

- *Legal benefits*—free legal advice offered to employees. In many cases, though, if you have a complicated legal problem, you'll just get a referral to a law firm and have to pay regular fees yourself.

- *Commuter subsidies*—company-subsidized commutation vouchers, tokens, or tickets to make commuting to work less expensive or completely free.

- *Financial counseling (also called preretirement)*—a growing trend, especially as companies cut back on retirement benefits and employees are forced to make more investment decisions on their own. This benefit sounds better than it usually is. More often than not, the counseling consists of one day of seminars explaining investment basics, how to get the most out of company savings plans, and general financial planning tips.

- *Executive development programs*—a perk given, as the name denotes, to executives only. Generally the program is designed to polish executives' management skills.

## Some Final Thoughts About Benefits

■ **A lower salary with substantial benefits can be worth more than a higher salary, in terms of its dollar value as a package.**

Perks and benefits add up. Most large corporations offer a complete and comprehensive benefits package with all or most of the benefits outlined above. Other benefits, which are not standard but may offer you comparable advantages, include company cars, subsidized cafeterias, company travel packages, and product discounts. All of these may be worth hundreds or even thousands of dollars per year in nonsalary benefits. Remember to factor in the tax consequences of these benefits; benefits such as company cars are taxable as income on your tax statements.

**TIP: When making a job-change decision, consider what you might lose or have to start paying for if you left: extra commuting, lost**

benefits, the need for a new wardrobe, more or less travel, stricter expense reimbursement, etc. If you're moving, factor in the moving costs beyond the amount the company is willing to assume. Amortize these costs over the expected duration of your stay with the company, and then subtract each year's amount from the salary you've been offered and compare it with your current salary. This is a good way to assess if you've been offered enough.

■ **Also ask about benefits if you work *part-time*.**

New laws and changing trends have brought benefits to part-timers as well. For example, some major "temp" firms now include vacation time as a standard benefit for people who work with them for at least a year, in addition to other benefits.

## NEGOTIATING FOR A BETTER OFFER

After you've looked at the components of a job offer, you'll have some decisions to make. If you absolutely don't like the company and the position, in one sense you're very lucky: It's an easy decision, just don't accept the offer.

In another scenario, you may either like the offer or like it enough to consider it . . . but there's a catch. The salary is too low, or the benefits aren't comprehensive, or certain aspects of the job need alteration. In this instance, you should try to negotiate for a better offer. Easily said, but much harder to do. Negotiating is difficult.

Most negotiations die before they start. The applicant boldly states, "I want 10 percent more," and the interviewer explains that due to "company policy" he can't pay any more than the first figure. The applicant panics, mumbles "Oh," and that's that. Often he or she then goes home and describes how hard it was to get the interviewer to budge: "I tried and I argued but they didn't give an inch. And you know how tough I can be. . . ." Almost everyone describes his or her negotiating experiences in very graphic and very false terms. Most people fail, and do so meekly. Many successful interviewers and even high-level managers fall completely apart on salary negotiations.

The rest of this chapter is a brief summary designed to *prevent* you from falling apart, to get you past an interviewer's objections, and to help you conclude your negotiations successfully.

## THE BASICS OF NEGOTIATING

### Rule #1: Negotiate from Strength

Negotiate when the time is right, when it's easiest for *you* to get what you want.

Your strongest negotiating period is just after you've received an offer (or when it's obvious that the interviewer wants to hire you) but *before* you have accepted the position. This brief period is the best time to negotiate for maximum benefit. The interviewer wants you and you haven't yet committed yourself to anything. Most of the time you'll be negotiating for a better base salary, but make certain that other aspects of the offer are satisfactory as well. If you see any other problems with the quality of your future employment, *now* is the time to push for a better deal.

### Rule #2: Know What You Want—Set Your Negotiating Targets

Before you open your mouth, *know* what you want and what compromises you'd be willing to make. As a good poker player would, set your own *internal* strategy and guidelines, and know how far you're willing to risk things.

Set your negotiating limits. Know the approximate salary level you want or feel you deserve and settle on a reasonable target salary for yourself based on the company's salary ranges and those of the industry. Don't be unrealistic. Generally, at the lower- and middle-management levels, you can reasonably hope to get 10%–20% more than what the interviewer offers you. If the company is offering $25,000 and you're looking for $40,000, realize that your job hunt is probably off-center. You're either setting your career sights too low or your salary sights too high. Unless something is wrong, you can't reasonably hope to negotiate up to that salary.

If you want to negotiate other employment terms, follow the same procedure. Have your limits in mind. Know what you want, what you expect, what you'll settle for.

In all cases, except when you're trying to start over in a new career, aim for a higher salary than your previous job. You want your resume to show upward movement.

### Rule #3: Do Your Homework

Good negotiating means preparation. When the interviewer asks "Why?" you must have reasons. When the interviewer says the company "never" pays more, you should be able to mention or suggest exceptions. This means doing some research. Check trade magazines, talk to people at the company or in the same industry. Get the facts before you start negotiating.

### Rule #4: Know How Far You're Willing to Go

After setting your salary target, establish how much you need or want this job. If you don't need or want the job, you can obviously go much further than you would if you were desperate to have it. Whatever the case, be prepared to show the interviewer that you are a successful, aggressive applicant in demand by other firms or organizations. Project the image that, although you want this position, you don't *need* it. You're willing to make some compromises, but you expect the same from the interviewer. Naturally, this is much easier if the job doesn't interest you that much.

### Rule #5: Study the Interviewer

Make a mental list of the interviewer's motivation for hiring you: What does he or she want or need? What can he or she negotiate, and what must be taken to upper management for approval? Also, what kind of person are you dealing with? Studying the interviewer can give you clues on how best to proceed.

### Rule #6: Help the Interviewer

Be prepared to project a helpful attitude, one in which you show that you want to work *with* the interviewer and arrive at a mutually beneficial conclusion. Before the interview, think of ways to convince the interviewer that you should be getting what you want.

### Rule #7: Be Prepared to Be Tough

Or firm, if you prefer. Help the interviewer, yes, but be ready for a civilized fight. Beneath the polite words between you and the interviewer is a disagreement. He or she is seeking to get you for less, you are seeking more. This means a fight—usually polite, usually couched in respectful "suggestions" or "ideas," but a fight nonetheless.

### Rule #8: Ask Questions

Keep the interviewer on the defensive by asking questions. Many salespeople go a step further and keep on asking questions that require a "yes" answer, figuring that sooner or later the succession of yeses will make it psychologically difficult for the interviewer to refuse. ("Don't you give incremental increases? Isn't my experience above average for the firm?" etc.) Keep the interviewer agreeing with you and he or she will almost be impelled to comply with your request for more money.

## WHAT YOU CAN NEGOTIATE FOR

■ **In general, the lower the position, the less negotiating flexibility you have, since the benefits for low-level jobs are usually standardized and salaries and job descriptions are more fixed.**

With lower-level positions, the interviewer doesn't have as much "give" or leeway in what more he or she can offer you. Also, it's best to face facts: At lower levels you are usually less valuable to the company; if you don't say yes to their offer, they can easily hire someone else. Be careful. Some people get so enthusiastic about tough negotiating techniques that they end up negotiating their way out of a job. Start by being *reasonable*.

*You can reasonably ask for:*

- an incremental increase in salary

- more vacation time

- a faster career track

> **TIP: If you're young, very often companies that won't part with an extra dime in salary will yield on giving you a faster career track. That translates into more dollars later. One woman wasted hours negotiating for a small $1,000 increase in salary at a rigid Fortune 500 giant. "It was the principle of the thing," she explained. Later she discovered she had won the battle but lost the war. Her experience could have qualified her for a faster career track, which would have gotten her a raise of several thousand dollars in just a few years. She had defeated herself.**

■ **At higher levels, the opportunities for compromise are greater, the methods of agreement are more complex, and the chances of having a successful negotiation are good.**

In addition to a higher salary, those going for higher-level positions may wish to negotiate an employment contract or a termination agreement that will establish a guaranteed duration to the job and continuation of income. Benefits, including stock and bonuses, are also important considerations. In these cases, you should first research the company norms (what most people are paid) and what the "star" employees receive, and then decide what you think you can get if you push for it.

## SUCCESSFUL NEGOTIATING

■ **First get the interviewer to state the salary.**

Sometimes you will be pleasantly surprised and the interviewer will name a figure *higher* than you expected. If this happens, keep calm and proceed to argue for a figure 10%–20% higher, secure in the knowledge that, at the very worst, you're getting more than you bargained for. Even if you lose, you win. Normally, though, the figure is less than your target. In that case, it's time to *really* start negotiating.

■ **The best opening ploy was stated before:** *Help the interviewer* **by appearing cooperative and giving reasons for what you want.**

Tell the interviewer what salary you had in mind. Give a higher figure than you expect to get, but not much more than 25% over the figure the interviewer stated. Don't stop there. In the same breath, give the reasons *why* you deserve a higher salary. In this way you'll establish that you're making a reasonable demand, one that will convince the interviewer and the interviewer's *superiors* that indeed you deserve more than "company policy" dictates. *Remember:* Often the interviewer's hands are tied. If he or she offers you more money, it will have to be explained to senior management. Try to make your case before the interviewer reports back with smokescreens such as "company policy" or "cost-cutting measures."

**EXAMPLE: "Hmm. There's a bit of a difference here. My target salary *range* was $40,000 to $45,000, which is in keeping**

with the unusual breadth of experience I've acquired. It's also in keeping with a normal 15 percent increase over my current position, which underutilizes all my talents."

■ *Don't* back yourself into a corner by stating one salary figure, unless you're prepared to give up the job or be embarrassed.

Many inexperienced negotiators commonly do this. They start out tough, and then crumple.

> EXAMPLE: *Applicant:* "I need a salary of $45,000. I can't accept anything less."
>
> *Interviewer:* "I'm sorry. Our salary levels aren't that high. I can't offer you more than $40,000. Maybe you should look elsewhere."
>
> The applicant can hold out, or give up. Most applicants give up.

Avoid this situation by giving the interviewer a salary range. Anticipate the interviewer's objections by giving reasons to prove that you are a special case. Offer the interviewer a *way out*. Give reasons the interviewer can use to justify the higher salary to upper management or to him- or herself.

*Some good reasons:*

• *You're unusually capable.* You're far and above the best candidate for the job, ready and able to hit the ground running and add significantly to the bottom line. This is the "superstar" reason, in which you state the excellent contributions you can make and then show why it's worth it to pay you more.

> EXAMPLE: "Thank you for the offer. As you know, I have the background and expertise to take this section of the firm and cut costs significantly without hurting efficiency. But I feel strongly that this unique expertise is worth more. I'm wondering if there's a way to tie in my cost-savings to an incremental bonus system? That way, I'll be getting what I'm worth, and your firm will still be saving dollars."

• *You're more experienced.* You have far more experience than is usual for the position. This experience will enable you to make a more significant contribution to the company than the average employee. Therefore, you're worth more. Give examples.

> **EXAMPLE:** "As we discussed earlier, my background is particularly extensive, more so than that of the usual candidate for this job. This means I'm bringing more to the job. Doesn't the company make salary adjustments for MBAs with additional degrees in the field? [If not, why not?]"

> **TIP:** This approach works well with bureaucratic organizations such as the government. Because an entering job level or grade level is usually determined by the extent of formal education or number of years of employment, you should try to convince the interviewer that your background fulfills the bureaucratic requirements for a higher civil service grade.

- *"It's only fair."* The salary range for this position throughout the industry is closer to your figure than the interviewer's. In other words, why is the interviewer offering you a below-par salary? Politely put the interviewer on the defensive.

> **EXAMPLE:** "Let me start by saying that this position really interests me. It offers me the sort of business challenge that I enjoy and one where I know I can contribute significantly to the bottom line. But my research and interviewing experience show that the salary level appears to be a bit below the norm. Is this company policy, or is there a bonus system that we haven't yet discussed?"

- *"I don't need this job anyway."* You're very interested in the unique challenges of this position, but you're also quite happy in your current position. You had assumed you would be offered the usual 10%–20% increase as an incentive for leaving your job.

  *Note:* This tactic is best used by people already in a good position.

> **EXAMPLE:** "As I said in the interview, the scope and challenges of this position make it very appealing. But I view this job as a step up from my current position, and feel that the salary should be set accordingly at a higher range—in keeping with what I can accomplish. Here's the problem: I'm trying to think of a way to accept it, but frankly I'm not certain the financial rewards make it worthwhile. I think you can understand why it would be difficult to

leave a successful position without having a reasonable salary increase."

---

## GET YOUR OFFER IN WRITING

■ **Once you've reached an agreement, be sure to get an offer letter or contract.**

The hard-and-fast rule for middle managers and above—never quit your current job until you've got an offer letter in your hand. If you're just starting out, a large firm will often give you one, a smaller firm may not. In general, you should be most concerned with offer letters and contracts if you're a middle manager or above, although at all levels they can be valuable.

If you're unemployed, still ask for an offer letter or contract. It's rare that a company will renege on an offer. Even so, you're always best off to get it in writing. More important, an offer letter will set forth the offer clearly. Once you see it in black and white, you can more easily decide whether it's the job for you.

Offer letters are common for middle-level managers. Higher-level managers typically get contracts that are more specific in terms of entry and exit terms and compensation.

*A good offer letter should include:*

- a complete job description, including title, in which duties and responsibilities are explained (and, if possible, it should include to whom you'll report and those who will report to you)

- your compensation—salary, bonus, and benefits

■ **Contracts, generally offered to upper-level executives and other professionals, are more specific than offer letters. They generally include:**

- the term of the contract (the length of time the contract is in effect—usually three to five years), including any renewal provisions

- a job description—duties and responsibilities spelled out, including title, the person to whom you'll report, those who will report to you, etc.

- termination clauses—the reasons for which you can be dismissed, the severance package you'll receive (severance pay, continuation of benefits, etc.)

- noncompete or confidentiality clauses

- your compensation—salary, bonus, and benefits, usually more specifically spelled out than in an offer letter

Should you get a contract? Whenever possible, a contract makes good sense. As you can see, it spells out legally precisely what your job entails, what your compensation is, the reasons you can be dismissed, and so forth. As mentioned above, with rare exceptions, if you're an upper-level executive or professional, you'll be offered a contract. Often you'll be offered one if you're a middle-level executive as well.

If you are not offered a contract, it's up to you to decide whether to ask for one. The bottom line—push for one if there is any reason for you to worry about the offer or the length of your tenure. For example, ask for one if the company is known for frequent firings, if it is headed for a merger (or, conversely, going to be acquiring another company), or if it is in an industry that has been marked by mergers and acquisitions or by recent downsizings. In addition, if the company always gives contracts, or if contracts are typically given at your level in your industry, you should expect one.

If, however, you discover at the outset of your negotiations that a company is loath to give contracts for some reason, do get an offer letter. Usually there shouldn't be much difficulty. The reason? Offer letters are perceived as less threatening, but they do basically the same thing as a contract—that is, outline the basic job agreement. One point—if you decide to go for an offer letter in lieu of a contract, be sure it includes a few lines on severance.

If you are getting a contract, you'll want to negotiate its terms carefully. Here are a few points that you should aim for in your contract:

- *Be sure that entry and exit terms are clearly spelled out.* Entry terms to try for: sign-on bonuses, performance bonuses (stock options, etc.). Exit terms to try for: severance pay for a year or more, benefits to continue throughout that period.

- *Try for automatic renewal of the contract, or at least automatic one-year renewal.* This will extend the length of time that the contract covers you, and thus protects you and the agreement you've hammered out with management.

- *Make sure the section outlining your job duties and responsibilities is as specific as possible.* Vague phrases can mean your job duties change in midstream.

- *In the section explaining why your employer can fire you, again aim for specificity if possible.* Usually you'll get a clause saying you can be fired for cause—and sometimes "cause" is explained. Problem: Often "just cause" is vague, ultimately permitting management to fire you for almost anything. Get "cause" delineated as precisely as possible. Also ask for written warnings and written notice of the reasons for your firing.

- *Be aware of the noncompete clause your employer may insert.* This will state something to the effect that you can't work for a competitor for the term of the contract, and often for a number of years after the term of the contract. When possible, get this clause stricken; otherwise try to limit the breadth of the clause. (It prohibits only full-time work, or doesn't apply if you're fired.)

# *Appendix: Sources*

## INTRODUCTION

The following is a listing of sources that should make your job hunt more effective—industry-specific, career-specific, and regional directories, publications, associations, and other job hunting tools that can help you in different phases of your job hunt.

Keep in mind: This list *doesn't* take the place of your own research or information gathering. We strongly recommend that you seek out the specific sources that meet your particular needs. But this list should give you a head start—and help make your job hunt a little easier.

*First, though, a few notes:*

- The following sources are divided into several categories: *general sources* (a few sources in addition to those already listed in Chapter 3, "Research"); *sources for career specialties* (ranging from accounting to writing, and helpful to those of you seeking sources in specific careers or occupations); *industry-specific sources* (ranging from advertising to utilities, and useful for locating information on specific industries); and finally, *regional sources* (with sources for each state and the District of Columbia). In some cases, there are overlaps. But in general, to get the most out of the source listings, you should look in both the career and industry listings. For example, if you're interested in becoming a journalist, check both "Writers, Editors, and Journalists" in the careers section and "Publishing" in the industry section.

- For more general business directories and periodicals, see Chapter 3, "Research," pages 77–112, and for general business associations, check the "Managerial" section of this Appendix, on page 313.

- In most cases, the associations included in the following are national and have regional offices around the country. Call the main number for more information on this.

- Again, remember that this source listing is not complete. We've focused on the larger associations, directories, and publications in each area. There may well be smaller ones that will work even better in your job hunt. For these, check your public library—using the research methods outlined in Chapter 3, "Research."

- Finally, good luck, and we hope that the following sources get you closer to your objective—the job you want!

## GENERAL SOURCES

*Dun's Career Guide*
Dun's Marketing Services
3 Sylvan Way
Parsippany, NJ 07054
800/526-0651
—Lists employers, hiring areas, contact names, etc.

*Job Finder* series *(Non-Profit's Job Finder, Professional's Job Finder, Private Sector Job Finder)*
Planning/Communications
7215 Oak Ave.
River Forest, IL 60305
800/829-5220
—Tells you where to look for thousands of job openings. Chockful of valuable, up-to-date information.

*Job Hunter's Sourcebook*
Gale Research, Inc.
835 Penobscot Bldg.
Detroit, MI 48226
800/877-4253

*Jobs '95 ('96, '97,* etc.)
Fireside/Simon & Schuster
1230 Ave. of the Americas
New York, NY 10020
212/976-7000
—Annual guide listing thousands of company addresses, reference sources, databases, and more. Also includes breakdown of trends by occupation, industry, and region.

*National Business Employment Weekly*
420 Lexington Ave.
New York, NY 10170
212/808-6791
—Contains *Wall Street Journal* help-wanted ads, articles on job hunting techniques, hot careers, employment trends, etc.

## SOURCES FOR CAREER SPECIALTIES

## ACCOUNTING

### Associations
*American Accounting Association*
5717 Bessie Dr.
Sarasota, FL 34223
813/921-7747
—Publishes the *Accounting Review.*

*American Institute of Certified Public
  Accountants*
Harborside Financial Center
201 Plaza 3
Jersey City, NJ 07311-3881
201/938-3000
—Publishes journal with many job listings.

*National Society of Public Accountants*
1010 N. Fairfax St.
Alexandria, VA 22314
703/549-6400
—Publishes journal with job listings,
  member's directory, etc.

### Directories
*Accountants Directory*
American Business Directories, Inc.
American Business Information, Inc.
5711 S. 86th Circle
PO Box 27347
Omaha, NE 68127
402/593-4600
—Broken into seven parts; cost of entire
  U.S. directory is $3,700; each part is less
  —for example, the Northeast directory
  of 23,000 is $735, or about three cents
  per name.

*Firm on Firm Directory*
American Institute of Certified Public
  Accountants
Harborside Financial Center
201 Plaza 3
Jersey City, NJ 07311-3881
201/938-3000
—Lists thousands of firms. Phone for

information; must be ordered by fax or
mail.

*National Directory of Accounting Firms
  and Accountants*
Gale Research, Inc.
835 Penobscot Bldg.
Detroit, MI 48226-4904
800/877-GALE
—Costs about $125.

### Periodicals
*Accounting Today*
425 Park Ave.
New York, NY 10166
212/371-9400
—Biweekly, covers most accounting
  topics.

*CPA Journal*
200 Park Ave., 10th fl.
New York, NY 10166
212/973-8300
—Monthly journal, mainly New York–
  oriented.

*CPA Letter*
American Institute of Certified Public
  Accountants
Harborside Financial Center
201 Plaza 3
Jersey City, NJ 07311-3881
201/938-3000

*Journal of Accountancy*
American Institute of Certified Public
  Accountants
Harborside Financial Center
201 Plaza 3
Jersey City, NJ 07311-3881
201/938-3000

*National Public Accountant*
National Society of Public Accountants
1010 N. Fairfax St.
Alexandria, VA 22314
703/549-6400

## ADMINISTRATIVE ASSISTANTS, SECRETARIES, CLERICAL WORKERS, TRAVEL AND HOTEL ADMINISTRATIVE WORKERS

### Associations
*Airline Employees Association*
6520 Cicero Ave.
Bedford Park, IL 60638
708/563-9999

*American Hotel and Motel Association*
1201 New York Ave., NW
Suite 600
Washington, DC 20005-3931
202/289-3100
—Publishes career brochures, runs special educational program for entry-level applicants, etc.

*American Society of Corporate Secretaries*
1270 Ave. of the Americas
New York, NY 10020
212/765-2620

*National Association of Executive Secretaries*
900 S. Washington St.
Falls Church, VA 22046
703/237-8616

*National Association of Legal Secretaries*
2250 E. 73rd St.
Suite 550
Tulsa, OK 74136
918/493-3540

*Professional Secretaries International*
10502 NW Ambassador Dr.
PO Box 20404
Kansas City, MO 64195
816/891-6600
—Publishes *The Secretary Magazine,* etc.

### Periodicals
*Secretary*
2800 Shirlington Rd.
Arlington, VA 22206
703/998-2534
—Monthly association magazine for career secretaries.

*The Secretary Magazine*
Professional Secretaries International
10502 NW Ambassador Dr.
PO Box 20404
Kansas City, MO 64195
816/891-6600

## ARTISTS AND DESIGNERS

### Associations
*American Council for the Arts*
1285 Ave. of the Americas, 3d fl.
New York, NY 10018
212/245-6655
—Publishes career guide, etc.

*American Institute of Graphic Arts*
1059 Third Ave.
New York, NY 10021
212/752-0813

*American Society of Interior Designers*
608 Massachusetts Ave., NE
Washington, DC 20002
202/546-3480
—Publishes career pamphlets, etc.

*Graphic Artists Guild*
11 W. 20th St., 8th fl.
New York, NY 10011
212/463-7730
—Publishes periodical, directory, etc.

*Industrial Designers Society of America*
1142 Walker Rd.
Suite E
Great Falls, VA 22066
703/759-0100
—Placement service, publishes magazine, directory, etc.

*National Computer Graphics Association*
2722 Merrilee Dr.
Reston, VA 22031
703/698-9600

*Printing Industries of America*
100 Daingerfield Rd.
Alexandria, VA 22314
703/519-8100
—Maintains referral service for members, includes wide variety of jobs in design and printing.

## Directories
*American Art Directory*
Reed Reference Publishing
121 Chanlon Rd.
New Providence, NJ 07974
800/521-8110
—Lists thousands of museums, schools, libraries, etc.

*Artist's Market*
Writer's Digest Books
1507 Dana Ave.
Cincinnati, OH 45207
513/531-2222
—Lists hundreds of markets for art and design work.

*Creative Black Book*
Macmillan Creative Services Group
115 Fifth Ave.
New York, NY 10003
212/254-1330

*Design Firm Directory*
Wefler & Associates
PO Box 1167
Evanston, IL 60204
708/475-1866
—Lists all types of design firms.

*Graphic Artist's Guild Directory*
Graphic Artists Guild
11 W. 20th St., 8th fl.
New York, NY 10011
212/463-7730

*Graphic Arts Blue Book*
AF Lewis and Co., Inc.
79 Madison Ave.
New York, NY 10016
212/679-0770

## Periodicals
*AIGA Journal*
American Institute of Graphic Arts
1059 Third Ave.
New York, NY 10021
212/752-0813

*American Artist*
BPI Communications
1515 Broadway
New York, NY 10036
212/764-7300

*Artweek*
12 S. First St.
Suite 520
San Jose, CA 95113
408/279-2293

*Communication Arts*
410 Sherman Ave.
PO Box 10300
Palo Alto, CA 94303
415/326-6040

*Computer Graphics World*
Penwell Directories
PO Box 21278
Tulsa, OK 74121
918/835-3161

*Design News*
Cahners Publishing Company
275 Washington St.
Newton, MA 02158
617/964-3030

*Graphic Arts Monthly*
249 W. 17th St.
New York, NY 10011
212/645-0067
800/637-6089

*HOW*
1507 Dana Ave.
Cincinnati, OH 45207
513/531-2222
—Bimonthly magazine for graphic artists.

*Industrial Design*
250 W. 57th St.
New York, NY 16107
212/956-0535

*Interior Design*
249 W. 17th St.
New York, NY 10011
212/464-0067
800/542-8138
—Monthly for designers and design administrators.

*Print*
3200 Tower Oaks Blvd.
Rockville, MD 20853
800/222-2654

## ENGINEERING, COMPUTERS, AND HIGH-TECH

### Associations
*Air and Waste Management Association*
PO Box 2861
Pittsburgh, PA 15230
412/232-3444
—Publishes periodical with job openings, directory, etc.

*American Association of Engineering Societies*
1111 19th St., NW
Suite 608
Washington, DC 20036
202/296-2237
—An association of many other engineering associations, publishes salary surveys, etc.

*American Chemical Society*
1155 16th St., NW
Washington, DC 20036
800/227-5558

—Publishes various periodicals with job listings (see separate listings), maintains job bank, listing service, counseling services, etc.

*American Institute of Aeronautics and Astronautics*
370 L'Enfant Promenade, SW
Washington, DC 20024
202/646-7400
—Newsletter with job listings, special newsletter for students with employment information, etc.

*American Institute of Architects*
1735 New York Ave., NW
Washington, DC 20006
202/626-7300
—Publishes periodical directories, operates member's referral service.

*American Institute of Chemical Engineers*
345 E. 47th St.
New York, NY 10017
212/705-7663
—Publishes periodical with job openings, placement referral service, etc.

*American Society of Civil Engineers*
345 E. 47th St.
New York, NY 10017
212/705-7496
—Publishes periodical with job openings, directories, job service for members, etc.

*American Society of Engineering Education*
1818 N St., NW
Suite 600
Washington, DC 20036
202/331-3500
—Publishes periodical with job openings, directories.

*American Society of Information Science*
8720 Georgia Ave.
Suite 501
Silver Spring, MD 20910-3602
301/495-0900
—Publishes newsletter devoted to careers and job openings.

*American Society of Mechanical Engineers*
345 E. 47th St.
New York, NY 10017
212/705-7722
—Publishes periodical with job openings.

*Environmental Careers Organization*
286 Congress St.
Boston, MA 02210
617/426-4375
—Publishes special career publications, places students and recent grads in short-term professional positions, career conferences, etc.

*IEEE Computer Society*
1730 Massachusetts Ave., NW
Washington, DC 20036
202/371-0101
—Publishes members-only periodical with job openings, etc.

*Institute of Electrical and Electronics Engineers (IEEE)*
345 E. 47th St.
New York, NY 10017
212/705-7900
—Publishes periodical with job openings, annual directory of members, career/ employment guide, etc.

*Junior Engineering Technical Society*
1420 King St.
Suite 405
Alexandria, VA 22314
703/548-JETS
—A clearinghouse for career information on most engineering careers, with various programs, guidance, etc. For information, send self-addressed stamped envelope and ask to receive order form.

*National Society of Professional Engineers*
1420 King St.
Alexandria, VA 22314
703/684-2800
—Publishes directory, etc.

## Directories
*CPC Annual*
College Placement Council, Inc.
62 Highland Ave.
Bethlehem, PA 18017
215/868-1421
—Organizations with job opportunities.

*Directory of Chemical Engineering Consultants*
American Institute of Chemical Engineers
345 E. 47th St.
New York, NY 10017
212/705-7663

*Directory of Engineers in Private Practice*
National Society of Professional Engineers
1420 King St.
Alexandria, VA 22314
703/684-2800

*Peterson's Job Opportunities for Engineering, Science, and Computer Graduates*
Peterson's Guides, Inc.
PO Box 2123
Princeton, NJ 08543-2123
609/243-9111
800/338-3282
—Lists hundreds of corporations and government agencies that are hiring, includes detailed information.

## Periodicals
*Architectural Record*
PO Box 564
Highstown, NJ 08520
800/257-9402
—Monthly professional journal with some job listings.

*Chemical & Engineering News*
345 E. 47th St.
New York, NY 10017
212/705-7663
—Excellent industry roundups are particularly valuable as overviews for career changers and new entrants, classifieds include many job openings.

*Chemical Engineering Progress*
American Institute of Chemical Engineers
345 E. 47th St.
New York, NY 10017
212/705-7338

*Civil Engineering*
345 E. 47th St.
New York, NY 10017
212/705-7496
—Monthly association magazine with
many job listings.

*Engineering News-Record*
McGraw-Hill, Inc.
1221 Ave. of the Americas
New York, NY 10020
212/512-2000
800/262-4729
—Good help-wanted section, publishes
top companies' listings.

*Environment Today*
1483 Chain Bridge Rd.
McLean, VA 22101
703/448-0336
—Eight issues per year for environmental
engineers.

*Graduating Engineer*
Peterson's/COG Publishing
16030 Ventura Blvd.
Suite 560
Encino, CA 91436
818/789-5371
—Career advice, special issues such as
high-tech careers, women and minority
hiring trends, etc.

*Hazmat World*
233 N. Michigan
24th fl.
Chicago, IL 60601
312/938-2300
—Monthly for hazardous waste specialists.

*High Technology Careers*
Westech Publishing Co.
4701 Patrick Henry Dr.
Suite 1901
Santa Clara, CA 95054
408/970-8800

—High-tech industry tabloid with
hundreds of high-tech listings.

*IEEE Spectrum*
345 E. 47th St.
New York, NY 10017
212/705-7016
—Many job listings.

*Mechanical Engineering*
345 E. 47th St.
New York, NY 10017
212/705-7782
—Monthly, carries many job listings.

# HEALTH CARE

## Associations
*American Academy of Physician Assistants*
950 N. Washington St.
Alexandria, VA 22314
703/836-2272

*American College of Healthcare Executives*
840 N. Lake Shore Dr.
Chicago, IL 60611
312/943-0544
—Publishes members-only journal with
job listings, directory, etc.

*American Dental Association*
211 E. Chicago Ave.
Chicago, IL 60611
312/440-2736
—Publishes periodicals with job listings,
career booklets, etc.

*American Dental Hygienists Association*
444 N. Michigan Ave.
Suite 3400
Chicago, IL 60611
312/440-8900
—Publishes monthly periodical, accredits
hygienists, etc.

*American Dietetic Association*
216 W. Jackson Blvd.
Suite 800
Chicago, IL 60606
312/899-0040
—Publishes periodical career and
educational information, etc.

*American Health Information Management
Association*
919 N. Michigan Ave.
Chicago, IL 60611
312/787-2672
—Publishes journal with job listings,
directory, referral service, educational
programs.

*American Hospital Association*
840 N. Lake Shore Dr.
Chicago, IL 60611
312/280-6000
—Primarily for administrators, publishes
periodical with job openings, directory
with thousands of hospitals.

*American Medical Association*
535 N. Dearborn St.
Chicago, IL 60610
312/464-5000
—Premier U.S. medical association, many
affiliations and numerous services,
including job placement; publishes
periodical with job listings, etc.

*American Medical Technologists*
Registered Medical Assistant
710 Higgins Rd.
Park Ridge, IL 60068
708/823-5169
—For medical lab technologists, medical
assistants, etc.; offers placement
services, various member services.

*American Nurses Association*
600 Maryland Ave., SW
Suite 100W
Washington, DC 20024-2571
202/554-4444
—Offers numerous services, operates
placement service, publishes periodical
with job openings, etc.

*American Physical Therapy Association*
1111 N. Fairfax St.
Alexandria, VA 22314
703/684-2782
800/999-2782
—Publishes periodical with job listings,
annual conference with placement
services, career information.

*American Public Health Association*
1015 15th St., NW
Washington, DC 20005
202/789-5600
—Publishes journal, directory, has
placement service for members.

*American Society for Medical Technology*
7910 Woodmont Ave.
Suite 1301
Bethesda, MD 20814
301/657-2768
—For medical lab technicians, has
placement service, etc.

*American Society for Radiologic
Technologists*
15000 Central Ave., SE
Albuquerque, NM 87123
505/298-4500
—Publishes periodicals with job listings,
etc.

*Healthcare Financial Management
Association*
2 Westbrook Corporate Ctr.
Suite 700
Westchester, IL 60154
708/531-9600
—Publishes periodical with listings,
maintains job database for members.

*National Association for Emergency
Medical Technicians*
9140 Ward Pkwy.
Kansas City, MO 64114
816/444-3500
—Offers placement service, etc.

## Directories

*Hospital Phone Book*
Reed Reference Publishing
121 Chanlon Rd.
New Providence, RI 07974
800/521-8110
—Thousands of numbers, etc., of hospitals
nationwide.

*Nursing Career Directory*
Springhouse Corp.
1111 Bethlehem Pike
Springhouse, PA 19477
215/646-8700

*Nursingworld Journal Professional Career
Guide*
Prime National Publishing Co.
470 Boston Post Rd.
Weston, MA 02193
617/899-2702

*US Medical Directory*
Reed Reference Publishing
121 Chanlon Rd.
New Providence, RI 07974
800/521-8110
—Extensive listing of health-care facilities
and practitioners.

## Periodicals

*American Journal of Nursing*
555 W. 57th St.
New York, NY 10019
212/582-8820
—Monthly for members of the American
Nurses Association.

*AORN*
2170 S. Parker Rd.
Denver, CO 80231
303/755-6300
—Monthly association magazine for
operating-room nurses, with job listings.

*DVM: The Newsmagazine of Veterinary
Medicine*
131 E. First
Duluth, MN 55802
800/346-0085
—Monthly, includes job listings.

*Emergency: The Journal of Emergency
Services*
6300 Yarrow Dr.
Carlsbad, CA 92009
619/438-2511
—Monthly journal for EMTs, paramedics.

*Healthcare Financial Management*
2 Westbrook Corp. Ctr.
Westchester, IL 60154
708/531-9600
—Monthly for managers and workers in
health care.

*Hospitals*
737 N. Michigan Ave.
Chicago, IL 60611
312/440-6800
—Semimonthly for hospital
administrators.

*Journal of the American Dental
Association*
211 E. Chicago Ave.
Chicago, IL 60611
312/440-2736
—Nine issue/year periodical for members
of the association, carries job listings.

*Nursing 95*
1111 Bethlehem Pike
Springhouse, PA 19477
215/646-8700
—Monthly.

## INTERNATIONAL/NONPROFIT

## Periodicals

*Community Jobs*
ACCESS
30 Irving Place
9th fl.
New York, NY 10003
212/475-1001
—Lists nonprofit job openings.

*The Economist*
10 Rockefeller Plz.
New York, NY 10020
212/541-5730
—London-based internationally oriented
  newsmagazine, has a few job listings,
  valuable for insight into world affairs.

*Federal Career Opportunities*
PO Box 1059
Vienna, VA 22185-0200
703/281-0200
—Biweekly listing all types of U.S.
  government jobs, including some
  overseas.

*International Employment Gazette*
1525 Wade Hampton Blvd.
Greenville, SC 29609
800/882-9188
—Biweekly with hundreds of listings,
  including some multinational business
  jobs.

*International Employment Hotline*
PO Box 3030
Oakton, VA 22124
703/620-1972
—Job listings for overseas jobs, includes
  some private sector as well as
  governmental.

*International Jobs Bulletin*
University Placement
Woody Hall B-208
Southern Illinois at Carbondale, IL 62901
618/453-2391
—Bimonthly listing about 100 international
  jobs of various types.


## MANAGERIAL

### Associations
*American Management Association*
135 W. 50th St.
New York, NY 10020
212/586-8100
—The major association for managers,
  offers numerous programs, has many

offices worldwide, bookstore,
information service, etc.

*American Planning Association*
1313 E. 60th St.
Chicago, IL 60637
312/955-9100
—Publishes periodical with job listings,
  referral service, etc., for members.

*American Society for Public
  Administration*
1120 G St., NW
Washington, DC 20005
202/626-2711

*Financial Management Association*
University of South Florida
College of Business Administration
Tampa, FL 33640-5500
813/974-2084
—Publishes periodical with job listings.

*Institute of Real Estate Management*
430 N. Michigan Ave.
7th fl.
Chicago, IL 60611
312/661-1930
—Placement service for members, etc.

*International Facility Management
  Association*
1 Greenway Plz.
11th fl.
Houston, TX 77046
713/623-IFMA

*International Personnel Association*
1617 Duke St.
Alexandria, VA 22314
703/549-7100
—Periodicals for members, with job
  listings.

*Society for Human Resource Management*
606 N. Washington St.
Alexandria, VA 22314
703/548-3440
—Publishes periodical with job listings,
  maintains HRM-net job bank of jobs
  listed in periodical.

## Directories

*AMA's Executive Employment Guide*
American Management Association
135 W. 50th St.
New York, NY 10020
212/586-8100
Fax: 212/903-8163
—Free to AMA members; lists search
firms, job registries, etc.

*AMBA's MBA Employment Guide*
Association of MBA Executives
227 Commerce St.
East Haven, CT 06512
203/467-8870
—For $10 each, sends a listing of
corporations in three states of choice for
one functional area.

*Macmillan Directory of Leading Private
Companies*
Reed Reference Publishing
PO Box 31
121 Chanlon Rd.
New Providence, RI 07974
800/521-8110 or 800/323-6772
—Expensive but a good source for hard-
to-find private firms.

*Peterson's Job Opportunities for Liberal
Arts Graduates*
Peterson's Guides, Inc.
PO Box 2123
Princeton, NJ 08543-2123
609/243-9111
800/338-3282
—Lists hundreds of corporations and
organizations that are hiring, including
detailed information.

## Periodicals

*FE/Financial Executive*
PO Box 1938
Morristown, NJ 07962
201/898-4600
—Bimonthly.

*Forty-Plus Newsletter*
Forty Plus of New York
15 Park Row
New York, NY 10038
212/233-6086
—Particularly for job hunters over 40.

*HR Magazine*
606 N. Washington St.
Alexandria, VA 22314
703/548-3440
—Monthly for human resources
executives, particularly those in
compensation, benefits, and training.

*INC*
38 Commercial Wharf
Boston, MA 02110
617/248-8000
—Invaluable for targeting fast-moving
corporations that may be hiring.

*Industry Week*
1100 Superior Ave.
Cleveland, OH 44114
216/696-7000
—Semimonthly, covers industrial
management.

*Journal of Commerce*
2 World Trade Center
New York, NY 10048
212/837-7000
—Daily business newspaper.

*National Business Employment Weekly*
420 Lexington Ave.
New York, NY 10170
212/808-6791
—Weekly that includes all ads from *The
Wall Street Journal,* as well as career-
oriented articles.

*Personnel Journal*
ACC Communications
245 Fischer Ave. B-2
Costa Mesa, CA 92626
714/751-1863
—Monthly for human resources pros.

# SCIENCE

## Associations

*American Chemical Society*
1120 Vermont Ave., NW
Washington, DC 20005
800/227-5558
—Publishes various periodicals with job listings, such as the *Journal of Agricultural and Food Chemistry* and *Chemical and Engineering News,* career brochures, and salary surveys; maintains job clearinghouse, listing service, counseling service, and more.

*American Geological Institute*
4220 King St.
Alexandria, VA 22302
703/379-2480
—Publishes magazine with job listings, etc.

*American Institute of Architects*
1735 New York Ave., NW
Washington, DC 20006
202/626-7300
—Publishes periodical with employment information, directory, etc.

*American Institute of Biological Sciences*
730 11th St., NW
Washington, DC 20001
202/628-1500
—Publishes career brochures, periodical with job listings; offers member placement services; also runs *BioTron,* a computerized bulletin board service that includes job opportunities. Phone number is 202/628-AIBS.

*American Institute of Physics*
335 E. 45th St.
New York, NY 10017
212/661-9404
500 Sunnyside Blvd.
Woodbury, NY 11797
516/576-2200
—Publishes periodicals with job listings, surveys, etc.

## Directories

*Conservation Directory*
National Wildlife Foundation
1400 16th St., NW
Item 79561
Washington, DC 20036
703/790-4402
800/432-6564
—Lists hundreds of state and federal government agencies, nonprofit organizations, educational institutions, etc. (with addresses, phone numbers), all involved in conservation, that may provide job leads.

*Peterson's Job Opportunities for Engineering, Science, and Computer Graduates*
Peterson's Guides, Inc.
PO Box 2123
Princeton, NJ 08543-2123
609/243-9111
800/338-3282
—Lists hundreds of corporations and government agencies that are hiring; includes detailed information on positions available, etc.

## Periodicals

*Chemical & Engineering News*
345 E. 47th St.
New York, NY 10017
212/705-7663
—Magazine does excellent industry roundups, particularly useful as overviews for entry-level job hunters; extensive classifieds.

*High Technology Careers*
Westech Publishing Co.
4701 Patrick Henry Dr., Ste. 1901
Santa Clara, CA 95054
408/970-8800
—High-tech industry tabloid that includes listings of hundreds of high-tech job openings.

*Physics Today*
335 E. 45th St.
New York, NY 10017
212/661-9404
—Monthly association magazine; in
addition to state-of-the-profession type
of articles that may be useful in a job
hunt, also has numerous job listings.

*Science*
1333 H St., NW
Washington, DC 20005
202/326-6500
—Well-known weekly science magazine;
includes job listings.

## SOCIAL SERVICES/LEGAL

### Associations
*American Association for Counseling and
Development*
5999 Stevenson Ave.
Alexandria, VA 22304
703/823-9800
800/545-2223
—Major association in certifying
counselors; holds workshops, etc.;
publishes periodical with job openings
and more.

*American Occupational Therapy
Association*
PO Box 1725
Rockville, MD 20849-1725
800/366-9799
—Offers educational and career
information.

*American Planning Association*
1313 E. 60th St.
Chicago, IL 60637
312/955-9100
—Publishes periodical with member
listings, directory.

*American Psychological Association*
750 First St., NE
Washington, DC 20002
202/336-5500
—Publishes periodical with job listings,
directories, etc.

*American Society of Criminology*
1314 Kinnear Rd.
Ste. 212
Columbus, OH 43212
614/292-9207
—Publishes periodical with job openings,
directory, placement service for
members, etc.

*American Speech-Language-Hearing
Association*
10801 Rockville Pike
Rockville, MD 20852
301/897-5700
—Publishes periodical with job listings,
employment referral, career/educational
information, etc.

*Legal Assistant Management Association*
638 Prospect Ave.
Hartford, CT 06105
203/586-7507

*National Association of Legal Assistants*
1516 S. Boston
Ste. 200
Tulsa, OK 74119
918/587-6828

*National Association of Social Workers*
750 First St., NE
Washington, DC 20002
202/408-8600
—Publishes periodical with job listings,
etc.

*National Court Reporters Association*
8224 Old Courthouse Rd.
Vienna, VA 22182-3808
703/556-6272
—Publishes employment periodical with
many job listings.

*National Paralegal Association*
PO Box 406
Solebury, PA 18963
215/297-8333
Fax: 215/297-8358
—Publishes and sells many different
directories, salary surveys, rental
mailing lists, placement networks, etc.

## Directories
*Law Firm Yellow Pages*
Monitor Publishing Co.
104 Fifth Ave.
2d fl.
New York, NY 10011
212/627-4140

## Periodicals
*American Lawyer*
600 Third Ave.
New York, NY 10016
212/973-2800
—"Insider's" view of legal industry—filled
   with employment ads.

*Community Jobs*
ACCESS
30 Irving Place
9th fl.
New York, NY 10003
212/475-1001
—Monthly nonprofit sector jobs magazine,
   lists hundreds of job openings.

*Corrections Today*
8025 Laurel Lakes Ct.
Laurel, MD 20797
301/206-5100
—Invaluable for anyone considering a
   corrections career.

*NASW News*
750 First St., NE
Washington, DC 20002
202/408-8600
—Association magazine for social
   workers; includes numerous job listings.

*National and Federal Legal Employment
   Report*
Federal Reports
1010 Vermont Ave., NW
Ste. 408
Washington, DC 20005
202/393-3311
—Monthly publication listing hundreds of
   legal jobs, chiefly in government.

*National Employment Listing Service*
Sam Houston State University
Criminal Justice Center
Huntsville, TX 77341-2296
409/294-1692
—Monthly listing of job openings in all
   areas of law enforcement and
   corrections; also includes social work
   positions.

*National Law Journal*
111 Eighth Ave.
New York, NY 10011
212/741-8300
—Weekly publication for lawyers, includes
   numerous job openings.

*Opportunity in Public Interest Law*
ACCESS
30 Irving Place
9th fl.
New York, NY 10003
212/475-1001
—Lists hundreds of legal jobs in
   government.

*Social Service Jobs*
10 Angelica Dr.
Framingham, MA 01701
508/626-8644
Fax: 508/626-9389
—Biweekly listing jobs in social services—
   counselors, psychologists, etc.

# TEACHERS, LIBRARIANS, HISTORIANS, AND SOCIAL SCIENTISTS

## Associations
*American Alliance for Health, Physical
   Education, Recreation and Dance*
1900 Association Dr.
Reston, VA 22091
703/476-3400
—Publishes periodical with job listings;
   offers placement service.

**American Association for Counseling and Development**
5999 Stevenson Ave.
Alexandria, VA 22304
703/823-9800
800/545-2223
—Major association in certifying counselors; holds workshops, etc.; publishes periodical with job openings and more.

**American Association for Higher Education**
1 Du Pont Circle
Ste. 360
Washington, DC 20036
202/293-6440

**American Association of Museums**
1225 I St., NW
Washington, DC 20005
202/289-1818
—Publishes periodical with job openings; offers placement services, etc.

**American Association of School Administrators**
1801 N. Moore St.
Arlington, VA 22209
703/528-0700
—Publishes periodical with job listings, etc.

**American Association of School Librarians**
50 E. Huron St.
Chicago, IL 60611
312/944-6780

**American Association of University Professors**
1012 14th St., NW
Ste. 500
Washington, DC 20005
202/737-5900

**American Economic Association**
2014 Broadway
Ste. 305
Nashville, TN 37203
615/322-2595
—Publishes periodical with job openings; operates placement service; etc.

**American Economic Development Council**
9801 W. Higgins Rd.
Rosemont, IL 60018-4726
708/692-9944
—Publishes periodical; offers job referrals for members; etc.

**American Federation of Teachers**
555 New Jersey Ave., NW
Washington, DC 20001
202/879-4400

**American Library Association**
50 E. Huron St.
Chicago, IL 60611
800/545-0243
—Publishes periodical with job listings. Also maintains phone numbers and information on state library job hot lines —tape-recorded messages that list library job openings for some states. Call for specific phone numbers. The ALA also maintains the special *Grapevine* job database.

**American Society for Information Science**
8720 Georgia Ave.
Ste. 501
Silver Springs, MD 20910
301/495-0900
—Publishes periodical with job openings, operates member placement service, etc.

**American Sociological Association**
1722 N St., NW
Washington, DC 20036
202/833-3410
—Publishes periodical with job listings, directory, etc.

**Association for School, College, and University Staffing**
1600 Dodge Ave.
Evanston, IL 60201-3451
708/864-1999
—Publishes *Job Search Handbook,* with articles on job hunting and job listings.

*College and University Personnel
  Association*
1233 20th St., NW
Ste. 301
Washington, DC 20036
202/429-0311
—Puts out major salary survey, offers
  professional development programs,
  etc.

*Modern Language Association*
10 Astor Pl.
New York, NY 10003-6981
—Publishes job listings for English as well
  as foreign-language teachers.

*National Art Education Association*
1916 Association Dr.
Reston, VA 22091
703/860-8000
—Maintains placement service for
  members.

*National Association for the Education of
  Young Children*
1509 16th St., NW
Washington, DC 20036-1426
202/232-8777

*National Council of Teachers of English*
1111 W. Kenyon Rd.
Urbana, IL 61801
217/328-3870

*National Council of Teachers of
  Mathematics*
1906 Association Dr.
Reston, VA 22091
703/620-9840
—Publishes journal with job listings.

*National Science Teachers Association*
1840 Wilson Blvd.
Arlington, VA 22201
703/243-7100
—Publishes periodical with job listings,
  directory, etc.

*Special Library Association*
1700 18th St., NW
Washington, DC 20009
202/234-4700
—Publishes periodical with job openings,
  has resume referral service, tape-
  recorded job openings.

## Directories

*American Library Association—Handbook
  of Organization and Membership
  Directory*
American Library Association
50 E. Huron St.
Chicago, IL 60611
800/545-2433

*American Library Directory*
Reed Reference Publishing
PO Box 31
New Providence, NJ 07974-9904
800/521-8110

*Directory of Federal Libraries*
Oryz Press
4041 N. Central
Ste. 700
Phoenix, AZ 85012-3397
800/279-6799

*Directory of Special Libraries and
  Information Centers*
Gale Research, Inc.
835 Penobscot Bldg.
Detroit, MI 48226
800/877-GALE

*Guide to Library Placement Sources*
American Library Association
50 E. Huron St.
Chicago, IL 60611
800/545-2433
—Valuable centralized sources listing
  associations and organizations
  nationwide that offer placement services
  for librarians.

*Opportunities Abroad for Educators:
  Fulbright Teacher Exchange Program*
E/ASX, Room 3513
U.S. Information Agency
Washington, DC 20547
202/619-4555
—Lists countries and positions available,
  includes application and describes
  program, updated yearly.

*WILSONLINE: Education Index*
(computer database)
H. W. Wilson Company
950 University Ave.
Bronx, NY 10452
800/367-6770
—Computer database with extensive
  listing of education periodicals.

## Periodicals
*ABA Journal*
750 N. Lake Shore Dr.
Chicago, IL 60611
312/988-5000

*American Educator*
555 New Jersey Ave., NW
Washington, DC 20001
202/879-4420

*American Libraries*
50 E. Huron St.
Chicago, IL 60611
312/944-6780
800/545-2433
—Monthly American Library Association
  magazine; job ads can be obtained three
  weeks in advance of publication—call
  for details.

*American Teacher*
555 New Jersey Ave., NW
Washington, DC 20001
202/879-4400

*Chronicle of Higher Education*
1255 23rd St., NW
Washington, DC 20037
or

PO Box 1955
Marion, OH 43306-2055
202/466-1000
—Monthly magazine for college faculty
  and administrators; includes numerous
  job listings.

*Current Openings in Education in USA*
Education Information Service
PO Box 662 D
Newton, MA 02161
617/237-0887

*Library Journal*
249 W. 17th St.
New York, NY 10011
212/463-6822
800/669-1002
—Numerous job listings.

*Teacher*
4301 Connecticut Ave., NW
Ste. 432
Washington, DC 20008
202/686-0800

*Wilson Library Bulletin*
950 University Ave.
Bronx, NY 10452
212/588-8400
800/367-6770

## TECHNICAL

## Associations
*Air Traffic Control Association*
2300 Clarendon Blvd.
Ste. 711
Arlington, VA 22201
703/522-5717
—Publishes periodical.

*Association of Manufacturing Technicians*
7901 Westpark Dr.
McLean, VA 22102
703/893-2900

*Computer-Aided Manufacturing
    International*
1250 E. Copeland Rd.
Ste. 500
Arlington, TX 76011-8909
817/860-1654

*Electronics Technicians Association
    International*
602 N. Jackson St.
Greencastle, IN 46135
317/653-8262
—Publishes periodical with a few job
    openings; offers referral service for
    members, certification tapes, etc.

*Future Aviation Professionals of America*
4959 Massachusetts Blvd.
Atlanta, GA 30337
800/JET-JOBS

*International Society of Certified
    Electronics Technicians*
2708 W. Berry
Ft. Worth, TX 76109
817/921-9101
—Publishes periodical with job openings,
    etc.

*Professional Aviation Maintenance
    Association*
500 Northwest Plz.
Ste. 1016
St. Ann, MO 63704
314/739-2580

*Society of Motion Picture and Television
    Engineers*
595 W. Hartsdale Ave.
White Plains, NY 10607
914/761-1100

## Periodicals
*Airport Maintenance Technology*
1233 Janesville Ave.
Ft. Atkinson, WI 53538
414/563-6388

*Computer Aided Engineering*
Penton Publishing
1100 Superior Ave.
Cleveland, OH 44114
216/696-7000

## WRITERS, EDITORS, AND JOURNALISTS

## Associations
*Editorial Free-lancers Association*
PO Box 2050
Madison Sq. Station
New York, NY 10159
212/929-5400
—For annual fee, members can use listing
    service, which lists full- and part-time
    jobs for editors, writers, indexers, etc.

*Writers Guild of America, West*
8955 Beverly Blvd.
Los Angeles, CA 90048
310/205-2502

## Periodicals
*Editor and Publisher*
11 W. 19th St.
New York, NY 10011
—Weekly magazine for newspaper editors.

# INDUSTRY-SPECIFIC SOURCES

## ADVERTISING AND PUBLIC RELATIONS

### Associations

*American Advertising Federation*
1101 Vermont Ave.
Ste. 500
Washington, DC 20005
202/898-0089

*American Association of Advertising Agencies*
666 Third Ave.
New York, NY 10017
212/682-2500

*Association of National Advertisers*
155 E. 44th St.
New York, NY 10017
212/697-5950

*International Advertising Association*
342 Madison Ave.
Ste. 2000
New York, NY 10017
212/557-1133

*Public Relations Society of America*
33 Irving Pl.
New York, NY 10003
212/995-2230
—Provides job hot line (212/995-0476) with job listings and information on resume forwarding for these jobs.

### Directories

*AAAA Roster and Organization*
American Association of Advertising Agencies
666 Third Ave.
New York, NY 10017
212/682-2500

*Directory of Minority Public Relations Professionals*
Public Relations Society of America
33 Irving Pl.
New York, NY 10003
212/995-2230

*Macmillan Directory of International Advertisers and Agencies*
Reed Reference Publishing
121 Chanlon Rd.
New Providence, NJ 07974
800/521-8110

*O'Dwyer's Directory of Corporate Communications*
271 Madison Ave.
New York, NY 10016
212/679-2471

*O'Dwyer's Directory of Public Relations Executives*
271 Madison Ave.
New York, NY 10016
212/679-2471

*O'Dwyer's Directory of Public Relations Firms*
271 Madison Ave.
New York, NY 10016
212/679-2471

*Public Relations Consultants Directory*
American Business Directories, Inc.
5707 S. 86th Cir.
Omaha, NE 68127
402/331-7169

*Standard Directory of Advertising Agencies*
Reed Reference Publishing
121 Chanlon Rd.
New Providence, NJ 07974
800/521-8110

## Periodicals

*Advertising Age*
220 E. 42nd St.
New York, NY 10017
212/210-0100
—Weekly tabloid covering the ad industry.
Excellent help-wanted section.

*Adweek*
1515 Broadway
New York, NY 10036
212/536-5336
—Weekly covering ad industry. Like *Ad
Age,* has a strong help-wanted section.

*O'Dwyers PR Marketplace*
271 Madison Ave.
New York, NY 10016
212/679-2471
—Biweekly newsletter listing job openings
and business opportunities for PR
practitioners.

*Public Relations Journal*
Public Relations Society of America
33 Irving Pl.
New York, NY 10003
212/995-2230
—Monthly magazine sent free to PRSA
members, but available for a yearly
subscription fee to nonmembers; annual
*Register* issue lists members and
affiliations, plus addresses.

## AEROSPACE

### Associations

*Aerospace Industries Association*
1250 I St., NW
Washington, DC 20005
202/371-8500

*American Institute of Aeronautics and
Astronautics*
370 L'Enfant Promenade, SW
Washington, DC 20024
202/646-7400

—Puts out *AIAA Bulletin,* which includes
employment listings, and the *AIAA
Student Journal,* which is aimed at
aerospace students and includes articles
on job hunting and entry-level career
opportunities.

*General Aviation Manufacturers
Association*
1400 K St., NW
Washington, DC 20005
202/393-1500

### Directories

*Aerospace Facts and Figures*
Aerospace Industries Association
1250 I St., NW
Washington, DC 20005
202/371-8500

*International ABC Aerospace Directory*
Jane's Information Group
1340 Braddock Pl.
Ste. 300
PO Box 1436
Alexandria, VA 22313-2036
703/683-3700

*World Aviation Directory*
Aviation Week Group
McGraw-Hill, Inc.
1200 G St., NW
Washington, DC 20005
202/383-3700

### Periodicals

*Aerospace Daily*
McGraw-Hill, Inc.
1200 G St., NW
Washington, DC 20005
202/383-3700

*Aerospace Engineering*
400 Commonwealth Dr.
Warrendale, PA 15096
412/772-7114
—Puts out monthly by the Society of
Aerospace Engineers; geared to design
engineers, technical managers, etc.

*Aviation Week and Space Technology*
1221 Ave. of the Americas
New York, NY 10020
212/512-6942
—Weekly considered by many to be the industry "bible"; covers all phases of aerospace, including commercial, defense, and space; includes classified ads.

*Defense News* and *Space News*
6883 Commercial Dr.
Springfield, VA 22159
703/658-8400
—Two magazines covering the defense industry and space industry.

# AUTOMOTIVE

## Associations
*American Automobile Manufacturers Association, Inc.*
7430 Second Ave.
Detroit, MI 48202
313/872-4311

*American International Automobile Dealers Association*
8400 Westpark Dr.
McLean, VA 22102
703/821-7000

*National Automotive Dealers Association*
8400 Westpark Dr.
McLean, VA 22102
703/821-7000

*Society of Automotive Engineers*
400 Commonwealth Dr.
Warrendale, PA 15096
412/776-4841

## Directories
*Automotive News Market Data Book*
Automotive News
1400 Woodbridge Ave.
Detroit, MI 48207
313/446-6000

—Annual special issue of *Automotive News* that includes extensive listings of auto manufacturers, suppliers, etc.

*Ward's Automotive Yearbook*
Ward's Communications, Inc.
28 W. Adams St.
Detroit, MI 48226
313/962-4433

## Periodicals
*Automotive Industries*
2600 Fisher Bldg.
Detroit, MI 48202
313/875-2090

*Automotive Marketing*
Chilton Way
Radnor, PA 19089
215/964-4395

*Automotive News*
1400 Woodbridge Ave.
Detroit, MI 48207
313/446-6000
—Considered industry "bible," includes extensive help-wanted section.

# AVIATION

## Associations
*Air Line Employees Association*
5600 S. Central Ave.
Chicago, IL 60638-3797
312/767-3333
—Puts out monthly *Job Opportunity Bulletin* listing job openings in all areas of aviation.

*Air Traffic Control Association*
2300 Clarendon Blvd.
Ste. 711
Arlington, VA 22201
703/522-5717

*Air Transport Association of America*
1301 Pennsylvania Ave.
Ste. 1000
Washington, DC 20004
202/625-4000

*American Association of Airport
   Executives*
4212 King St.
Alexandria, VA 22302
703/824-0500
—Puts out publications including *Airport
Report,* which contains help-wanted ads.

*Future Aviation Professionals of America*
4959 Massachusetts Blvd.
Atlanta, GA 30032
404/997-8097
—Offers wide range of career assistance
for members; puts out different
publications that include job listings,
such as *Pilot Job Reports* and *Flight
Attendant Job Reports*; maintains
computerized job banks.

*General Aviation Manufacturers
   Association*
1400 K St., NW
Ste. 801
Washington, DC 20005
202/393-1500

*National Air Carrier Association*
1730 M St., NW
Washington, DC 20036
202/833-8200

*National Air Transportation Association*
4226 King St.
Alexandria, VA 22302
703/845-9000

*Regional Airline Association*
1101 Connecticut Ave., NW
Washington, DC 20036
202/857-1170

**Directories**
*Annual Report of the Commuter Regional
   Airline Industry*
Regional Airline Association
1101 Connecticut Ave., NW
Washington, DC 20036
202/857-1170

*Official Airline Guide: North American
   Edition* and *Worldwide Edition*
2000 Clearwater Dr.
Oak Brook, IL 60521
312/654-6000
800/323-3537

*World Aviation Directory*
McGraw-Hill, Inc.
1200 G St., 2d fl.
Washington, DC 20005
202/383-3700

## BANKING

**Associations**
*American Bankers Association*
1120 Connecticut Ave., NW
Washington, DC 20036
202/663-4000

*American League of Financial Institutions*
1709 New York Ave., NW
Ste. 801
Washington, DC 20006
202/628-5624
—Offers career placement assistance.

*Independent Bankers Association of
   America*
1 Thomas Cir., NW
Ste. 950
Washington, DC 20005
202/659-8111

*Mortgage Bankers Association of America*
1125 15th St., NW
Washington, DC 20005
202/861-6500

*National Association of Federal Credit
Unions*
3138 N. 10th St.
Ste. 300
Arlington, VA 22201
703/522-4770
—Publishes monthly *Jobs/OPS,* which lists
job opportunities; available (free) to
members only.

*National Bankers Association*
1802 T St.
Washington, DC 20009
202/588-5432
—Operates job referral service for
members.

## Directories
*American Banker Yearbook*
American Banker, Inc.
1 State St. Plz.
New York, NY 10003
212/803-6700

*American Financial Directory*
McFadden Business Publications
6195 Crooked Creek Rd.
Norcross, GA 30092-9986
404/448-1011
800/247-7376

*Moody's Bank and Financial Manual*
Moody's Investor Services, Inc.
99 Church St.
New York, NY 10007
212/553-0300

*Polk's Bank Directory*
R. L. Polk & Co.
PO Box 3051000
Nashville, TN 37230-5100
615/889-3350
800/827-2265

## Periodicals
*ABA Banking Journal*
345 Hudson St.
New York, NY 10014
212/620-7200

*American Banker*
1 State St. Plz.
New York, NY 10004
212/803-6700
—Daily newspaper for senior executives
and bank officers, often has good help-
wanted section.

## BROADCASTING

## Associations
*Broadcast Promotion and Marketing
Executives*
6255 Sunset Blvd.
Los Angeles, CA 90028
213/465-3777
—Operates job referral bank for members.

*International Radio and Television Society*
420 Lexington Ave.
Ste. 1714
New York, NY 10170
212/867-6650
—Sponsors summer internships for
college communications majors.

*National Academy of Television Arts and
Sciences*
111 W. 57th St.
New York, NY 10019
212/586-8424

*National Association of Black-Owned
Broadcasters*
1730 M St., NW
Washington, DC 20036
202/463-8970
—Maintains placement service and offers
workshops.

*National Association of Broadcasters*
1771 N St., NW
Washington, DC 20036
202/429-5300
—Operates job clearinghouse, placement
service for minorities; also puts out
career brochures, such as *Careers in
Radio* and *Careers in Television.*

*National Association of Public Television
 Stations*
1350 Connecticut Ave., NW
Washington, DC 20036
202/887-1700


*National Cable Television Association*
1724 Massachusetts Ave., NW
Washington, DC 20036
202/775-3550


*Radio Advertising Bureau*
304 Park Ave. So.
New York, NY 10010
212/254-4800


*Radio-Television News Directors
 Association*
1000 Connecticut Ave., NW
Washington, DC 20036
202/659-6510
—Puts out newsletter listing job openings
  —free to members, but available to
  nonmembers for subscription price.


*Television Bureau of Advertising*
477 Madison Ave.
New York, NY 10022
212/486-1111


## Directories
*Broadcasting & Cable Marketplace*
PO Box 31
New Providence, NJ 07974-9903
800/323-4345


*Broadcasting Yearbook*
Broadcasting Publications, Inc.
1705 DeSales St., NW
Washington, DC 20036
202/659-2340

*International Television and Video
 Almanac*
159 W. 53rd St.
New York, NY 10019


*Standard Rate & Data Service: Spot Radio*
 and *Spot Television Rates and Data* (2
 different books)
3004 Glenview Rd.
Wilmette, IL 60091
708/256-6067


*World Radio TV Handbook*
Billboard Publications, Inc.
1515 Broadway
New York, NY 10036
212/764-7300


## Periodicals
*Broadcasting*
1705 DeSales St., NW
Washington, DC 20036
202/659-2340
—Weekly covering all aspects of broadcast
  industry; contains strong help-wanted
  section.


*Electronic Media*
740 N. Rush St.
Chicago, IL 60611
312/649-5200
—Weekly covering all aspects of broadcast
  industry.


*Television Broadcast*
2 Park Ave.
New York, NY 10016
212/779-1919
—Monthly, covers both radio and
  television.


*Video Week*
Television Digest, Inc.
2115 Ward Court, NW
Washington, DC 20037
202/872-9200

# CHEMICALS

## Associations
*American Chemical Society*
1155 16th St., NW
Washington, DC 20036
202/872-4600
—Publishes *Chemical & Engineering News*
(listed below) as well as others; offers
career counseling, job clearinghouse,
and other employment programs for
members.

*American Institute of Chemists*
7315 Wisconsin Ave., NW
Ste. 502E
Bethesda, MD 20814
301/652-2447
—Publishes *The Chemist,* which includes
employment listings; operates job
placement service.

*Chemical Manufacturers Association*
2501 M St., NW
Washington, DC 20037
202/887-1100

## Directories
*Chemical Industry Directory*
State Mutual Book and Periodical Service
521 Fifth Ave.
New York, NY 10017
212/682-5844

*Chemicals Directory*
275 Washington St.
Newton, MA 02158
617/964-3030
—Relatively low cost makes this a good
basic source for a resume mailing list.

*Directory of Chemical Producers U.S.A.*
Stanford Research Institute International
333 Ravenswood Ave.
Menlo Park, CA 94025
415/859-3627

## Periodicals
*Chemical & Engineering News*
1155 16th Ave., NW
Washington, DC 20036
202/872-4600

*Chemical Engineering*
1221 Ave. of the Americas
New York, NY 10020
212/512-2849

*Chemical Week*
888 Seventh Ave.
New York, NY 10019
212/621-4900

*Modern Plastics*
1221 Ave. of the Americas
New York, NY 10020
212/512-6241

# COMPUTERS/ELECTRONICS

## Associations
*American Electronics Association*
PO Box 54990
Santa Clara, CA 95056
408/987-4200

*Association for Computing Machinery*
1515 Broadway
New York, NY 10036
212/869-7400
—Runs resume databank for members.

*Computer and Automated Systems
  Association of SME*
1 SME Dr.
Dearborn, MI 48128
313/271-1500

*Computer and Business Equipment
  Manufacturers Association*
1250 I St., NW
Washington, DC 20005
202/737-8888

Electronics Industries Association
2001 I St., NW
Washington, DC 20006
202/457-4900

IEEE Computer Society
1730 Massachusetts Ave., NW
Washington, DC 20036
202/371-0101

Information Industry Association
555 New Jersey Ave., NW
Washington, DC 20001
202/639-8262

Semiconductor Industry Association
4300 Stevens Creek Blvd.
Ste. 271
San Jose, CA 95129
408/246-2711

## Directories
Directory of Top Computer Executives
Applied Computer Research
PO Box 82266
Phoenix, AZ 85071-2266
602/995-5929

Who's Who in Electronics Regional Source
  Directory
2057 Aurora Rd.
Twinsburg, OH 44087
216/425-9000

## Periodicals
Computer World
375 Cochituate Rd.
Framingham, MA 01701
508/879-0700
—Weekly tabloid covering all aspects of
  computer industry.

Data Communications
1221 Ave. of the Americas
New York, NY 10020
212/512-6050
—Monthly magazine for those involved in
  computer network implementation and
  integration.

Datamation
249 W. 17th St.
New York, NY 10010
212/645-0067
—Semimonthly aimed at IS managers,
  manufacturers, etc. Puts out annual
  Datamation 100 issue listing top
  companies in field, includes addresses
  and profiles. Can be useful for resume
  mailing list.

EDN
275 Washington St.
Newton, MA 02158
617/964-3030
—Biweekly for electronics engineers,
  product designers, systems designers,
  etc.

Electronic Business
275 Washington St.
Newton, MA 02158
617/964-3030
—Semimonthly covering all phases of
  computer and electronics industry;
  annual Electronic Business 200 runs
  down top companies in industry.

Electronic News
488 Madison Ave.
New York, NY 10022
212/909-5900
—Weekly newspaper.

# CONSUMER PRODUCTS

## Associations
Association of Home Appliance
  Manufacturers
20 N. Wacker Dr.
Chicago, IL 60606
312/984-5800

Cosmetic Toiletry and Fragrance
  Association
1101 17th St., NW
Ste. 300
Washington, DC 20006
202/331-1770

*Electronic Industries Association*
2001 Pennsylvania Ave., NW
Washington, DC 20006-1813
202/457-4900

*National Housewares Manufacturers*
 *Association*
6400 Shafer Ct.
Ste. 650
Rosemont, IL 60018
708/292-4200

*Soap and Detergent Association*
475 Park Ave. S.
New York, NY 10016
212/725-1262

## Directories
*Appliance Manufacturer Annual Directory*
Corcoran Communications, Inc.
5900 Harper Rd.
Ste. 105
Solon, OH 44139
216/349-3060

*Electronic Market Data Book*
2001 Pennsylvania Ave., NW
Washington, DC 20006-1813
202/457-4900

*Household and Personal Products Industry*
 *Buyers Guide*
Rodman Publishing Corp.
17 S. Franklin Tpke.
Ramsey, NJ 07446
201/825-2552

## Periodicals
*Appliance*
1110 Jorie Blvd.
Oak Brook, IL 60522
708/9909-3484

*Appliance Manufacturer*
Corcoran Communications, Inc.
5900 Harper Rd.
Ste. 105
Solon, OH 44139
216/349-3060

*Drug & Cosmetic Industry*
Edgell Communications
7500 Old Oak Blvd.
Cleveland, OH 44130
216/243-8100

*Household and Personal Products Industry*
PO Box 555
Ramsey, NJ 07446
201/825-2552
—Monthly, good help-wanted section.

*Soap/Cosmetics/Chemical Specialties*
445 Broad Hollow Rd.
Melville, NY 11747
516/845-2700

# ENERGY

## Associations
*American Gas Association*
1515 Wilson Blvd.
Arlington, VA 22009
703/841-8600

*American Petroleum Institute*
1220 L St., NW
Ste. 900
Washington, DC 20005
202/682-8000

*National Coal Association*
1130 17th St., NW
Washington, DC 20036
202/463-2625

*National Petroleum Council*
1625 K St., NW
Washington, DC 20006
202/393-6100

## Directories
*Brown's Directory of North American &*
 *International Gas Companies*
131 W. First St.
Duluth, MN 55802
218/723-9200

*Oil & Gas Directory*
PO Box 130508
Houston, TX 77219
713/529-8789

*Whole World Oil Directory*
Reed Reference Publishing
121 Chanlon Rd.
New Providence, NJ 07974
800/323-6772

## Periodicals
*Coal*
29 N. Wacker Dr.
Chicago, IL 60606
312/726-8202
—Monthly magazine for coal industry
   executives in all areas, including
   administrative, engineering, and
   operations.

*Oil and Gas Journal*
PO Box 1260
Tulsa, OK 74101
918/835-3161
—Weekly magazine covering oil
   production, exploration, and marketing.

*Petroleum Marketing Management*
1801 Rockville Pike
Ste. 330
Rockville, MD 20852
301/984-7333
—Bimonthly for petroleum marketing
   professionals, including major company
   executives, independent marketers,
   distributors, etc.

*World Oil*
PO Box 2608
Houston, TX 77252
713/529-4301
—Monthly magazine for company owners,
   operating managers, geologists,
   production engineers, and drilling
   contractors.

# FASHION

## Associations
*American Apparel Manufacturers
   Association*
2500 Wilson Blvd.
Ste. 301
Arlington, VA 22201
703/524-1864

*Clothing Manufacturers Association of the
   USA*
1290 Ave. of the Americas
New York, NY 10104
212/757-6664

*International Association of Clothing
   Designers*
475 Park Ave. S.
New York, NY 10016
212/685-6602

## Directories
*AAMA Directory*
American Apparel Manufacturers
   Association
2500 Wilson Blvd.
Ste. 301
Arlington, VA 22201
703/524-1864

*Apparel Trades Book*
Dun & Bradstreet, Inc.
1 Diamond Hill Rd.
Murray Hill, NJ 07974
201/665-5000

*The Fashion Guide: International Designer
   Directory*
Fairchild Publications
7 W. 34th St.
New York, NY 10001
212/630-4000
800/247-6622

*The Fashion Resource Directory*
Fairchild Publications
7 W. 34th St.
New York, NY 10001
212/630-4000
800/247-6622

## Periodicals

*Apparel Industry Magazine*
6255 Barfield Rd.
Ste. 200
Atlanta, GA 30328-4300
404/252-8831
—Monthly magazine for people in all
aspects of apparel industry, including
designers, manufacturers, contractors,
suppliers.

*Bobbin*
PO Box 1986
Columbia, SC 29202
803/771-7500
—Monthly magazine for executives in
apparel manufacturing, textile milling,
retailing.

*Daily News Record*
7 W. 34th St.
New York, NY 10001
212/630-4000
800/247-6622
—Daily newspaper for apparel
manufacturers, wholesalers, buyers,
retailers, and jobbers.

*Footwear News*
7 W. 34th St.
New York, NY 10001
212/630-4000
800/247-6622
—Weekly newspaper covering footwear
industry for designers, buyers,
wholesalers, suppliers, etc.

*Women's Wear Daily*
7 W. 34th St.
New York, NY 10001
212/630-4000
800/247-6622
—Daily newspaper, considered the
industry "bible," covering women's
clothing industry.

## FILM AND ENTERTAINMENT

### Associations

*Academy of Motion Picture Arts and
   Sciences*
8949 Wilshire Blvd.
Beverly Hills, CA 90211
213/859-9619

*American Film Marketing Association*
12424 Wilshire Blvd.
Los Angeles, CA 90025
310/447-1555

*American Society of Cinematographers*
PO Box 2230
Los Angeles, CA 90213
213/876-5080
800/448-0145

*Directors Guild of America*
7920 Sunset Blvd.
Hollywood, CA 90046
310/289-2000

*Motion Picture Association of America*
1133 Ave. of the Americas
New York, NY 10036
212/840-6161

*National Academy of Recording Arts and
   Scientists*
3402 Pico Blvd.
Santa Monica, CA 90404
310/392-3777

*Recording Industry Association of America*
1020 19th St., NW
Washington, DC 20036
202/775-0101

*Society of Motion Picture and Television
   Engineers*
595 W. Hartsdale Ave.
White Plains, NY 10607
914/761-1100

## Directories

*Cash Box Annual World Wide Directory*
Cash Box
345 W. 58th St.
New York, NY 10019
212/245-4224

*International Motion Picture Almanac*
Quigley Publishing Co.
159 W. 53rd St.
New York, NY 10019
212/247-3100

*Radio & Records Ratings Report and Directory*
1930 Century Park W.
Los Angeles, CA 90067
310/553-4330

*Recording Engineer/Producer Black Book*
Intertec Publishing Corp.
9800 Metcalf
Overland Park, KS 66212-2215
913/341-1300

*Who's Who in the Motion Picture Industry*
Packard Publishing
PO Box 2187
Beverly Hills, CA 90213
213/854-0276

## Periodicals

*Back Stage*
1515 Broadway
New York, NY 10036
212/764-7300
—Weekly newspaper covering film production, entertainment, and television commercial production. Includes fairly extensive help-wanted ads.

*Billboard*
Billboard Publications, Inc.
1515 Broadway
New York, NY 10036
212/764-7300
—Covers music industry.

*Box Office*
6640 Sunset Blvd.
Ste. 100
Los Angeles, CA 90028
213/465-1186
—Aimed at people involved in film production and distribution, including theater owners, managers, operators, etc.

*Cash Box*
345 W. 58th St.
New York, NY 10019
212/245-4224
—Music industry magazine aimed at record manufacturers and distributors, music publishers, store owners, and recording artists.

*Daily Variety*
5700 Wilshire Blvd.
Los Angeles, CA 90036
213/857-6600

*Film Journal*
244 W. 49th St.
New York, NY 10019
212/246-6460

*Hollywood Reporter*
50755 Wilshire Blvd.
Los Angeles, CA 90036
213/525-2000

*Recording Engineer & Producer*
9800 Metcalf
Overland Park, KS 66212-2215
913/341-1300
—Covers music recording industry.

*Variety*
475 Park Ave. S.
New York, NY 10016
212/779-1100

# FINANCIAL SERVICES

## Associations

*Association for Investment Management
and Research*
PO Box 3668
Charlottesville, VA 22901
804/977-6600
—Operates free 24-hour job opportunities
hot line for members only.

*Commercial Finance Association*
225 W. 34th St.
Ste. 1815
New York, NY 10122
212/594-3490

*Financial Analysts Federation*
5 Boar's Head Lane
Charlottesville, VA 22903
804/980-3688
—Operates free 24-hour job opportunities
hot line for members only.

*Financial Executives Institute*
10 Madison Ave.
Morristown, NJ 07960
201/898-4600
—Offers members free career counseling,
job referrals, and other job hunting
services.

*Financial Managers Society*
85 Michigan Ave.
Ste. 500
Chicago, IL 60603
312/578-1300

*National Association of Credit
Management*
8815 Centre Park Dr.
Columbia, MD 21045
410/740-5560

*Securities Industry Association*
120 Broadway
New York, NY 10271
212/608-1500

## Directories

*Corporate Finance Sourcebook*
Reed Reference Publishing
121 Chanlon Rd.
New Providence, NJ 07974
800/323-6772

*Directory of American Financial
Institutions*
McFadden Business Publications
6195 Crooked Creek Rd.
Norcross, GA 30092
404/448-1011

*Moody's Bank & Finance Manual*
Moody's Investor Service
99 Church St.
New York, NY 10007
212/553-0300

*Securities Industry Yearbook*
Securities Industry Association
120 Broadway
New York, NY 10271
212/608-1500

## Periodicals

*Barron's National Business & Financial
Weekly*
200 Liberty St.
New York, NY 10281
212/416-2700
800/628-9320
—Weekly newspaper for finance
executives as well as investors in
general.

*Financial Services Report*
Philips Publishing
1201 Seven Locks Rd.
Ste. 300
Potomac, MD 20854
301/340-2100

*Financial World*
1328 Broadway
New York, NY 10001
212/594-5030
—Monthly aimed at commodities and
options traders.

*Institutional Investor*
488 Madison Ave.
New York, NY 10022
212/303-3300
—Monthly magazine aimed at people in
institutional investment, including
brokers, portfolio managers, financial
consultants, professional investors.

*Pensions & Investment Age*
220 E. 42nd St.
New York, NY 10017
212/210-0100
—Biweekly for pension plan managers,
executives, and administrators. Includes
help-wanted ads.

## FOOD AND BEVERAGE

### Associations
*American Bakers Association*
1350 I St., NW
Washington, DC 20005-3305
202/789-0300

*American Frozen Food Institute*
1764 Old Meadow Lane
McLean, VA 22102
703/821-0770

*Distilled Spirits Council of the United
    States*
1250 I St., NW
Ste. 900
Washington, DC 20005
202/628-3544

*Grocer Manufacturers Association*
1010 Wisconsin Ave., NW
Ste. 800
Washington, DC 20007
202/337-9400
—Puts out free annual directory.

*National Food Processors Association*
1401 New York Ave., NW
Ste. 400
Washington, DC 20005
202/639-5900

*National Soft Drink Association*
1101 16th St., NW
Washington, DC 20036
202/463-6732

### Directories
*American Frozen Food Industry Directory*
American Frozen Food Institute
1764 Old Meadow Lane
McLean, VA 22102
703/821-0770

*Food Engineer's Directory of US Food and
    Beverage Plants*
Chilton Book Co.
Chilton Way
Radnor, PA 19089
215/687-8200

*Hereld's 5000: The Directory of Leading
    U.S. Food, Confectionery, Beverage and
    Petfood Manufacturers*
200 Leeder Hill Dr.
Ste. 341
Hamden, CT 06517
203/281-6766

*Jobson's Handbook*
100 Ave. of the Americas
New York, NY 10013
212/274-7000
—Covers the alcoholic beverage industry.

### Periodicals
*Beverage World*
150 Great Neck Rd.
Great Neck, NY 11021
516/829-9210
—Monthly magazine for beverage industry
executives. Includes help-wanted ads.
Annual leading companies issue may be
useful for targeting a resume mailing
list.

*Food Business*
301 E. Erie St.
Chicago, IL 60611
312/664-2020

*Food Engineering*
Chilton Way
Radnor, PA 19089
215/964-4448
—Monthly aimed at range of food industry
  personnel, including food processors,
  equipment manufacturers, distributors,
  and retailers.

*Food Processing*
301 E. Erie St.
Chicago, IL 60611
312/664-2020
—Monthly magazine covering all aspects
  of food industry. Annual special issue
  useful for its industry roundup.

*Progressive Grocer*
263 Tresser Blvd.
Stamford, CT 06901-3218
203/325-3500
—Monthly magazine for grocery/
  supermarket executives, owners,
  operators, etc.

*Supermarket News*
7 W. 34th St.
New York, NY 10001
212/630-4230
800/247-2160
—Weekly tabloid for food store execs,
  managers, owners, etc.

## HEALTH SERVICES AND PHARMACEUTICALS

### Associations
*American Health Care Association*
1201 L St., NW
Washington, DC 20004-2037
202/783-2242

*American Hospital Association*
1840 N. Lake Shore Dr.
Chicago, IL 60611
312/280-6000
800/621-6902

*American Pharmaceutical Association*
2215 Constitution Ave., NW
Washington, DC 20037
202/628-4410

*Health Industry Distributors Association*
1200 G St., NW
Suite 400
Washington, DC 20005
202/783-8700
—Puts out low-cost annual directory.

*Healthcare Financial Management
  Association*
2 Westbrook Corporate Ctr.
Suite 700
Westchester, IL 60154
800/252-4362

*National Association of Pharmaceutical
  Manufacturers*
747 Third Ave.
New York, NY 10017
212/838-3720

*National Pharmaceutical Council*
1894 Preston White Dr.
Reston, VA 22091
703/620-5390

*Pharmaceutical Manufacturers Association*
1100 15th St., NW
Washington, DC 20005
202/835-3400

### Directories
*AHA Guide to the Health Care Field*
American Hospital Association
1840 N. Lake Shore Dr.
Chicago, IL 60611
312/280-6000
800/621-6902

*Billians Hospital Blue Book*
2100 Powers Ferry Rd.
Atlanta, GA 30339
404/955-5656
—Relatively low price, possibly useful for
  mailing lists.

*Biotechnology Directory*
49 W. 24th St.
New York, NY 10010
212/673-4400

*Dun's Guide to Healthcare Companies*
Dun's Marketing Services
3 Sylvan Way
Parsippany, NJ 07054-3896
201/605-6000

*Medical and Health Information Directory*
Gale Research, Inc.
835 Penobscot Bldg.
Detroit, MI 48226-4094
800/877-4253

*National Directory of Health Maintenance*
  *Organizations*
Group Health Association of America
1129 20th St., NW
Suite 600
Washington, DC 20036
303/778-3247

## Periodicals
*Healthcare Executive*
840 N. Lake Shore Dr.
Chicago, IL 60611
312/943-0544
—Bimonthly for health-care executives.

*Healthweek*
Box 10460
Eugene, OR 97401
503/343-1200
—Biweekly for health-service
  professionals, personnel at hospitals and
  HMOs, suppliers, nurses, physicians, etc.

*Modern Healthcare*
740 Rush St.
Chicago, IL 60606
312/649-5341
—Biweekly for health-service
  professionals.

*Pharmaceutical Processing*
PO Box 650
Morris Plains, NJ 07950
201/292-5100
—Monthly for people in pharmaceutical
  production, research and development,
  engineering, etc.

*Pharmaceutical Technology*
PO Box 10460
Eugene, OR 97401
503/343-1200

# HOSPITALITY (INCLUDING HOTELS AND RESTAURANTS)

## Associations
*American Hotel and Motel Association*
1201 New York Ave., NW
Washington, DC 20005
202/289-3100

*Hotel Sales and Marketing Association*
1300 L. St., NW
Ste. 800
Washington, DC 20005
202/789-0089

*International Food Service Executives*
  *Association*
1000 S. State Rd. 7
Ste. 103
Margate, FL 33068

*National Restaurant Association*
1200 17th St., NW
Ste. 800
Washington, DC 20036
202/331-5900

## Directories
*Chain Restaurant Operators: High Volume*
  *Independent Restaurants*
Lebhar-Friedman, Inc.
425 Park Ave.
New York, NY 10022
212/756-5000

*Directory of Hotel and Motel Systems;
    Hotel and Motel Red Book*
American Hotel Association Directory
    Corp.
1201 New York Ave., NW
Washington, DC 20005
202/289-3162

*Directory of Hotel/Motel Management
    Companies*
Advantstar
7500 Old Oak Blvd.
Cleveland, OH 44130
216/243-8100

*Foodservice Industry Directory*
National Restaurant Association
1200 17th St., NW
Suite 800
Washington, DC 20036
202/331-5900

*Who's Who in the Lodging Industry*
American Hotel and Motel Association
1201 New York Ave., NW
Washington, DC 20005
202/289-3100
—This relatively low-cost annual directory
    is also available on printed address
    labels.

## Periodicals
*Cornell Hotel and Restaurant
    Administration Quarterly*
Cornell University School of Hotel
    Administration
327 Statler Hall
Ithaca, NY 14853
607/255-5093

*Hotel and Motel Management*
7500 Old Oak Blvd.
Cleveland, OH 44130
216/243-8100
—Twenty-one-issue magazine aimed at
    hotel/motel executives.

*Hotels*
1350 E. Touhy Ave.
Des Plaines, IL 60018
708/635-8800

—Monthly aimed at hotel industry execs,
    developers, management firms, etc.

*Nation's Restaurant News*
425 Park Ave.
New York, NY 10022
212/756-5200
—Weekly tabloid for restaurant owners
    and food-service managers.

*Restaurant Business*
355 Park Ave. S.
New York, NY 10010
212/592-6500
—Eighteen-issue magazine for food-
    service-organization executives,
    manufacturers, and restaurant food
    distributors.

*Restaurant Hospitality*
1100 E. Superior Ave.
Cleveland, OH 44114
216/696-7000
—Monthly magazine for restaurant
    owners, managers, etc., aimed chiefly at
    table-service establishments.

*Restaurants and Institutions*
1350 E. Touhy Ave.
Des Plaines, IL 60018
708/635-8800
—Biweekly for hospitality industry
    managers.

# INSURANCE

## Associations
*American Insurance Association*
85 John St.
New York, NY 10038
212/669-0400

*Health Insurance Association of America*
1025 Connecticut Ave., NW
Ste. 1200
Washington, DC 20036
202/223-7780

*Insurance Information Institute*
110 William St.
New York, NY 10038
212/669-9200
—Members are insurance companies;
  group provides information to public,
  sponsors seminars, maintains library.

*Reinsurance Association of America*
1301 Pennsylvania Ave., NW
Suite 900
Washington, DC 20036
202/638-3690

## Directories
*Best's Insurance Reports*
Ambest Rd.
Oldwick, NJ 08858
908/439-2200

*Insurance Almanac*
Underwriter Printing & Publishing Co.
50 E. Palisades Ave.
Englewood, NJ 07631
201/569-8808
—Lists more than 3,000 insurance
  companies; national, state, and local
  insurance associations, agents, brokers,
  etc.

*Insurance Phone Book and Directory*
Reed Reference Publishing
121 Chanlon Rd.
New Providence, NJ 07974
800/323-6772

*Who's Who in Insurance*
Underwriter Printing & Publishing Co.
50 E. Palisades Ave.
Englewood, NJ 07631
201/569-8808
—Lists more than 5,000 individuals
  involved in the insurance industry;
  includes title, company affiliation,
  biographical information; may be useful
  in preparing for interviews.

## Periodicals
*American Agent and Broker*
330 N. Fourth St.
St. Louis, MO 63102
314/421-5445
—Monthly magazine for agents, brokers,
  department heads, and adjusters.

*Best's Review*
Ambest Rd.
Oldwick, NJ 08858
908/439-2200
—Monthly magazine; there are two
  different editions, *Life and Health* and
  *Property and Casualty.* Both are aimed at
  executives and include good help-
  wanted sections.

*Business Insurance*
740 Rush St.
Chicago, IL 60611
312/649-5200
—Weekly tabloid for those involved in
  corporate property, casualty, and
  employee insurance protection.

*Insurance Review*
110 William St.
New York, NY 10038
212/669-9200
—Monthly magazine for insurance
  industry executives and managers.

*National Underwriter*
43-47 Newark St.
Hoboken, NJ 07030
201/963-2300
—Weekly tabloid; there are two editions,
  *Life and Health* and *Property and
  Casualty,* both aimed at management.

## MANUFACTURING

## Associations
*American Hardware Manufacturers
  Association*
801 N. Plz. Dr.
Shaumberg, IL 60173
708/605-1025

*American Production and Inventory
    Control Society*
500 W. Annandale Rd.
Falls Church, VA 22046
703/237-8344

*Construction Industry Manufacturers
    Association*
111 E. Wisconsin Ave.
Milwaukee, WI 53202
414/272-0943

*Fabricators and Manufacturers Association
    International*
833 Featherstone Rd.
Rockford, IL 61107
815/399-8700

*National Association of Manufacturers*
1331 Pennsylvania Ave., NW
Ste. 1500, North Lobby
Washington, DC 20004-1703
202/637-3000

*Tooling and Manufacturing Association*
1177 S. Dee Rd.
Park Ridge, IL 60068
708/825-1120
—Offers job referral service and resume
  bank service for members.

## Directories
*American Manufacturers Directory*
American Business Directories
5711 S. 86th Cir.
Omaha, NE 68127
402/593-4600

*MacRAE's Blue Book, Inc.*
Business Research Publications, Inc.
817 Broadway
New York, NY 10003
212/673-4700
800/622-7237

*Moody's Industrial Manual*
Moody's Investor's Service, Inc.
99 Church St.
New York, NY 10007
212/553-0300

*Thomas Register of American
    Manufacturers; Thomas Register
    Catalog File*
Thomas Publishing Company
1 Penn Plz.
New York, NY 10119
212/290-7200

## Periodicals
*Design News*
275 Washington St.
Newton, MA 02158
617/964-3030
—Semimonthly magazine for design and
  technical engineers, managers, etc.

*Manufacturing Engineering*
PO Box 930
1 SME Dr.
Dearborn, MI 48121
313/271-1500
—Monthly put out by the Society of
  Manufacturing Engineers, aimed at
  engineers as well as plant managers,
  designers, technicians.

*Plant Services*
301 E. Erie St.
Chicago, IL 60611
312/644-2020
—Monthly for plant personnel in a range
  of fields, including maintenance,
  engineering, materials handling, and
  environment.

*Quality*
191 S. Gary Ave.
Wheaton, IL 60188
708/665-1000
—Monthly for managers, quality
  assurance engineers, inspectors, etc.

# METALS AND MINING

## Associations

*American Institute of Mining,*
  *Metallurgical, and Petroleum Engineers*
345 E. 47th St.
14th fl.
New York, NY 10017
212/705-7695

*American Iron and Steel Institute*
1101 17th St., NW
13th fl.
Washington, DC 20036
202/452-7100

*American Mining Congress*
1920 N St., NW
Washington, DC 20036
202/861-2800

*ASM International (American Society for*
  *Metals)*
9639 Kinsman
Materials Park, OH 44073
216/338-5151
—Publishes periodicals, which include
  help-wanted ads.

*Association of Iron and Steel Engineers*
3 Gateway Ctr.
Ste. 2350
Pittsburgh, PA 15222
412/281-6323

*Society of Mining Engineers*
Caller No. D
Littleton, CO 80127
303/973-9550
—Puts out monthly magazine.

*Steel Manufacturers Association*
1010 Wisconsin Ave.
Washington, DC 20036
202/452-7100

## Directories

*Directory of Iron and Steel Plants*
Association of Iron and Steel Engineers
3 Gateway Ctr.
Ste. 2350
Pittsburgh, PA 15222
412/281-6323

*Dun's Industrial Guide: The Metalworking*
  *Directory*
Dun's Marketing Services
3 Sylvan Way
Parsippany, NJ 07054-3896
201/605-6000

*Iron and Steel Works Directory of the*
  *United States and Canada*
American Iron and Steel Institute
1101 17th St., NW
13th fl.
Washington, DC 20036
202/452-7100

*Western Mining Directory*
Howell Publishing Company
PO Box 370510
Denver, CO 80237
303/770-6795
—Lists about 1,400 firms and
  organizations involved in mining in the
  West.

## Periodicals

*American Metal Market*
825 Seventh Ave.
New York, NY 10019
212/887-8550
—Daily newspaper covering the metals
  industry, aimed at executives, managers,
  etc.

*Engineering and Mining Journal*
29 N. Wacker Dr.
Chicago, IL 60606
312/726-2802
—Monthly.

*Iron Age*
191 S. Gary Ave.
Carol Stream, IL 60188
708/462-2286

*Mining World News*
90 W. Grove St.
Ste. 200
Reno, NV 89509
702/827-1115
—Monthly.

# PAPER AND FOREST PRODUCTS

## Associations
*Forest Products Research Society*
2801 Marshall Ct.
Madison, WI 53705
608/231-1361
—Puts out *Forest Products Journal.*

*Paper Industry Management Association*
2400 E. Oakton St.
Arlington Heights, IL 60005
708/956-0250
—Publishes *PIMA Magazine,* includes
  help-wanted section.

*Technical Association of the Pulp and
  Paper Industry*
15 Technology Pkwy. S.
Norcross, GA 30092
404/446-1400
—Puts out monthly magazine *TAPPI.*

## Directories
*Directory of the Forest Products Industry*
Miller Freeman Publications, Inc.
6600 Silacci Way
Gilroy, CA 95020
408/848-5296

*International Pulp and Paper Directory*
Miller Freeman Publications, Inc.
6600 Silacci Way
Gilroy, CA 95020
408/848-5296

*Lockwood-Post's Directory of the Paper,
  Pulp and Allied Trades*
Miller Freeman Publications, Inc.
6600 Silacci Way
Gilroy, CA 95020
408/848-5296

*Walden's ABC Guide and Paper Production
  Yearbook*
Walden-Mott Corporation
225 N. Franklin Tpk.
Ramsey, NJ 07446-1600
201/818-8630

## Periodicals
*Forest Industries*
600 Harrison St.
San Francisco, CA 94104
415/905-2200
—Monthly for forest industry executives,
  managers.

*Logger and Lumberman*
PO Box 489
Wadley, GA 30477
912/252-2537
—Monthly for forest industry managers,
  personnel.

*Pulp & Paper*
600 Harrison St.
San Francisco, CA 94104
415/905-2200
—Monthly for managers, supervisors,
  executives.

# PUBLISHING

## Associations
*American Business Press*
675 Third Ave.
Ste. 415
New York, NY 10017
212/661-6360
—Puts out monthly employment roundup
  with listings of jobs for members.

American Newspaper Association
11600 Sunrise Valley Dr.
Reston, VA 22091
703/648-1072
—Offers job hot line.

Association of American Publishers
220 E. 23rd St.
New York, NY 10010
212/689-8920

Magazine Publishers Association
575 Lexington Ave.
New York, NY 10022
212/752-0055

National Newspaper Association
1525 Wilson Blvd.
Ste. 550
Arlington, VA 22209
703/907-7900

## Directories
American Book Trade Directory
Reed Reference Publishing
121 Chanlon Rd.
New Providence, RI 07974
800/521-8110

Bacon's Publicity Checker
Bacon's Publishing Company
332 S. Michigan Ave.
Chicago, IL 60604
312/922-2400

Editor & Publisher International Yearbook
11 W. 19th St.
New York, NY 10011
212/675-4380

Editor & Publisher Market Guide
11 W. 19th St.
New York, NY 10011
212/675-4380

Gale Directory of Publications and
    Broadcast Media
Gale Research, Inc.
835 Penobscot Blding.
Detroit, MI 48226-4094
800/877-4253

Journalism Career and Scholarship Guide
The Dow Jones Newspaper Fund
PO Box 300
Princeton, NJ 08543
609/452-2820

Literary Marketplace; The Directory of
    American Book Publishing; International
    Literary Marketplace
Reed Reference Publishing
121 Chanlon Rd.
New Providence, NJ 07974
800/521-8110

Magazine Industry Marketplace
Reed Reference Publishing
121 Chanlon Rd.
New Providence, NJ 07974
800/521-8110

National Directory of Magazines
Oxbridge Communications
150 Fifth Ave.
New York, NY 10011
212/741-0231 (in New York)
800/955-0231

Publishers Directory
Gale Research, Inc.
835 Penobscot Bldg.
Detroit, MI 48226-4094
800/877-4253

Standard Periodical Directory
Gale Research, Inc.
835 Penobscot Bldg.
Detroit, MI 48226-4094
800/877-4253

Standard Periodical Directory
Oxbridge Communications
150 Fifth Ave.
New York, NY 10011
212/741-0231 (in New York)
800/955-0231

*Standard Rate & Data: Business
  Publications Rate and Data*
Standard Rate & Data Service
3004 Glenview Rd.
Wilmette, IL 60091
800/323-4588

*Ulrich's International Periodicals Directory*
Reed Reference Publishing
121 Chanlon Rd.
New Providence, NJ 07974
800/521-8110

## Periodicals
*Editor & Publisher*
11 W. 19th St.
New York, NY 10011
212/675-4380
—Weekly, with in-depth coverage of the
  newspaper industry and extensive help-
  wanted section.

*Magazine & Bookseller*
322 Eighth Ave.
New York, NY 10001
212/620-7330
—Monthly magazine for magazine and
  book retailers and wholesalers.

*Publishers Weekly*
249 W. 17th St.
New York, NY 10011
800/278-2991
—Weekly magazine, considered the
  industry "bible," covering all phases of
  book publishing, including production,
  design, sales, rights, and new book
  forecasts; extensive help-wanted
  section.

## REAL ESTATE AND CONSTRUCTION

## Associations
*American Society of Professional
  Estimators*
11141 Georgia Ave.
Ste. 412
Wheaton, MD 20902
301/929-8849

*American Subcontractors Association*
1004 Duke St.
Alexandria, VA 22314
703/684-3450

*Associated Builders and Contractors*
1300 N. 17th St.
Rosslyn, VA 22209
703/812-2000

*Associated General Contractors of America*
1957 E St., NW
Washington, DC 20006
202/393-2040

*Institute of Real Estate Management*
430 N. Michigan Ave.
Chicago, IL 60611
312/329-6000

*International Association of Corporate Real
  Estate Executives/National Association
  of Corporate Real Estate Executives*
4400 Columbia Dr.
Ste. 100
West Palm Beach, FL 33409
407/683-8111
—Publishes members-only newsletters,
  which contain job opportunities listings.

*National Association of Home Builders*
15th and M Sts., NW
Washington, DC 20005
202/822-0200

*National Association of Realtors*
430 N. Michigan Ave.
Chicago, IL 60611
312/329-8449
—Publishes *Real Estate Today.*

*National Constructors Association*
1730 M St., NW
Ste. 900
Washington, DC 20036
202/466-8880

## Directory
*The Real Estate Sourcebook*
Reed Reference Publishing
121 Chanlon Rd.
New Providence, NJ 07974
800/323-6772

## Periodicals
*Builder*
National Association of Home Builders
15th and M Sts., NW
Washington, DC 20005
202/822-0200

*Building Design and Construction*
PO Box 5080
Des Plaines, IL 60017-5080
708/635-8800
—Aimed at those involved in commercial
building, including engineers, general
contractors, subcontractors, architects.

*Buildings*
PO Box 1888
Cedar Rapids, IA 52406
319/364-6167
—Monthly magazine for developers,
building managers and owners,
management firms, etc.

*Engineering News-Record*
1221 Ave. of the Americas
New York, NY 10020
212/512-3549
—Weekly covering engineering, heavy and
industrial construction, etc., aimed
primarily at construction executives,
engineers, architects, contractors. Good
help-wanted section.

*Environmental Protection*
PO Box 2573
Waco, TX 76702
817/776-9000
—Covers pollution control, waste control
management, and hazardous waste
disposal.

*Environmental Waste Management*
243 W. Main St.
Kutztown, PA 19530
215/683-5098
—Monthly magazine for environmental
waste professionals—transporters,
shippers, generators, disposers, and
equipment manufacturers.

*Highway and Heavy Construction*
PO Box 5080
Des Plaines, IL 60017-5080
708/635-8800

*Journal of Property Management*
Institute of Real Estate Management
430 N. Michigan Ave.
Chicago, IL 60611
312/329-6000
—Association members-only magazine
that includes good help-wanted section.

*Nation's Building News*
National Association of Home Builders
15th and M Sts., NW
Washington, DC 20005
202/822-0200

*Professional Builder/Remodeler*
PO Box 5080
Des Plaines, IL 60017-5080
708/635-8800
—Magazine aimed at professionals in
construction, contracting, architecture,
etc.

*Water Engineering & Management*
380 Northwest Hwy.
Des Plaines, IL 60016
708/298-6622
—Monthly publication for designers,
construction personnel, and others in
waste water and water engineering.

# RETAILING
## (See also listings under Fashion.)

## Associations
*International Association of Chain Stores*
3800 Moor Pl.
Alexandria, VA 22305
703/683-3136

*International Council of Shopping Centers*
5665 Fifth Ave.
New York, NY 10022
212/421-8181

*International Mass Retail Association*
1901 Pennsylvania Ave.
10th fl.
Washington, DC 20006
202/861-0774

*National Retail Federation*
100 W. 31st St.
New York, NY 10001
212/631-7400

## Directories
*Directory of Consumer Electronics, Photography, and Major Appliance Retailers and Distributors*
Chain Store Guide Information Services
425 Park Ave.
New York, NY 10022
212/756-5252

*Directory of Department Stores*
Chain Store Guide Information Services
425 Park Ave.
New York, NY 10022
212/756-5252

*Directory of General Merchandise/Variety Chains and Specialty Stores*
Chain Store Guide Information Services
425 Park Ave.
New York, NY 10022
212/756-5252

*Fairchild's Financial Manual of Retail Stores*
Fairchild Publications
7 W. 34th St.
New York, NY 10001
212/630-4000
800/247-6622

## Periodicals
*Chain Store Age Executive*
425 Park Ave.
New York, NY 10022
212/756-5252
—Monthly magazine aimed at retail executives, managers, buyers, etc., at general merchandise, specialty chain, and department stores. Annual year-end roundups include rankings of top stores in different retail categories.

*Children's Business*
7 W. 34th St.
New York, NY 10001
212/630-4230
—Covers children's apparel and accessories.

*Discount Merchandiser*
233 Park Ave. S.
New York, NY 10003
212/979-4800
—Monthly magazine for discount store executives, managers, buyers, etc.

*Discount Store News*
425 Park Ave.
New York, NY 10022
212/756-5252
—Biweekly for discount store managers, operators, planners, merchandisers, etc.

*Drug Store News*
425 Park Ave.
New York, NY 10022
212/756-5252
—Biweekly for chain and independent drugstore execs, managers, pharmacists, manufacturers.

*HFD Retailing Home Furnishings*
7 W. 34th St.
New York, NY 10001
212/630-4800
—Weekly tabloid covering home
furnishings retailing.

*Mass Market Retailers*
220 Fifth Ave.
New York, NY 10001
212/213-6000
—Biweekly for headquarters execs of
chain drugstores, discount stores, and
supermarkets.

*Sportstyle*
7 W. 34th St.
New York, NY 10001
212/630-4230
—Semimonthly publication for sporting
goods and activewear retailers,
wholesalers, and manufacturers.

*STORES*
100 W. 31st St.
New York, NY 10001
212/244-8777
—Monthly magazine published by the
National Retail Federation, aimed at
retail executives. Annual directory issues
offer listings of leading stores.

# TELECOMMUNICATIONS

## Associations
*International Communications Association*
12750 Merritt Dr.
Ste. 710
Dallas, TX 75287
214/233-3889

*Telecommunications Association*
701 N. Haven Ave.
Ste. 200
Ontario, CAN 91764-4925
909/945-1122

*United States Telephone Association*
1401 H St., NW
Ste. 600
Washington, DC 20005
202/326-7300

## Directories
*The Mobil Communications Directory*
Phillips Publishing, Inc.
1201 Seven Locks Rd.
Ste. 300
Potomac, MD 20854
800/326-8638

*Statistics of the Local Exchange Carriers*
United States Telephone Association
1401 H. St., NW
Ste. 600
Washington, DC 20005
202/326-7300
—Lists top 150 U.S. telephone companies
and over 600 local exchange carriers.

*Telecommunications Directory*
Gale Research, Inc.
835 Penobscot Bldg.
Detroit, MI 48226
800/877-8638

*Telephone Engineer & Management
Directory*
Advanstar Communications
131 W. First St.
Duluth, MN 55802
218/723-9470

*Telephone Industry Directory and
Sourcebook*
Phillips Publishing, Inc.
1201 Seven Locks Rd.
Ste. 300
Potomac, MD 20854
301/340-2100

## Periodicals

*America's Network*
233 N. Michigan Ave.
2 Illinois Center
24th fl.
Chicago, IL 60601
312/938-2378
—Semimonthly magazine for telephone company managers, engineers, executives, etc.

*Communications Magazine*
6300 S. Syracuse Way
Ste. 650
Englewood, CO 80111
303/220-0600
—Monthly magazine for telecommunications professionals, including those in sales, management, and technical positions.

*Telecommunications*
685 Canton St.
Norwood, MA 02062
617/769-9750
—Monthly magazine for telecommunications engineers and managers involved in telecommunications buying or specifications.

*Telephony*
55 E. Jackson Blvd.
Chicago, IL 60604
312/922-2435
—Weekly magazine for engineers, specifiers, buyers, etc.

# TRANSPORTATION

## Associations

*American Bureau of Shipping*
2 World Trade Ctr.
106th fl.
New York, NY 10048
212/839-5000

*American Maritime Association*
485 Madison Ave.
15th fl.
New York, NY 10022
212/319-9217

*American Trucking Association*
2200 Mill Rd.
Alexandria, VA 22314
708/838-1700
—Puts out weekly publication *Transport Topics,* which includes a strong help-wanted section and is available to nonmembers as well as members.

*Association of American Railroads*
American Railroad Building
50 F St., NW
Washington, DC 20001
202/639-2100

*Industrial Truck Association*
1750 K St., NW
Ste. 460
Washington, DC 20006
202/296-9880

*National Association of Fleet Administrators/National Association of Fleet Managers*
120 Wood Ave. S.
Iselin, NJ 08830
908/494-8100

*National Motor Freight Traffic Association*
2200 Mill Rd.
Alexandria, VA 22314
703/838-1821

*Transportation Institute*
5201 Auth Way
Fall Springs, MD 20746
202/347-2590

## Directories

*American Motor Carrier Directory*
K-III Press, Inc.
424 W. 33rd St.
New York, NY 10001
212/714-3100

*Directory of Truckload Carriers*
Optimum Transportation Services
210 Teaberry Ln.
Clarks Summit, PA 18411
717/586-9023

*Moody's Transportation Manual*
99 Church St.
New York, NY 19997
212/553-0300

*National Tank Truck Carrier Directory*
2200 Mill Rd.
Alexandria, VA 22314
703/838-1960

*Official Railway Guide—North American*
  *Freight Service Edition*
K-III Press, Inc.
424 W. 33rd St.
New York, NY 10001
212/714-3100

## Periodicals
*American Shipper*
PO Box 4728
Jacksonville, FL 32201
904/355-2601
—Monthly magazine aimed at those in the
  shipping industry, including ship and
  barge operators, traffic and export
  managers, manufacturers, and service
  agencies.

*Commercial Carrier Journal*
201 King of Prussia Rd.
Radnor, PA 19089
215/964-4523
—Monthly publication for executives in
  truck fleets, long and short haul, volume
  buses, etc.

*Distribution*
201 King of Prussia Rd.
Radnor, PA 19089
215/964-4384
—Monthly magazine for traffic and
  transportation managers and executives,
  shippers, packers, etc.

*Inbound Logistics*
5 Penn Plz.
8th fl.
New York, NY 10001
212/629-1560
—Monthly magazine for people in inbound
  freight transportation.

*Pro Trucker*
610 Colonial Park Dr.
Roswell, GA 30075
404/587-0311
—Monthly magazine for professional
  drivers, fleet operators, etc.

*Progressive Railroading*
230 W. Monroe
Ste. 2210
Chicago, IL 60606
312/629-1200
—Monthly magazine for railroad
  operations and maintenance officials,
  etc.

*Railway Age*
345 Hudson St.
New York, NY 10014
212/620-7200
—Monthly magazine covering railroads
  and rapid transit systems.

*Shipping Digest*
51 Madison Ave.
New York, NY 10010
212/689-4411
—Weekly magazine aimed at executives
  involved in overseas exporting.

# TRAVEL

## Associations
*American Society of Travel Agents*
1101 King St.
Alexandria, VA 22314
703/739-2782

*Institute of Certified Travel Agents*
148 Linden St.
PO Box 612059
617/237-0280


*Travel Industry Association of America*
1133 21st St.
Washington, DC 20036
202/293-1433


## Directory
*World Travel Directory*
Travel Weekly
Reed Travel Group
500 Plaza Dr.
Secaucus, NJ 07096
201/902-2000


## Periodicals
*Business Travel News*
600 Community Dr.
Manhasset, NY 11030
516/562-5000
—Thirty-six-issue magazine for those in
corporate travel—including corporate
travel managers, agencies with business
travel practice, and more general travel
companies, such as airlines.


*Travel Agent*
801 Second Ave.
New York, NY 10017
212/370-5050
—Weekly magazine for travel agents, tour
operators, executives, and others in the
travel industry.


*Travel Trade*
15 W. 44th St.
New York, NY 10036
212/730-6600
—Weekly periodical for travel agency
personnel (salespeople, executives,
reservation clerks, etc.) as well as tour
operators, resort personnel, and related
areas.

*Travel Weekly*
500 Plaza Dr.
Secaucus, NJ 07096
201/902-2000
—Weekly tabloid covering all aspects of
the travel industry, aimed at agency
personnel, sales and promotion staffers,
tour operators, hospitality industry
personnel, and more. The industry
"bible."


# UTILITIES

## Associations
*American Public Gas Association*
PO Box 11094D
Lee Hwy.
Ste. 102
Fairfax, VA 22030
703/352-3890


*American Public Power Association*
2301 M St., NW
Washington, DC 20037
202/467-2970


*National Rural Electric Cooperative
   Association*
1800 Massachusetts Ave., NW
Washington, DC 20036
202/857-9500
—Maintains resume listing service for
members.


*National Utility Contractors Association*
4301 N. Fairfax Dr.
Ste. 360
Arlington, VA 22203-1627
703/358-9300

## Directories
*American Public Gas Association Directory*
American Public Gas Association
PO Box 11094D
Lee Hwy.
Ste. 102
Fairfax, VA 22030
703/352-3890

*Directory of Gas Utility Companies*
Midwest Oil Register, Inc.
1120 E. Fourth St.
Tulsa, OK 74120-3220
918/582-2000

*Electrical World Directory of Electric
    Utilities*
McGraw-Hill, Inc.
1221 Ave. of the Americas
New York, NY 10020
212/391-4570

*Moody's Public Utility Manual*
99 Church St.
New York, NY 10007
212/553-0300

## Periodicals
*Electrical World*
11 W. 19th St.
New York, NY 10011
212/337-4072

—Monthly magazine for electric utility
    executives, managers, engineers, and
    related areas, including students.

*Public Power*
American Public Power Association
2301 M St., NW
Washington, DC 20037
202/467-2900

*Public Utilities Fortnightly*
2111 Wilson Blvd.
Arlington, VA 22201
703/243-7000
—Semimonthly for utility executives,
    managers, engineers, and other
    personnel.

*Transmission & Distribution*
707 Westchester Ave.
Ste. 101
White Plains, NY 10604
914/949-8500
—Monthly magazine for electric utilities
    executives, engineers, etc.

# REGIONAL SOURCES (BY STATE)

## ALABAMA

### Business Periodical
*Business Alabama Monthly*
PMT Publishing
2465 Commercial Park Dr.
Mobile, AL 36606
205/473-6269
—Puts out annual "Top Public
    Companies" issue, listing leading area
    companies.

### Directories
*Alabama Business Directory*
American Business Directories
5711 S. 86th Cir.
PO Box 27347
Omaha, NE 68127
402/593-4600

*Alabama Directory of Mining and
    Manufacturing*
Harris Publishing Company
2057 Aurora Rd.
Twinsburg, OH 44087
216/425-5900
800/888-5900

*Alabama Industrial Directory*
Alabama Development Office
c/o State Capitol
Montgomery, AL 36130
205/263-0048

*Alabama Manufacturers Register*
Manufacturers' News, Inc.
1633 Central St.
Evanston, IL 60201
708/864-7000

*Southeastern Regional Manufacturers
    Directory*
George D. Hall Co.
50 Congress St.
Boston, MA 02109
617/523-3745
—Includes Alabama, Georgia, and
    Mississippi.

## Government Employment Offices
*Office of Personnel Management*
520 Wynn Dr., NW
Huntsville, AL 35816
205/837-0894
—Federal job-service center.

*Employment Service*
Dept. of Industrial Relations
649 Monroe St.
Montgomery, AL 36130
205/242-8055
—State job-service center.

## ALASKA

## Business Periodical
*Alaska Business*
PO Box 241288
Anchorage, AK 99524
907/276-4373

## Directory
*Alaska Business Directory*
American Business Directories
5711 S. 86th Cir.
PO Box 27347
Omaha, NE 68127
402/593-4600

## Government Employment Offices
*Office of Personnel Management*
222 W. Seventh Ave.
PO Box 22
Anchorage, AK 99513
907/271-5821
—Federal job-service center.

*Employment Service*
Employment Security Div.
PO Box 25509
Juneau, AK 99802
907/465-2712
—State job-service center.

## ARIZONA

## Business Periodicals
*Arizona Business Gazette*
PO Box 1950
Phoenix, AZ 85004
602/271-7300

*The Business Journal*
2910 N. Central Ave.
Phoenix, AZ 85012
602/230-8400

## Directories
*Arizona Business Directory*
American Business Directories
5711 S. 86th Cir.
PO Box 27347
Omaha, NE 68127
402/593-4600

*Arizona Industrial Directory*
Manufacturers' News, Inc.
1633 Central St.
Evanston, IL 60201
708/864-7000

## Government Employment Offices
*Office of Personnel Management*
3225 N. Central Ave.
Ste. 1415
Phoenix, AZ 85012
602/640-4800
—Federal job-service center.

*Department of Employment Security*
PO Box 6123
Site Code 730A
Phoenix, AZ 85005
602/542-4016
—State job-service center.

## ARKANSAS

### Business Periodical
*Memphis Business Journal*
Mid-South Communications, Inc.
88 Union
Ste. 102
Memphis, TN 38103
901/523-1000
—Covers business in Memphis area, including western Tennessee.

### Directories
*Arkansas Business Directory*
American Business Directories
5711 S. 86th Cir.
PO Box 27347
Omaha, NE 68127
402/593-4600

*Directory of Arkansas Manufacturers*
Arkansas Industrial Development
  Foundation
PO Box 1784
Little Rock, AR 72203
501/682-1121

### Government Employment Offices
*Office of Personnel Management*
—Federal job-service center; see Texas listing.

*Employment Security Division*
PO Box 2981
Little Rock, AR 72203
501/682-2127
—State job-service center.

## CALIFORNIA

### Business Periodicals
*Long Beach Business*
2599 E. 28th St.
Long Beach, CA 90806
310/988-1222

*Los Angeles Business Journal*
5700 Wilshire Blvd.
Ste. 170
Los Angeles, CA 90036
213/549-5225

*San Diego Business Journal*
4909 Murphy Canyon Rd.
San Diego, CA 92123
619/277-6359

*San Francisco Business Times*
275 Battery St.
San Francisco, CA 94111
415/989-2522

### Directories
*California Business Directory*
American Business Directories
5711 S. 86th Cir.
PO Box 27347
Omaha, NE 68127
402/593-4600

*California Manufacturers Register*
Database Publishing Co.
523 Superior Ave.
Newport Beach, CA 92663
800/888-8434

*San Diego County Business Directory*
Database Publishing Co.
523 Superior Ave.
Newport Beach, CA 92663
800/888-8434

*Southern California Business Directory and
  Buyers Guide*
Database Publishing Co.
523 Superior Ave.
Newport Beach, CA 92663
800/888-8434

### Government Employment Offices
*Office of Personnel Management*
211 Main St.
San Francisco, CA 94105
415/744-5260
—Regional OPM headquarters.

*Office of Personnel Management*
Greater Los Angeles job hot line:
   818/575-6510
—Federal job-service center.

*Office of Personnel Management*
1029 J. St.
2d fl.
Sacramento, CA 95814
(mail only)
Street address:
4695 Watt Ave.
North Highlands, CA
—Federal job-service center.

*Office of Personnel Management*
Federal Bldg.
Rm. 4-S-9
880 Front St.
San Diego, CA 92188
619/557-6165
—Federal job-service center.

*Office of Personnel Management*
PO Box 7405
San Francisco, CA 94120
(mail only)
Street address:
211 Main St.
2d fl., Rm. 235
San Francisco, CA 94105
415/744-5627
—Federal job-service center.

*Job Service Division*
Employment Development Dept.
800 Capitol Mall
Sacramento, CA 95814
916/227-0300
—State job-service center.

## COLORADO

### Business Periodicals
*Boulder County Business Report*
4885 Riverbend Rd.
Ste. D
Boulder, CO 80301
303/440-4950

*Denver Business Journal*
1700 Broadway
Ste. 515
Denver, CO 80290
303/837-3500

### Directory
*Colorado Business Directory*
American Business Directories
5711 S. 86th Cir.
PO Box 27347
Omaha, NE 68127
402/593-4600

### Government Employment Offices
*Office of Personnel Management*
PO Box 25167
Denver, CO 89225
(mail only)
Street address:
12345 W. Alameda Pkwy.
Lakewood, CO
303/969-7050
—Federal job-service center.

*Employment Program*
Div. of Employment and Training
600 Grant St.
9th fl.
Denver, CO 80203-3528
303/837-3805
—State job-service center.

## CONNECTICUT

### Directories
*Connecticut Business Directory*
American Business Directories
5711 S. 86th Cir.
PO Box 27347
Omaha, NE 68127
402/593-4600

*Connecticut, Rhode Island Directory of
   Manufacturers*
Commerce Register, Inc.
190 Godwin Ave.
Midland Park, NJ 07432
201/445-3000

*Connecticut Service Directory*
George D. Hall Co.
50 Congress St.
Boston, MA 02109
617/523-3745

*Directory of Connecticut Manufacturers*
George D. Hall Co.
50 Congress St.
Boston, MA 02109
617/523-3745

*MacRAE's State Industrial Directory—*
*Connecticut, Rhode Island*
MacRAE's Blue Book, Inc.
817 Broadway
New York, NY 10003
212/673-4700
800/MAC-RAES

## Government Employment Offices
*Office of Personnel Management*
—Federal job-service center; see
Massachusetts listing.

*Job Service*
Connecticut Labor Dept.
200 Folly Brook Blvd.
Wethersfield, CT 06109
203/566-5160
—State job-service center, lists local state
job offices.

*State Recruitment and Testing Center*
1 Hartford Sq. E.
Ste. 101A
Hartford, CT 06106
203/566-2501

## DELAWARE

### Directories
*Delaware Business Directory*
American Business Directories
5711 S. 86th Cir.
PO Box 27347
Omaha, NE 68127
402/593-4600

*Delaware Directory of Commerce &*
*Industry*
Manufacturers' News, Inc.
1633 Central St.
Evanston, IL 60201
708/864-7000

*The Delaware Valley Corporate Guide*
Corfacts, Inc.
50 Rte. 9 N.
Morganville, NJ 07751
908/972-2500

*Directory of Central Atlantic States*
*Manufacturers*
George D. Hall Co.
50 Congress St.
Boston, MA 02109
617/523-3745
—Includes Maryland, Delaware, Virginia,
West Virginia, North Carolina, and South
Carolina.

*MacRAE's State Industry Directory—*
*Maryland/DC/Delaware*
MacRAE's Blue Book, Inc.
817 Broadway
New York, NY 10003
212/673-4700
800/MAC-RAES

## Government Employment Offices
*Office of Personnel Management*
—Federal job-service center; see
Philadelphia, PA, listing.

*Employment and Training Division*
Delaware Dept. of Labor
PO Box 9499
Newark, DE 19711
302/368-6911
—State job-service center.

## DISTRICT OF COLUMBIA

### Business Periodical
*Regardie's Business Washington*
1010 Wisconsin Ave., NW
Washington, DC 20007
202/343-0410

## Directories

*Dalton's Baltimore-Washington
  Metropolitan Directory*
Dalton's Directory
410 Lancaster Ave.
Haverford, PA 19041
215/649-2680
800/221-1050

*MacRAE's State Industrial Directory—
  Maryland/DC/Delaware*
MacRAE's Blue Book, Inc.
817 Broadway
New York, NY 10003
212/673-4700
800/MAC-RAES

*Washington, DC, Business Directory*
American Business Directories
5711 S. 86th Cir.
PO Box 27347
Omaha, NE 68127
402/593-4600

## Government Employment Offices

*Office of Personnel Management*
1900 E St., NW
Rm. 1416
Washington, DC 20415
202/653-8468
—Federal job-service center.

*Office of Job Service*
Dept. of Employment Services
500 C St., NW
Rm. 317
Washington, DC 20001
202/724-7050
—State job-service center.

## FLORIDA

## Business Periodicals

*Florida Trend*
PO Box 611
St. Petersburg, FL 33731
813/821-5800

*Miami Today*
PO Box 1368
Miami, FL 33101
305/579-0211

*Orlando Magazine*
PO Box 2207
Orlando, FL 32802
407/539-3939

*South Florida Business Journal*
1050 Lee Wagner Blvd.
Ft. Lauderdale, FL 33315
305/359-2100

*Tampa Bay Business*
PO Box 24185
Tampa, FL 33623
813/289-8225

## Directories

*Florida Business Directory*
American Business Directories
5711 S. 86th Cir.
PO Box 27347
Omaha, NE 68127
402/593-4600

*Florida Manufacturers Register*
Manufacturer's News, Inc.
1633 Central St.
Evanston, IL 60201
708/864-7000

## Government Employment Offices

*Office of Personnel Management*
Commodore Bldg.
Ste. 125
3444 McCrory Pl.
Orlando, FL 32803-3701
407/648-6148
—Federal job-service center.

*Dept. of Labor and Employment Security*
1320 Executive Ctr. Dr.
300 Atkins Bldg.
Tallahassee, FL 32301
904/488-7228
—State job-service center.

## GEORGIA

### Business Periodicals
*Atlanta Business Chronicle*
1801 Peachtree St., NE
Ste. 150
Atlanta, GA 30309
404/249-1000

*Georgia Trend*
1770 Indian Trail Rd.
Ste. 440
Norcross, GA 30093
404/806-6900

### Directories
*Georgia Business Directory*
American Business Directories
5711 S. 86th Cir.
PO Box 27347
Omaha, NE 68127
402/593-4600

*Georgia Manufacturers Register*
Manufacturers' News, Inc.
1633 Central St.
Evanston, IL 60201
708/864-7000

*Georgia Manufacturing Directory*
Dept. of Industry, Trade and Tourism
Marquis II Tower
Ste. 1100
285 Peachtree Center Ave.
PO Box 56706
Atlanta, GA 30343
404/656-3607

*Southeastern Regional Manufacturers
   Directory*
George D. Hall Co.
50 Congress St.
Boston, MA 02109
617/523-3745
—Includes Alabama, Georgia, and
  Mississippi.

### Government Employment Offices
*Office of Personnel Management*
Richard B. Russell Federal Bldg.
75 Spring St., SW
Atlanta, GA 30303-3109
—Federal job-service center.

*Employment Service*
148 International Blvd. N.
Rm. 400
Atlanta, GA 30303
404/656-3017
—State job-service center.

## HAWAII

### Business Periodicals
*Hawaii Business*
PO Box 913
Honolulu, HI 96808
808/946-3978

*Pacific Business News*
PO Box 833
Honolulu, HI 96808
808/521-0021

### Directories
*Directory of Manufacturers*
Chamber of Commerce of Hawaii
735 Bishop St.
Honolulu, HI 96813
808/545-4300

*Hawaii Business Directory*
American Business Directories
5711 S. 86th Cir.
PO Box 27347
Omaha, NE 68127
402/593-4600

### Government Employment Offices
*Office of Personnel Management*
Federal Bldg.
Rm. 5316
300 Ala Moana Blvd.
Honolulu, HI 96850
808/541-2791
(for outer islands and Pacific area: 808/541-
  2784)
—Federal job-service center.

Employment Service Division
Dept. of Labor and Industrial Relations
830 Punchbowl St.
Rm. 12
Honolulu, HI 96813
808/586-8711
—State job-service center.

# IDAHO

## Business Periodical
Idaho Business Review
4218 Emerald St.
PO Box 7193
Boise, ID 83707
208/336-3768

## Directories
Idaho Business Directory
American Business Directories
5711 S. 86th Cir.
PO Box 27347
Omaha, NE 68127
402/593-4600

Idaho Manufacturing Directory
Center for Business Development and
    Research
College of Business and Economics
University of Idaho
Moscow, ID 83483
208/885-6611

Inland Northwest Manufacturing Directory
Spokane Area Economic Development
    Council
N. 221 Wall
Ste. 310
Box 203
Spokane, WA 99210
509/624-9285
—Covers western Montana, northern
    Idaho and Oregon, and eastern
    Washington.

# ILLINOIS

## Business Periodicals
Crain's Chicago Business
740 N. Rush St.
Chicago, IL 60611
312/649-5370
—Publishes yearly directory of leading
    area companies.

The Wall Street Journal (Midwestern
    Edition)
Dow Jones & Co.
1 S. Wacker Dr.
Chicago, IL 60606
312/750-4000

## Directories
Harris Illinois Industrial Directory
Harris Publishing Company
2057 Aurora Rd.
Twinsburg, OH 44087
216/425-5900
800/888-5900

Illinois Business Directory
American Business Directories
5711 S. 86th Cir.
PO Box 27347
Omaha, NE 68127
402/593-4600

Illinois Manufacturers Register
Manufacturers' News, Inc.
1633 Central St.
Evanston, IL 60201
708/864-7000

Illinois Services Register
Manufacturers' News, Inc.
1633 Central St.
Evanston, IL 60201
708/864-7000

## Government Employment Office
*Office of Personnel Management*
(Regional federal office)
175 W. Jackson Blvd.
Rm. 530
Chicago, IL 60604
312/353-2922
312/353-6192 (job-service line)
—Federal job-service center; for Madison and St. Clair, see Missouri listing.

## INDIANA

### Business Periodical
*Indiana Business*
1200 Waterway Blvd.
Indianapolis, IN 46202
317/692-1200

### Directories
*Harris Indiana Industrial Directory*
Harris Publishing Company
2057 Aurora Rd.
Twinsburg, OH 44087
216/425-5900
800/888-5900

*Indiana Business Directory*
American Business Directories
5711 S. 86th Cir.
PO Box 27347
Omaha, NE 68127
402/593-4600

*Indiana Manufacturers Directory*
Manufacturers' News, Inc.
1633 Central St.
Evanston, IL 60201
708/864-7000

### Government Employment Office
*Office of Personnel Management*
—See Michigan listing or call 313/226-6950.

## IOWA

### Business Periodical
*Business Record*
100 Fourth St.
Des Moines, IA 50309
515/288-3336

### Directories
*Directory of Iowa Manufacturers*
Harris Publishing Company
2057 Aurora Rd.
Twinsburg, OH 44087
216/425-5900
800/888-5900

*Iowa Business Directory*
American Business Directories
5711 S. 86th Cir.
PO Box 27347
Omaha, NE 68127
402/593-4600

*Iowa Manufacturers Register*
Manufacturers' News, Inc.
1633 Central St.
Evanston, IL 60201
708/864-7000

### Government Employment Offices
*Office of Personnel Management*
—Federal job-service center; see listing for Missouri; phone 816/426-7757.

*Job Service Program Bureau*
Department of Job Service
818 Fifth Ave.
Des Moines, IA 50309
515/283-5208
—State job-service center.

## KANSAS

### Business Periodical
*Wichita Business Journal*
American City Business Journal
110 S. Main St.
Ste. 202
Wichita, KS 67202
316/267-6406

### Directory
*Kansas Business Directory*
American Business Directories
5711 S. 86th Cir.
PO Box 27347
Omaha, NE 68127
402/593-4600

### Government Employment Offices
*Office of Personnel Management*
—Federal job-service center; see Missouri listing.

*Division of Employment and Training*
Dept. of Human Resources
401 SW Topeka Blvd.
Topeka, KS 66603-3182
913/296-5317
—State job-service center.

## KENTUCKY

### Business Periodical
*Business First*
111 W. Washington St.
PO Box 40201
Louisville, KY 40202-1311
502/583-1731

### Directories
*Harris Kentucky Industrial Directory*
Harris Publishing Company
2057 Aurora Rd.
Twinsburg, OH 44087
216/425-5900
800/888-5900

*Kentucky Business Directory*
American Business Directories
5711 S. 86th Cir.
PO Box 27347
Omaha, NE 68127
402/593-4600

*Kentucky Directory of Manufacturers*
Department of Business and Industry
Capital Plaza Tower
Frankfort, KY 40601
502/564-4886

*Kentucky Manufacturers Register*
Manufacturers' News, Inc.
1633 Central St.
Evanston, IL 60201
708/864-7000

### Government Employment Offices
*Office of Personnel Management*
—See Ohio listing.

*Dept. for Employment Services*
275 E. Main St.
2d fl.
Frankfort, KY 40621
502/564-5331
—State job-service center.

## LOUISIANA

### Business Periodical
*Baton Rouge Business Report*
Louisiana Business, Inc.
PO Box 1949
Baton Rouge, LA 70821
504/928-1700

### Directories
*Directory of Louisiana Manufacturers*
Department of Economic Development
PO Box 94185
Capitol Station
Baton Rouge, LA 70804-9185
504/342-5383

*Greater Baton Rouge Manufacturers Directory*
Greater Baton Rouge Chamber of Commerce
564 Laurel St.
PO Box 3217
Baton Rouge, LA 70821
504/381-7125

*Louisiana Business Directory*
American Business Directories
5711 S. 86th Cir.
PO Box 27347
Omaha, NE 68127
402/593-4600

*Louisiana Manufacturers Register*
Manufacturers' News, Inc.
1633 Central St.
Evanston, IL 60201
708/864-7000

## Government Employment Offices
*Office of Personnel Management*
8610 Broadway
Ste. 305
San Antonio, TX 78217
210/805-2402
—Federal job-service center.

*Employment Service*
Office of Employment Security
PO Box 94094
Baton Rouge, LA 70804-9094
504/342-3016
—State job-service center.

## MAINE

### Directories
*MacRAE's State Directories—Maine/New Hampshire/Vermont*
MacRAE's Blue Book, Inc.
817 Broadway
New York, NY 10003
212/673-4700
800/MAC-RAES

*Maine Business Directory*
American Business Directories
5711 S. 86th Cir.
PO Box 27347
Omaha, NE 68127
402/593-4600

*Maine, Vermont, New Hampshire Directory of Manufacturers*
Commerce Register, Inc.
190 Godwin Ave.
Midland Park, NJ 07432
201/445-3000

## Government Employment Offices
*Office of Personnel Management*
—Federal job-service center; see New Hampshire listing.

*Job Service Division*
Bureau of Employment Security
PO Box 309
Augusta, ME 04330
207/287-3431

## MARYLAND

### Business Periodicals
*Baltimore Business Journal*
117 Water St.
Baltimore, MD 21202
410/576-1161

*Warfield's Baltimore*
11 E. Saratoga St.
Baltimore, MD 21202
410/725-1717

### Directories
*Dalton's Baltimore-Washington Metropolitan Directory*
Dalton's Directory
410 Lancaster Ave.
Haverford, PA 19041
215/649-2680
800/221-1050

*Directory of Central Atlantic States
   Manufacturers*
George D. Hall Co.
50 Congress St.
Boston, MA 02109
617/523-3745
—Includes Maryland, Delaware, Virginia,
West Virginia, North Carolina, and South
Carolina.

*Harris Directory of Maryland
   Manufacturers*
Harris Publishing Company
2057 Aurora Rd.
Twinsburg, OH 44087
216/425-5900
800/888-5900

*MacRAE's State Directories—Maryland/
   DC/Delaware*
MacRAE's Blue Book, Inc.
817 Broadway
New York, NY 10003
212/673-4700
800/MAC-RAES

*Maryland Business Directory*
American Business Directories
5711 S. 86th Cir.
PO Box 27347
Omaha, NE 68127
402/593-4600

## Government Employment Offices
*Office of Personnel Management*
Garmatz Federal Bldg.
101 W. Lombard St.
Baltimore, MD 21201
410/962-3822
—Federal job-service center.

*Maryland Dept. of Employment and
   Economic Development*
1100 N. Eutaw St.
Rm. 701
Baltimore, MD 21201
410/333-5187
—State job-service center.

# MASSACHUSETTS

## Business Periodical
*Boston Business Journal*
200 High St.
4th fl.
Boston, MA 02210
617/330-1000
—Weekly.

## Directories
*Directory of Massachusetts Manufacturers*
George D. Hall Co.
50 Congress St.
Boston, MA 02109
617/523-3745

*Directory of New England Manufacturers*
George D. Hall Co.
50 Congress St.
Boston, MA 02109
617/523-3745

*MacRAE's State Directories—
   Massachusetts/Rhode Island*
MacRAE's Blue Book, Inc.
817 Broadway
New York, NY 10003
212/673-4700
800/MAC-RAES

*Massachusetts Business Directory*
American Business Directories
5711 S. 86th Cir.
PO Box 27347
Omaha, NE 68127
402/593-4600

*Massachusetts Directory of Manufacturers*
Commerce Register, Inc.
190 Godwin Ave.
Midland Park, NJ 07432
201/445-3000

*Massachusetts Service Directory*
George D. Hall Co.
50 Congress St.
Boston, MA 02109
617/523-3745

## Government Employment Offices
*Office of Personnel Management*
Thomas P. O'Neill Federal Bldg.
10 Causeway St.
Boston, MA 02222-1031
617/565-5900
—Federal job-service center.

*Dept. of Employment Security and
  Training*
Charles F. Hurley Bldg.
Government Ctr.
Boston, MA 02114
617/727-6660

## MICHIGAN

## Business Periodicals
*Corporate Detroit*
26111 Evergreen Rd.
Ste. 303
Southfield, MI 48076
313/357-8300

*Crain's Detroit Business*
1400 Woodbridge St.
Detroit, MI 48207
313/446-6032

*Michigan Business*
2611 Evergreen Rd.
Ste. 303
Southfield, MI 48076-4499
313/357-8300

## Directories
*Harris Michigan Industrial Directory*
Harris Publishing Company
2057 Aurora Rd.
Twinsburg, OH 44087
216/425-5900
800/888-5900

*Michigan Business Directory*
American Business Directories
5711 S. 86th Cir.
PO Box 27347
Omaha, NE 68127
402/593-4600

## Government Employment Offices
*Office of Personnel Management*
477 Michigan Ave.
Rm. 565
Detroit, MI 48226
313/226-6950
—Federal job-service center.

*Bureau of Employment Service*
Employment Security Division
7310 Woodward Ave.
Detroit, MI 48202
313/876-5309
—State job-service center.

## MINNESOTA

## Business Periodicals
*Corporate Report Minnesota*
5500 Wayzata Blvd.
Minneapolis, MN 55416
612/591-2700

*Minneapolis/St. Paul Business*
5500 Wayzata Blvd.
Minneapolis, MN 55416
612/591-2701

## Directories
*Minnesota Business Directory*
American Business Directories
5711 S. 86th Cir.
PO Box 27347
Omaha, NE 68127
402/593-4600

*Minnesota Manufacturers Directory*
George D. Hall Co.
50 Congress St.
Boston, MA 02109
617/523-3745

*Minnesota Manufacturers Register*
Manufacturers' News, Inc.
1633 Central St.
Evanston, IL 60201
708/864-7000

## Government Employment Offices
*Office of Personnel Management*
Federal Bldg.
Rm. 501
Ft. Snelling
Twin Cities, MN 55111
612/725-3430
—Federal job-service center.

*Job Service and UI Operations*
690 American Center Bldg.
150 E. Kellogg
St. Paul, MN 55101
612/296-3627
—State job-service center.

## MISSISSIPPI

### Business Periodical
*Mississippi Business Journal*
Venture Publications
PO Box 4566
Jackson, MS 39296
601/352-9035

### Directories
*Mississippi Business Directory*
American Business Directories
5711 S. 86th Cir.
PO Box 27347
Omaha, NE 68127
402/593-4600

*Southeastern Manufacturers Directory*
George D. Hall Co.
50 Congress St.
Boston, MA 02109
617/523-3745
—Includes Alabama, Georgia, and
  Mississippi.

### Government Employment Offices
*Office of Personnel Management*
—See Alabama listing.

*Employment Service Division*
Employment Service Commission
PO Box 1699
Jackson, MS 39215-1699
601/354-8711
—State job-service center.

## MISSOURI

### Business Periodicals
*Kansas City Business Journal*
324 E. 11th St.
Ste. 800
Kansas City, MO 64106
816/421-5900

*St. Louis Business Journal*
PO Box 647
St. Louis, MO 63188
314/421-6200

### Directories
*Harris Missouri Directory of Manufacturers*
IDC (div. of Harris Publishing Company)
2057 Aurora Rd.
Twinsburg, OH 44087
216/425-5900
800/888-5900

*Missouri Business Directory*
American Business Directories
5711 S. 86th Cir.
PO Box 27347
Omaha, NE 68127
402/593-4600

*Missouri Manufacturers Directory*
Manufacturers' News, Inc.
1633 Central St.
Evanston, IL 60201
708/864-7000

### Government Employment Offices
*Office of Personnel Management*
Federal Bldg.
Rm. 134
Kansas City, MO 64106
816/426-5702

—Federal job-service center—for counties west of and including Mercer, Grundy, Livingston, Carroll, Saline, Pettis, Benton, Hickory, Dallas, Webster, Douglas, and Ozark.

*Office of Personnel Management*
Old Post Office Bldg.
815 Olive St.
Rm. 400
St. Louis, MO 63101
314/539-2285
—Federal job-service center for all Missouri counties not listed above.

*Employment Service*
Division of Employment Security
PO Box 59
Jefferson City, MO 65104
314/751-3790
—State job-service center.

# MONTANA

## Business Periodical
*Montana Business Quarterly*
University of Montana
Bureau of Business and Economic Research
Missoula, MT 59812
406/243-5113

## Directories
*Inland Northwest Manufacturing Directory*
Spokane Area Economic Development Council
N. 221 Wall
Ste. 310
PO Box 203
Spokane, WA 99210
509/624-9285
—Covers western Montana, northern Idaho and Oregon, and eastern Washington.

*Montana Business Directory*
American Business Directories
5711 S. 86th Cir.
PO Box 27347
Omaha, NE 68127
402/593-4600

*Montana Manufacturers Directory*
Montana Dept. of Commerce
Small Business Development Center
Federal Bldg. 301
S. Park, Drawer 10054
Helena, MT 59626
406/449-5381

## Government Employment Offices
*Office of Personnel Management*
—Federal job-service center; see Colorado listing; call 303/969-7050.

*Job Service/Employment and Training Division*
PO Box 201505
Helena, MT 59620-1505
406/447-3200
—State job-service center.

# NEBRASKA

## Directories
*Directory of Nebraska Manufacturers*
Dept. of Economic Development
PO Box 94666
Lincoln, NE 68509
402/471-3111

*Nebraska Business Directory*
American Business Directories
5711 S. 86th Cir.
PO Box 27347
Omaha, NE 68127
402/593-4600

## Government Employment Offices
*Office of Personnel Management*
—Federal job-service center; see Missouri listing.

*Job Service*
Nebraska Dept. of Labor
550 S. 16th St.
Lincoln, NE 68509
402/471-9824
—State job-service center.

## NEVADA

### Business Periodicals
*Las Vegas Business*
5300 W. Sahara Ave.
Las Vegas, NV 89102
702/871-6780

*Nevada Business Journal*
3800 Howard Hughes Pkwy.
Las Vegas, NV 89109
702/735-7003

### Directory
*Nevada Business Directory*
American Business Directories
5711 S. 86th Cir.
PO Box 27347
Omaha, NE 68127
402/593-4600

### Government Employment Offices
*Office of Personnel Management*
—Federal job-service center; see
   Sacramento, California, listing.

*Employment Service*
Employment Security Dept.
500 E. Third St.
Carson City, NV 89713
702/687-4650
—State job-service center.

## NEW HAMPSHIRE

### Business Periodical
*Business New Hampshire Magazine*
404 Chestnut St.
Ste. 201
Manchester, NH 03101-1803
603/626-6354

### Directories
*MacRAE's State Directories—Maine/New
   Hampshire/Vermont*
MacRAE's Blue Book, Inc.
817 Broadway
New York, NY 10003
212/673-4700
800/MAC-RAES

*Maine, Vermont, New Hampshire
   Directory of Manufacturers*
George D. Hall Co.
50 Congress St.
Boston, MA 02109
617/523-3745

*New Hampshire Business Directory*
American Business Directories
5711 S. 86th Cir.
PO Box 27347
Omaha, NE 68127
402/593-4600

*New Hampshire Manufacturing Directory*
Tower Publishing Co.
34 Diamond St.
PO Box 7720
Portland, ME 04112
207/774-9813

### Government Employment Offices
*Office of Personnel Management*
—See Massachusetts listing.

*Employment Service Bureau*
Dept. of Employment Security
32 S. Main St.
Concord, NH 03301
603/224-3311
—State job-service center.

## NEW JERSEY

### Business Periodical
*New Jersey Business*
New Jersey Business and Industry
   Association
310 Passaic Ave.
Fairfield, NJ 07004
201/882-5004

## Directories
*Business Journal's Directory of
    Manufacturing*
Corfacts-Business Journal of New Jersey
Business Information Div.
50 Rte. 9 N.
Morganville, NJ 07751
800/678-2565

*Directory of New Jersey Manufacturers*
George D. Hall Co.
50 Congress St.
Boston, MA 02109
617/523-3745

*MacRAE's State Industrial Directory—New
    Jersey*
MacRAE's Blue Book, Inc.
817 Broadway
New York, NY 10003
212/673-4700
800/MAC-RAES

*New Jersey Business Directory*
American Business Directories
5711 S. 86th Cir.
PO Box 27347
Omaha, NE 68127
402/593-4600

*New Jersey Directory of Manufacturers*
Commerce Register, Inc.
190 Godwin Ave.
Midland Park, NJ 07432
201/445-3000

*New Jersey Service Directory*
George D. Hall Co.
50 Congress St.
Boston, MA 02109
617/523-3745

## Government Employment Offices
*Office of Personnel Management*
—See Massachusetts listing.

*New Jersey Dept. of Labor*
Labor Bldg.
CN 058
Trenton, NJ 08652
609/292-2400
—State job-service center.

# NEW MEXICO

## Business Periodical
*New Mexico Business Journal*
2323 Aztec Rd., NE
Albuquerque, NM 87107
505/889-2911

## Directories
*New Mexico Business Directory*
American Business Directories
5711 S. 86th Cir.
PO Box 27347
Omaha, NE 68127
402/593-4600

*New Mexico Manufacturing Directory*
Economic Development and Tourism Dept.
1100 St. Francis Dr.
Santa Fe, NM 87503
505/827-0300

## Government Employment Offices
Office of Personnel Management
Federal Building
421 Gold Ave. W
Albuquerque, NM 87102
505/766-5583
—Federal job-service center.

*Employment Service Employment Security
    Dept.*
PO Box 1928
Albuquerque, NM 87103
505/841-8437
—State job-service center.

# NEW YORK

## Business Periodicals
*Business NY*
152 Washington Ave.
Albany, NY 12210
518/465-7511

*Crain's New York Business*
220 E. 42nd St.
New York, NY 10017
212/210-0270
—Puts out annual directory listing top
companies in New York.

*Long Island/Business*
2150 Smithtown Ave.
Ronkonkoma, NY 11779
516/737-1700
—Puts out annual special issue, "Long
Island Executive Register," which lists
area businesses and includes contact
names.

*Westchester Business Journal*
Westfair Communications
22 Sawmill River Rd.
Hawthorne, NY 10532
914/347-5200

## Directories
*Dalton's New York Metropolitan Directory*
Dalton's Directory
410 Lancaster Ave.
Haverford, PA 19041
215/649-2680
800/221-1050

*MacRAE's State Industrial Directory—New
York State*
MacRAE's Blue Book, Inc.
817 Broadway
New York, NY 10003
212/673-4700
800/MAC-RAES

*New York Business Directory*
American Business Directories
5711 S. 86th Cir.
PO Box 27347
Omaha, NE 68127
402/593-4600

*New York Manufacturers Directory*
George D. Hall Co.
50 Congress St.
Boston, MA 02109
617/523-3745

*New York Metropolitan Directory of
Manufacturers*
Commerce Register, Inc.
190 Godwin Ave.
Midland Park, NJ 07432
201/445-3000

*New York Upstate Directory of
Manufacturers*
Commerce Register, Inc.
190 Godwin Ave.
Midland Park, NJ 07432
201/445-3000

## Government Employment Offices
*Office of Personnel Management*
Jacob K. Javits Federal Bldg.
26 Federal Plz.
New York, NY 10278
212/264-0422
—Federal job-service center.

*Office of Personnel Management*
James M. Hanley Federal Bldg.
100 S. Clinton St.
Syracuse, NY 13260
315/423-5660
—Federal job-service center.

*Job Service Division*
New York State Dept. of Labor
State Campus
Bldg. 12
Albany, NY 12240
518/457-2612
—State job-service center.

# NORTH CAROLINA

## Business Periodicals
*Business NC*
5435-77 Center Dr.
Ste. 50
Charlotte, NC 28217
704/523-6987

*Carolina Business*
PO Box 1088
New Bern, NC 28561
919/633-5106

## Directories
*Directory of Central Atlantic States
  Manufacturers*
George D. Hall Co.
50 Congress St.
Boston, MA 02109
617/523-3745
—Includes Maryland, Delaware, Virginia,
  North Carolina, and South Carolina.

*Directory of North Carolina Manufacturers*
George D. Hall Co.
50 Congress St.
Boston, MA 02109
617/523-3745

*North Carolina Business Directory*
American Business Directories
5711 S. 86th Cir.
PO Box 27347
Omaha, NE 68127
402/593-4600

## Government Employment Offices
*Office of Personnel Management*
4407 Bland Rd.
Ste. 200
Raleigh, NC 27609
919/790-2822
—Federal job-service center.

*Employment Security Commission of
  North Carolina*
PO Box 27625
Raleigh, NC 27611
919/733-7522
—State job-service center.

## NORTH DAKOTA

## Directories
*MacRAE's State Directories—North
  Dakota/South Dakota*
MacRAE's Blue Book, Inc.
817 Broadway
New York, NY 10003
212/673-4700
800/MAC-RAES

*North Dakota Business Directory*
American Business Directories
5711 S. 86th Cir.
PO Box 27347
Omaha, NE 68127
402/593-4600

## Government Employment Offices
*Office of Personnel Management*
—Federal job-service center; see
  Minnesota listing.

*Employment and Job Training Division*
Job Service North Dakota
PO Box 5507
Bismarck, ND 58502
701/224-2842
—State job-service center.

## OHIO

## Business Periodicals
*Corporate Cleveland*
Business Journal Publishing
1720 Euclid Ave.
Cleveland, OH 44115
216/621-1644

*Crain's Cleveland Business*
700 St. Clair Ave. W.
Cleveland, OH 44113
216/522-1383

## Directories
*Harris Ohio Industrial Directory*
Harris Publishing Company
2057 Aurora Rd.
Twinsburg, OH 44087
216/425-5900
800/888-5900

*Ohio Business Directory*
American Business Directories
5711 S. 86th Cir.
PO Box 27347
Omaha, NE 68127
402/593-4600

*Ohio Directory of Manufacturers*
Commerce Register, Inc.
190 Godwin Ave.
Midland Park, NJ 07432
201/445-3000

*Ohio Manufacturers Register*
Manufacturers' News, Inc.
1633 Central St.
Evanston, IL 60201
708/864-7000

## Government Employment Offices
*Office of Personnel Management*
200 W. Second St.
Rm. 506
Dayton, OH 45402
513/225-2576
—Federal job-service center; see Michigan
   listing for counties north of and
   including Van Wert, Auglaize, Hardin,
   Marion, Crawford, Richland, Ashland,
   Wayne, Stark, Carroll, and Columbiana.

*Employment Service Division*
Bureau of Employment Services
145 S. Front St.
Rm. 640
Columbus, OH 43215
614/466-2421
—State job-service center.

## OKLAHOMA

## Business Periodical
*Tulsa Business Chronicle*
World Publishing Co.
315 S. Boulder
PO Box 1770
Tulsa, OK 74102
918/581-8560

## Directories
*Oklahoma Business Directory*
American Business Directories
5711 S. 86th Cir.
PO Box 27347
Omaha, NE 68127
402/593-4600

*Oklahoma Directory of Manufacturers and
   Processors*
Oklahoma Dept. of Commerce
PO Box 26980
Oklahoma City, OK 73126
405/843-9770

## Government Employment Offices
*Office of Personnel Management*
8610 Broadway
Ste. 305
San Antonio, TX 78217
210/805-2402
—Federal job-service center.

*Employment Service Employment Security
   Commission*
2401 N. Lincoln Blvd.
Oklahoma City, OK 73105
405/557-0200
—State job-service center.

## OREGON

## Business Periodicals
*The Business Journal*
American City Business Journals
PO Box 14490
Portland, OR 97214
503/274-8733

*Oregon Business*
921 SW Morrison
Ste. 407
Portland, OR 97205
503/223-0304

## Directories
*Directory of Oregon Manufacturers*
Economic Development Department
775 Summer St., NE
Salem, OR 97310
503/373-1200

*Inland Northwest Manufacturing Directory*
Spokane Area Economic Development
  Council
N. 221 Wall
Ste. 310
PO Box 203
Spokane, WA 99210
509/624-9285
—Covers western Montana, northern
  Idaho and Oregon, and eastern
  Washington.

*Oregon Business Directory*
American Business Directories
5711 S. 86th Cir.
PO Box 27347
Omaha, NE 68127
402/593-4600

## Government Employment Offices
*Office of Personnel Management*
Federal Bldg., Rm 376
1220 SW Third Ave.
Portland, OR 97204
503/326-3141
—Federal job-service center.

*Employment Service*
875 Union St., NE
Salem, OR 97311
503/378-3213
—State job-service center.

# PENNSYLVANIA

## Business Periodicals
*Allegheny Business*
471 Lincoln Ave.
Pittsburgh, PA 15202
412/734-2300

*Philadelphia Business Journal*
400 Market St.
Ste. 300
Philadelphia, PA 19106
215/238-1450

*Pittsburgh Business Times*
2313 E. Carson St.
Ste. 200
Pittsburgh, PA 15203
412/481-6397

## Directories
*Dalton's Philadelphia Metropolitan
  Directory*
Dalton's Directory
410 Lancaster Ave.
Haverford, PA 19041
215/649-2680
800/221-1050

*Harris Pennsylvania Industrial Directory*
Harris Publishing Company
2057Aurora Rd.
Twinsburg, OH 44087
216/425-5900
800/888-5900

*MacRAE's State Industrial Directory—
  Pennsylvania*
MacRAE's Blue Book, Inc.
817 Broadway
New York, NY 10003
212/673-4700
800/MAC-RAES

*Pennsylvania Business Directory*
American Business Directories
5711 S. 86th Cir.
PO Box 27347
Omaha, NE 68127
402/593-4600

*Pennsylvania Directory of Manufacturers*
Commerce Register, Inc.
190 Godwin Ave.
Midland Park, NJ 07432
201/445-3000

*Pennsylvania Manufacturers Register*
Manufacturers' News, Inc.
1633 Central St.
Evanston, IL 60201
708/864-7000

## Government Employment Offices
*Office of Personnel Management*
Federal Bldg.
600 Arch St.
Philadelphia, PA 19106
—Regional OPM office.

*Office of Personnel Management*
Federal Bldg.
Rm. 168
PO Box 761
Harrisburg, PA 17108
717/782-4494
—Federal job-service center.

*Office of Personnel Management*
Wm. J. Green, Jr. Federal Bldg.
600 Arch St.
Rm. 1416
Philadelphia, PA 19106
215/597-7440
—Federal job-service center.

*Office of Personnel Management*
Federal Bldg.
1000 Liberty Ave.
Rm. 119
Pittsburgh, PA 15222
412/644-2755
—Federal job-service center.

*Bureau of Job Service*
Labor 7 Industry Bldg.
Rm. 1115
Seventh and Forster Sts.
Harrisburg, PA 17121
717/787-3354
—State job-service center.

# RHODE ISLAND

## Business Periodical
*Providence Business News*
Herald Press, Inc.
300 Richmond St.
Providence, RI 02903
401/273-2201

## Directories
*Connecticut, Rhode Island Directory of
  Manufacturers*
Commerce Register, Inc.
190 Godwin Ave.
Midland Park, NJ 07432
201/445-3000

*MacRAE's State Industrial Directory—
  Massachusetts/Rhode Island*
MacRAE's Blue Book, Inc.
817 Broadway
New York, NY 10003
212/673-4700
800/MAC-RAES

*Rhode Island Business Directory*
American Business Directories
5711 S. 86th Cir.
PO Box 27347
Omaha, NE 68127
402/593-4600

*Rhode Island Directory of Manufacturers*
Dept. of Economic Development
7 Jackson Walkway
Providence, RI 02903
401/277-2601

## Government Employment Offices
*Office of Personnel Management*
—Federal job-service center; see
  Massachusetts listing.

*Job Service Division*
Dept. of Employment Security
101 Friendship St.
Providence, RI 02903
401/277-3722
—State job-service center.

# SOUTH CAROLINA

## Directories
*Directory of Central Atlantic States
  Manufacturers*
George D. Hall Co.
50 Congress St.
Boston, MA 02109
617/523-3745

—includes Maryland, Delaware, Virginia, North Carolina, and South Carolina.

*MacRAE's State Industrial Directory—North Carolina/South Carolina/Virginia*
MacRAE's Blue Book, Inc.
817 Broadway
New York, NY 10003
212/673-4700
800/MAC-RAES

*South Carolina Business Directory*
American Business Directories
5711 S. 86th Cir.
PO Box 27347
Omaha, NE 68127
402/593-4600

## Government Employment Offices
*Office of Personnel Management*
—Federal job-service center; see North Carolina listing.

*Employment Service*
PO Box 995
Columbia, SC 29202
803/737-2400
—State job-service center.

## SOUTH DAKOTA

### Directories
*MacRAE's State Directories—North Dakota/South Dakota*
MacRAE's Blue Book, Inc.
817 Broadway
New York, NY 10003
212/673-4700
800/MAC-RAES

*South Dakota Business Directory*
American Business Directories
5711 S. 86th Cir.
PO Box 27347
Omaha, NE 68127
402/593-4600

*South Dakota Manufacturers & Processors Directory*
Governor's Office of Economic Development
711 Wells Ave.
Pierre, SD 57501-3369
605/773-5032

### Government Employment Offices
*Office of Personnel Management*
—Federal job-service center; see Minnesota listing.

*South Dakota Dept. of Labor*
700 Governors Dr.
Pierre, SD 57501
605/773-3101
—State job-service center.

## TENNESSEE

### Business Periodicals
*Memphis Business Journal*
Mid-South Communications
88 Union
Ste. 102
Memphis, TN 38103
901/523-1000

*Nashville Business Journal*
Mid-South Communications
PO Box 23229
Nashville, TN 37202
615/254-9154

### Directory
*Tennessee Business Directory*
American Business Directories
5711 S. 86th Cir.
PO Box 27347
Omaha, NE 68127
402/593-4600

### Government Employment Offices
*Office of Personnel Management*
200 Jefferson Ave.
Ste. 1312
Memphis, TN 38103-2335
901/544-3956
—Federal job-service center.

*Employment Service*
Dept. of Employment Security
500 James Robertson Pkwy.
Nashville, TN 37245-0900
615/741-0922
—State job-service center.

## TEXAS

### Business Periodicals
*Dallas Business Journal*
4131 N. Central Expwy.
Dallas, TX 75204
214/520-1010

*Houston Business Journal*
1 W. Loop S.
Houston, TX 77027
713/688-8811

### Directories
*Directory of Texas Manufacturers*
University of Texas at Austin
Bureau of Business Research
PO Box 7459
Austin, TX 78713
512/471-1616

*Texas Business Directory*
American Business Directories
5711 S. 86th Cir.
PO Box 27347
Omaha, NE 68127
402/593-4600

*Texas Manufacturers Register*
Manufacturers' News, Inc.
1633 Central St.
Evanston, IL 60201
708/864-7000

### Government Employment Offices
*Office of Personnel Management*
1100 Commerce
Rm. 6812
Dallas, TX 75242
214/767-8035

—Federal job-service center—mail or
phone only.

*Office of Personnel Management*
8610 Broadway
Rm. 305
San Antonio, TX 78217
210/805-2402
—Federal job-service center—mail or
phone only.

*Employment Service*
Texas Employment Commission
101 E. 15th St.
Austin, TX 78778-001
512/463-2222
—State job-service center.

## UTAH

### Directories
*Utah Business Directory*
American Business Directories
5711 S. 86th Cir.
PO Box 27347
Omaha, NE 68127
402/593-4600

*Utah Directory of Business and Industry*
Dept. of Employment Security
Div. of Economic Development
324 State St.
Ste. 200
Salt Lake City, UT 84111
801/538-8700

### Government Employment Offices
*Office of Personnel Management*
—Federal job-service center; see Colorado
listing; call 303/969-7050.

*Employment Services/Field Oper.*
Dept. of Employment Security
164 Social Hall Ave.
Salt Lake City, UT 84147
801/533-2400

# VERMONT

## Business Periodical
*Vermont Business*
2 Church St.
Burlington, VT 05401-4445
802/863-8038

## Directories
*MacRAE's State Directories—Maine/New Hampshire/Vermont*
MacRAE's Blue Book, Inc.
817 Broadway
New York, NY 10003
212/673-4700
800/MAC-RAES

*Maine, Vermont, New Hampshire Directory of Manufacturers*
Commerce Register, Inc.
190 Godwin Ave.
Midland Park, NJ 07432
201/445-3000

*Vermont Business Directory*
American Business Directories
5711 S. 86th Cir.
PO Box 27347
Omaha, NE 68127
402/593-4600

## Government Employment Offices
*Office of Personnel Management*
—Federal job-service center; see Massachusetts listing.

*Employment Service*
Dept. of Employment and Training
PO Box 488
Montpelier, VT 05602
800/229-0311
—State job-service center.

# VIRGINIA

## Business Periodical
*Virginia Business*
411 E. Franklin St.
Richmond, VA 23219
804/649-6000

## Directories
*Directory of Central Atlantic States Manufacturers*
George D. Hall Co.
50 Congress St.
Boston, MA 02109
617/523-3745

*MacRAE's State Directories—North Carolina/South Carolina/Virginia*
MacRAE's Blue Book, Inc.
817 Broadway
New York, NY 10003
212/673-4700
800/MAC-RAES

*Virginia Business Directory*
American Business Directories
5711 S. 86th Cir.
PO Box 27347
Omaha, NE 68127
402/593-4600

## Government Employment Offices
*Office of Personnel Management*
Federal Bldg.
Rm. 220
200 Granby St.
Norfolk, VA 23510-1886
804/441-3355
—Federal job-service center.

*Employment Service*
Virginia Employment Commission
PO Box 1358
Richmond, VA 23211
804/786-7097
—State job-service center.

## WASHINGTON

### Business Periodical
*Sound Business*
3000 Northrup Way
Bellevue, WA 98004
206/827-9900

### Directories
*Inland Northwest Manufacturing Directory*
Spokane Area Economic Development
  Council
N. 221 Wall
Ste. 310
PO Box 203
Spokane, WA 99210
509/624-9285
—Covers western Montana, northern
  Idaho and Oregon, and eastern
  Washington.

*Washington Business Directory*
American Business Directories
5711 S. 86th Cir.
PO Box 27347
Omaha, NE 68127
402/593-4600

*Washington Manufacturers Register*
Database Publishing Co.
523 Superior Ave.
Newport Beach, CA 92663
800/888-8434

### Government Employment Offices
*Office of Personnel Management*
Federal Bldg, Rm. 110
915 Second Ave.
Seattle, WA 98174
206/220-6400
—Federal job-service center.

*Employment Security Dept.*
212 Maple Pk.
Olympia, WA 98507-9046
206/753-5116

## WEST VIRGINIA

### Directories
*Directory of Central Atlantic States
  Manufacturers*
George D. Hall Co.
50 Congress St.
Boston, MA 02109
617/523-3745

*Harris West Virginia Manufacturing
  Directory*
Harris Publishing Company
2057 Aurora Rd.
Twinsburg, OH 44087
216/425-5900
800/888-5900

*West Virginia Business Directory*
American Business Directories
5711 S. 86th Cir.
PO Box 27347
Omaha, NE 68127
402/593-4600

*West Virginia Manufacturers Register*
Manufacturers' News, Inc.
1633 Central St.
Evanston, IL 60201
708/864-7000

### Government Employment Offices
*Office of Personnel Management*
—Federal job-service center; see Ohio
  listing or call 513/225-2720.

*Employment Service Division*
Dept. of Employment Security
112 California Ave.
Charleston, WV 25305
304/558-1138
—State job-service center.

## WISCONSIN

### Business Periodicals
*The Business Journal Serving Greater
 Milwaukee*
American City Business Journals
2025 N. Summit Ave.
Milwaukee, WI 53202
414/278-7788

*Corporate Report Wisconsin*
PO Box 878
Memomonee Falls, WI 53052
414/255-9077

### Directories
*Classified Directory of Wisconsin
 Manufacturers*
WMC Service Corp.
501 E. Washington Ave.
PO Box 352
Madison, WI 53701-0352
608/258-3400

*Wisconsin Business Directory*
American Business Directories
5711 S. 86th Cir.
PO Box 27347
Omaha, NE 68127
402/593-4600

*Wisconsin Manufacturers Register*
Manufacturers' News, Inc.
1633 Central St.
Evanston, IL 60201
708/864-7000

*Wisconsin Services Directory*
WMC Service Corp.
501 E. Washington Ave.
PO Box 352
Madison, WI 53701-0352
608/258-3400

### Government Employment Office
*Office of Personnel Management*
—Federal job-service center—in counties
 of Grant, Iowa, Lafayette, Dane, Green,
 Rock, Jefferson, Walworth, Waukesha,
 Racine, Kenosha, and Milwaukee, see
 Illinois listing and call 312/353-6189; for
 all other Wisconsin counties, see
 Minnesota listing.

## WYOMING

### Directory
*Wyoming Business Directory*
American Business Directories
5711 S. 86th Cir.
PO Box 27347
Omaha, NE 68127
402/593-4600

### Government Employment Offices
*Office of Personnel Management*
—Federal job-service center; see Colorado
 listing; call 303/969-7050.

*Employment Service*
Employment Security Commission
PO Box 2760
Casper, WY 82602
307/235-3611
—State job-service center.

# *Index*

brief
brief